FACE TO FACE

FACE to FACE

PORTRAITS OF THE DIVINE IN EARLY CHRISTIANITY

ROBIN MARGARET JENSEN

FORTRESS PRESS / MINNEAPOLIS

Cover and book design: Zan Ceeley
About the cover art: Left: Detail of Jesus enthroned, ca. 400 C.E. Church of Santa Pudenziana, Rome. Middle: Detail of Dome mosaic, early 6th cen. C.E., Arian Baptistery, Ravenna. Right: Detail of Medallion portrait of Christ from arch of presbyterium, San Vitale, Ravenna. All photos are by Robin Margaret Jensen.

Library of Congress Cataloging-in-Publication Data
Jensen, Robin Margaret
  Face to face : portraits of the divine in early Christianity / Robin Margaret Jensen.
    p. cm.
  Includes bibliographical references and index.
  ISBN 0-8006-3678-3 (pbk. : alk. paper)—ISBN 0-8006-6092-7 (alk. paper)
  1. Jesus Christ—Art. 2. God—Art. 3. Saints in art. 4. Art, Early Christian. 5. Portraits, Roman. I. Title.
  N8050.J43 2004
  704.9'485'09021—dc22

                                                     2004012360

Manufactured in Canada.

09   08   07   06   05   1   2   3   4   5   6   7

To the memory of my parents,

ROBERT AND MARGARET JENSEN,

with confidence that they will one day

see God "face to face"

Contents

Preface

IN THE EARLY autumn of 1888, two years before his death and, despite the ravages of his final illness, experiencing one of his most productive periods, Vincent van Gogh wrote a few lines about the nature of portrait painting to his brother, Theo:

> Ah my dear brother, sometimes I know so well what I want. I can well do without God in both my life and also in my painting, but suffering as I am, I cannot do without something greater than myself, something which is my life—the power to create. And if, deprived of the physical power, one tries to create thoughts instead of children, one is still very much part of humanity. And in my pictures I want to say something consoling as music does. I want to paint men and women with a touch of the eternal, whose symbol was once the halo, which we try to convey by the very radiance and vibrancy of our colouring. . . . Ah portraiture, portraiture, with the mind, the soul of the model—that is what really must come, it seems to me.[1]

Vincent's insistence that a true portrait captures far more than a physical likeness by also portraying the mind and the soul of the model, is well illustrated by the work he produced around that time. Departing from a concentration on landscapes and still lifes, or anonymous scenes of workers and café sitters, he produced a series of memorable images including the portrait of the postman Joseph Roulin (Arles, August, 1888), the Arlésienne (Arles, November, 1888), the Woman Rocking a Cradle (Arles, December, 1888), the Head Warder at the Asylum of Saint-Rémy (St.-Rémy, 1889), and finally his own self-portrait, painted two months before his suicide (Auvers-sur-Oise, 1890). Through color, composition, and technique, Vincent here captured the distinct personality of each model, and time's passing has borne this out as a "touch of the eternal." These portraits say as much about the painter's skill and insight as they do about the model's personality or aspirations, and the faces of these ordinary persons indeed have become eternal in their way. Van Gogh's models appear on postcards sold in nearly every art book-shop in the world, their faces as familiar to us as certain celebrities or pop stars.

The fascination with trying to "capture the soul" of an individual by making a physical likeness coexists with art itself. From Egyptian mum-mies to Byzantine icons to the work of such twentieth-century photog-raphers as Alfred Steigleitz, Richard Avedon, and Diane Arbus, portraits have been private and intimate, public and monumental, huge and tiny, religious and secular. They might show the whole human form or merely a disembodied face. Sometimes portraits had utilitarian pur-poses such as recording the physical appearance of princess candidates for dynastic marriage; others guarded the family as tutelary spirits or mediated the divine presence of a deity. Essentially, they portrayed the appearance of an individual (human, divine, or imagined) produced from life or from memory, so as to allow identification, aid the memory, reveal key aspects of the subject's character or personality, or invite devotion.

Portraits are potent and can be dangerous. Persons who have become ostracized or unpopular may have their images cut out, painted over, or digitally removed. Portrait statues of former rulers and dictators have been toppled or decapitated as a means of erasing their memory and indicating their impotence. In some cultures, taking a photograph of an unsuspecting stranger is not only rude but equivalent to stealing. To own an image is to rob identity or to gain access to the inner being, pos-sibly for evil purpose. Portraits also present a moment of a life from a certain viewpoint, which may be revealing, manipulative, truthful, ide-alizing, or distorting. Portraits honor, expose, examine, or express the reality of a human, physical existence. They can describe, exalt, or ridicule; they may inspire contemplation, derision, imitation, or devo-tion. They may be brutally honest or deeply sympathetic, their subjects shown as heroic, noble, saintly, stupid, weak, or evil. Likeness is not an easy thing to define, and its measure lies in the response of a viewer as much as in the skill or intentions of the artist. Whereas caricature cap-tures certain identifiable features and exaggerates them into humorous or mocking portrayals, idealizing images work in the opposite direction, but both can be likenesses. Picasso's portrait of Dora Mar in the cubist style is also a likeness on its own terms.

The matter of identification is key since the original and image are related but very different things. One is not contained within the other: the latter only refers to the former, or merely even to some aspect of that other's existence—merely a single moment in time, an episode of a life, but not the whole. Thus, the capturing of the soul is only for a specific fixed time and place and only according to the eye of a particular beholder (the artist and the viewer). Even so, some portraits have come to be indelibly associated with their model, like Gilbert Stuart's George Washington, or Hans Holbein's portrait of Henry VIII.

Portraits are relational, since the viewer meets the model face to face. And the face above all (in particular, the eyes) serves as the vulnerable conduit to the soul. Although portraits may include the rest of the body, the face also is the basis of the likeness. Eyes don't always meet the gaze of the viewer, since some portraits are in profile, but a faceless portrait is almost incomprehensible. Without the face, the portrait is incomplete, but a superficial facial image itself is not necessarily a portrait. The driver's license or identity card only roughly matches an external appearance and has a single function. A true portrait conveys something essential about its subject that transcends mere surface likeness. This is achieved through the use of color, composition, technique, or style, which includes such secondary details as costume, props, or setting that add important identifying as well as descriptive elements.

For some religious persons, the idea of making a portrait of God is utterly blasphemous. God is asserted to be invisible and beyond human comprehension. Nevertheless, Scriptures are filled with anthropomorphic descriptions of God and stories of God's appearance to humans in one form or another (a burning bush, an angelic visitor, the Ancient of Days on a throne). Moses is told that he cannot see God's face, but the Apostle Paul assures his readers that one day we will see God "face to face" (1 Cor 13:12). Jesus tells his disciples that if they have seen him they have seen the Father (John 14:9), even though the fourth evangelist still claims that "no one has ever seen God" (John 1:18). The Epistle to the Colossians calls Christ the "image of the invisible God" (1:15). And, even though it avoids any representation of the First Person of the Trinity, the Orthodox Church defends the importance of portrait icons on the basis that the incarnation of Christ gave God a "human face." These statements of faith all claim that verbal expression is not God's only means of self-revelation and that Christians might well claim that there is also a visual means of knowing and comprehending the Divine—having both ears to hear and eyes to see the "glory of the Lord" in and through the testimony of nature, history, and everyday human living.

Not only whether but how the image of God or Christ should be portrayed is a different problem, which has been deeply controversial and divisive in the history of Christianity. The problem of representing a divine nature, or even capturing a physical human likeness of that One who left no certain record of appearance or eyewitness description, might be insurmountable apart from an act of faith, a belief in the gift of a miraculous image, or the acceptance that a true likeness is not based on mundane historical data but can emerge out of tradition, personal religious experience, or even particular visionary experiences. And, if the record shows us anything, it is that a wide variety of different representations does not imply that all (but perhaps one) are wrong. It may be that all are right. The nearly infinite variety of portraits of Christ that have been created by Christians in all places and times may lead us to one almost paradoxical conclusion—that no one image can tell the whole story and that all can show us some aspect of the truth. In a sense, more is better. The existence of four separate canonical Gospels perhaps demonstrates this. But the same might be said of any human portrait as well. No one image can capture the whole of an individual's life and character. Every image leads us to the model, while at the same time it shows only an aspect or even a tiny glimpse of the reality of the individual.

Thus, the term "portrait" here has a very specific meaning—it aims, like van Gogh's paintings, to capture not only the external appearance but also the whole person, including the mind and soul, and to portray that "touch of eternity." Thus, the picture tells a story far more expansive and profound than it might seem on the surface. The beauty and the truth of these images have less to do with verisimilitude or even aesthetic judgments than with the way they affect their viewers. Such images lead viewers to a different kind of understanding of the subject, and perhaps even to the story arousing affection or devotion, and finally allow the observer both to sense the presence of the model and to be inspired to imitation of the virtues conveyed through the image. In this way, the faculty of sight is a potent means by which humans may come to encounter the holy and to be transformed by that encounter.

This book examines the power of images, especially in the early Christian tradition in the centuries just prior to the establishment of and controversies surrounding the place of the icon in liturgy and devotion. I contend that the seeds of what later would become the Orthodox defense of the icon already existed in early Christian teaching and that actual visual images were both used and appreciated, almost as soon as Christians had any distinct material culture of their own. The later rejection of visual images by the church at various times and places (in both East and West), even when prompted by legitimate fear of idolatry, usually misunderstood the nature of most of these images and failed to attend to the essential role of seeing in the Christian teaching about salvation.

I began this work three years ago as a Luce Fellow in Theology, funded by the Henry Luce Foundation through the Association of Theological Schools. In addition to the Foundation and the ATS, I wish to thank my teachers, Richard Brilliant, for stirring my interest in ancient portraiture, and Richard Norris, for his wise commentary on the problem of God's invisibility. Mary Charles Murray, Jaš Elsner, Tom Mathews, Corby Finney, and Graydon Snyder have also been important influences on me as well. The International Catacomb Society, Amy Hirschfeld, and my other colleagues on that Board have been immensely generous with their images and their time; Kate Layzer read and ably edited some of my first drafts; and Lee Jefferson proofread and indexed the final version. I am especially grateful to Zan Ceeley of Fortress Press for her work on the design of this book—an essential aspect of any book on the visual arts. I also want to thank Andover Newton Theological School for providing a sabbatical leave; Vanderbilt Divinity School for allowing me an initial leave from teaching after I joined its faculty; and my colleagues both in Boston and Nashville for stimulating conversations and support over the past decade. Finally, I want to thank my husband, Patout Burns, for being my conversation partner, travel companion, generous and patient editor, and handy reference service. He also should get the credit for many of the photographs in this book, but we usually cannot tell which one of us took which pictures, slides, or digital images in our collection.

Abbreviations

Ancient

Ad M. Caes.	Fronto, *Ad M. Caesarem* (To Marcus Aurelius)
Adv. Eun.	Basil of Caesarea, *Adversus Eunomium* (Against Eunomius)
Adv. Eun. Lib. 2	Gregory of Nyssa, *Adversus Eunomium liber 2* (Against Eunomius' Second Book)
Adv. nat.	Arnobius, *Adversus nationes* (Against the Nations)
Alex.	Plutarch, *Alexander*
Anima et res.	Gregory of Nyssa, *De anima et resurrectione* (On the Soul and the Resurrection)
Ann.	Tacitus, *Annales* (Annals)
Ant.	Josephus, *Antiquitates Judaicae* (Jewish Antiquities)
Apol.	John of Damascus, *Apologiae* (On the Divine Images: Three Apologies against Those Who Attack the Divine Images)
Apol.	Justin, *Apologia* (Defense)
Apol.	Tertullian, *Apologeticum* (Apology)
Auto.	Theophilus, *Ad Autolycum* (To Autolycus)
B. J.	Josephus, *Bellum Judaicum* (Jewish War)
Bell. Jug.	Sallust, *Bellum Jugurthinum* (The Jugurthine War)
C. Ap.	Josephus, *Contra Apionem* (Against Apion)
C. Ar.	Athanasius, *Orationes contra Arianos* (Discourse against the Arians)
Carm.	Fortunatus, *Carmina* (Poems)
Carm.	Paulinus, *Carmina* (Poems)
Carn. Chr.	Tertullian, *De carne Christi* (On the Flesh of Christ)
Cat.	Cyril of Jerusalem, *Catecheses* (Catechetical Lectures)
Catech. illum.	John Chrysostrom, *Catecheses ad illuminandos* (Baptismal Instructions)
C. Cels.	Origen, *Contra Celsum* (Against Celsus)
C. Eun.	Ps. Basil, *Contra Eunomium* (Against Eunomius)
C. Gent.	Athanasius, *Contra gentes* (Against the Pagans)
Cel. hier.	Pseudo-Dionysius, *De caelesti hierarchia* (On the Celestial Hierarchy)
Civ.	Augustine, *De civitate Dei* (City of God)
Codex Theo.	*Codex Theodosianus* (Theodosian Code)
Coll.	John Cassian, *Collationes* (Conferences)
Comm. Cant.	Origen, *Commentarius in Canticum* (Commentary on the Song of Songs)
Comm. Ezech.	Jerome, *Commentariorum in Ezechielem libri XVI* (Commentary on Ezekiel, Book 16)
Comm. Isa.	Eusebius, *Commentarius in Isaiam* (Commentary on Isaiah)
Comm. Matt.	Origen, *Commentarium in evangelium Matthaei* (Commentary on the Gospel of Matthew)
Conf.	Philo, *De confusione linguarum* (On the Confusion of Tongues)
Cons. ev.	Augustine, *De consensu evangelistarum* (Harmony of the Gospels)
Contempl.	Philo, *De vita contemplativa* (On the Contemplative Life)
Decal.	Philo, *De Decalogo* (On the Decalogue)

Dei cogn.	Dio Chrysostom, *De Dei cognitione* (On the Knowledge of God)
Deit.	Gregory of Nyssa, *De deitate Filii et Spiritus Sancti* (On the Divinity of the Son and the Holy Spirit)
Dem. Ev.	Eusebius, *Demonstratio evangelica* (Demonstration of the Gospel)
Dial.	Justin, *Dialogus cum Tryphone* (Dialogue with Trypho)
Div. nom.	Pseudo-Dionysius, *De divinis nominibus* (On the Divine Names)
Ecc. hier.	Pseudo-Dionysius, *De ecclesiastica hierarchia* (On the Ecclesiastical Hierarchy)
Enarrat. Ps.	Augustine, *Enarrationes in Psalmos* (Exposition of the Psalms)
Enn.	Plotinus, *Enneades*
Ep.	Augustine, *Epistulae* (Letters)
Ep.	Basil, *Epistulae* (Letters)
Ep.	Cyprian, *Epistulae* (Letters)
Ep.	Gregory I, *Epistulae* (Letters)
Ep.	Paulinus, *Epistulae* (Letters)
Ep.	Pliny, *Epistulae* (Letters)
Ep.	Serenus *Epistulae* (Letters)
Ep. ad Avitum	Jerome, *Epistula ad Avitum* (Letter to Avitus)
Ep. Ferrandus	Fulgentius of Ruspe, *Epistula ad Ferrandum* (Letter to Ferrandus)
Epid.	Irenaeus, *Epideixis tou apostolikou kērygmatos* (Demonstration of the Apostolic Preaching)
Exp. Ps.	John Chrysostom, *Expositiones in Psalmos* (Exposition of the Psalms)
Expl. Dan.	Jerome, *Explanatio in Danielem* (Commentary on Daniel)
Fid. symb.	Augustine, *De fide et symbolo* (On Faith and the Symbol)
Fide orth.	John of Damascus, *De fide orthodoxa* (On the Orthodox Faith)
Fort.	Cyprian, *Ad Fortunatum* (To Fortunatus: Exhortation to Martyrdom)
Fr.	Euripides, *Fragmenta* (Fragments)
Frag. ep.	Julian (Emperor), *Fragmentum Epistolae* (Fragment of a Letter to a Priest)
Fug.	Philo, *De Fuga et inventione* (On Flight and Finding)
Giants	Philo, *On Giants*
Haer.	Irenaeus, *Adversus haereses* (Against Heresies)
Her.	Ovid, *Heroides*
Heracl.	Lucian, *Heracles*
Hist.	Eusebius, *Historia ecclesiastica* (History of the Church)
Hist.	Nicephorus, *Opuscula Historica* (Brief History)
Hist.	Philostorgius, *Historia ecclesiastica* (History of the Church)
Hist.	Polybius, *Historiae* (Histories)
Hist.	Socrates, *Historia ecclesiastica* (History of the Church)
Hist.	Tacitus, *Historiae* (Histories)
Hist.	Theodorus Lector, *Historia ecclesiastica* (History of the Church)
Hist. Aug. Sev. Alex.	Lampridius, *Historia Augusta, Severus Alexander* (Life of the Emperor Severus Alexander)
Hom.	Basil, *Homiliae* (Homilies)
Hom.	Gregory the Great, *Homiliae* (Homilies)
Hom.	Gregory Nazianzen, *Homiliae* (Homilies)
Hom.	Ps. Basil, *Homiliae* (Homilies)
Hom. 1 Cor.	John Chrysostom, *Homiliae in epistulam i ad Corinthios* (Homily on the First Epistle to the Corinthians)
Hom. 56 Matt.	John Chrysostom, *Homiliae in Matthaeum* (Homilies on Matthew)
Hom. encom. in Melet.	John Chrysostom, *Homilia encomium in Melitium* (Homily in Praise of Meletius)
Hom. Exod.	Origen, *Homiliae in Exodum* (Homilies on Exodus)
Hom. Gen.	Origen, *Homiliae in Genesim* (Homilies on Genesis)
Hom. Heb.	John Crysostom, *Homiliae in epistulam ad Hebraeos* (Homilies on the Epistle to the Hebrews)
Hom. Num.	Origen, *Homiliae in Numeros* (Homilies on Numbers)
Idol.	Tertullian, *De idololatria* (On Idolatry)
Imag.	Lucian, *Imagines* (Essays on Portraiture)
Inc.	Athanasius, *De incarnatione* (On the Incarnation)

Jul.	Suetonius, *Divus Julius* (Divine Julius)
Laps.	Cyprian, *De lapsis* (On the Lapsed)
Laud. Theod.	Gregory of Nyssa, *Laudatio S. Theodori* (In Praise of St. Theodore)
Leg.	Athenagoras, *Legatio Pro Christianis* (Supplication for the Christians)
Liber pont.	*Liber Pontificalis* (Book of the Popes)
Marc.	Porphyry, *Ad Marcellum* (To Marcellus)
Marc.	Tertullian, *Adversus Marcionem* (Against Marcion)
Mart.	Tertullian, *Ad Martyras* (To the Martyrs)
Mor.	Plutarch, *Moralia* (Morals)
Mor. eccl.	Augustine, *De moribus ecclesiae catholicae* (Morals of the Catholic Church)
Mort.	Lactantius, *De mortibus persecutorum* (On the Deaths of Persecutors)
Myst. theo.	Pseudo-Dionysius, *De mystica theologia* (On Mystical Theology)
Nat.	Pliny, *Naturalis historia* (Natural History)
Nat. d.	Cicero, *De natura deorum* (On the Nature of the Gods)
Num	Plutarch, *Numa* (Numa)
Oct.	Minucius Felix, *Octavius*
Opif.	Philo, *De opificio mundi* (On the Creation of the World)
Or.	Evagrius, *De oratione* (Chapters on Prayers)
Or.	Libanius, *Orationes* (Orations)
Or.	Gregory of Nazianzus, *Orationes* (Orations)
Obit. Bas.	Gregory of Nazianzus, *De obitu Basilii* (Funeral Oration for Basil)
Paed.	Clement of Alexandria, *Paedagogus* (Christ the Teacher)
Pamm.	Jerome, *Ad Pammachium* (To Pammachius against John of Jerusalem)
Pan.	Epiphanius, *Panarion* (Medicine Chest)
Pereg.	Egeria, *Peregrinatio* (Pilgrimage or Itinerary)
Peri.	Prudentius, *Peristephanon liber* (The Book of the Martyrs' Crowns)
Poet.	Aristotle, *Poetica* (Poetics)
Post.	Philo, *De posteritate Caini* (On the Posterity of Cain)
Praep. Ev.	Eusebius, *Praeparatio Evangelica* (Preparation for the Gospel)
Prac.	Evagrius Ponticus, *Practicos* (Practicos)
Prax.	Tertullian, *Adversus Praxeas* (Against Praxeas)
Princ.	Origen, *De Principiis* (On First Principles)
Pro Imag.	Lucian, *Pro Imaginibus* (Essays on Portraiture Defended)
Prot.	Clement, *Protrepticus* (Exhortation to the Greeks)
Pud.	Tertullian, *De pudicitia* (On Modesty)
R.	Rabbi
Ref.	Hippolytus, *Refutatio omnium haeresium* (Refutation of All Heresies)
Ref.	Theodore the Studite, *Refutationes* (Refutations of the Iconoclasts)
Scorp.	Tertullian, *Scorpiace* (Antidote for the Scorpion's Sting)
Serm.	Augustine, *Sermones* (Sermons)
Serm.	Leo, *Sermones* (Sermons)
Spect.	Tertullian, *De spectaculis* (On the Shows)
Spir. Sanct.	Basil of Caesarea, *Spiritus Sanctus* (The Holy Spirit)
Stat.	Chrysostom, *Ad populum Antiochenum de statuis* (On the Statues)
Stoic. rep.	Plutarch, *De Stoicorum repugnantiis* (Stoic Self-Contradictions)
Strom.	Clement, *Stromateis* (Miscellanies)
Test.	Epiphanius, *Testamentum* (Testament)
Tib.	Suetonius, *Tiberius*
Tract. Ev. Jo.	Augustine, *In Evangelium Johannis tractatus* (Tractates on the Gospel of John)
Trad. Ap.	Hippolytus, *Traditio apostolica* (Apostolic Tradition)
Trin.	Augustine, *De Trinitate* (On the Trinity)
Trin.	Novatian, *De Trinitate* (On the Trinity)
Ver. rel.	Augustine, *De vera religione* (On True Religion)
Vit. Apoll.	Philosotratus, *Vita Apollonii* (Life of Apollonius of Tyana)
Vit. Const.	Eusebius, *Vita Constantini* (Life of Constantine)
Vit. Plot.	Porphyry, *Vita Plotini* (Life of Plotinus)

Modern

AB	*Art Bulletin*
ACW	Ancient Christian Writers
AH	*Art History*
AJA	*American Journal of Archaeology*
ANF	*Ante-Nicene Fathers*
ANRW	*Aufstieg und Niedergang der römischen Welt*
ARTS	*Art, Religion, and Theological Studies*
BAR	*Biblical Archaeology Review*
BRev	*Bible Review*
Bull Roy Bel	*Bulletin Académie Royale de Belgique*
Cah.Arch.	Cahiers Archéologiques
CCSL	Corpus Christianorum: series latina
CisSt	*Cistercian Studies*
CWS	Classics of Western Spirituality
DOP	*Dumbarton Oaks Papers*
FC	Fathers of the Church
GCS	Die griechischen christlichen Schrifsteller
HDR	Harvard Dissertations in Religion
HTR	*Harvard Theological Review*
IEJ	*Israel Exploration Journal*
JBL	*Journal of Biblical Literature*
JECS	*Journal of Early Christian Studies*
JR	*Journal of Religion*
JSJ	*Journal for the Study of Judaism*
JSJSup	Supplements to the *Journal for the Study of Judaism*
JTS	*Journal of Theological Studies*
LCL	Loeb Classical Library
MDAI	*Mitteilungen des Deutschen archäologischen Instituts*
MEFR	*Mélanges d'archéologie et d'histoire de l'école français de Rome*
NPNF²	*Nicene and Post-Nicene Fathers*, Series 2
PBSR	*Papers of the British School at Rome*
PG	Patrologiae cursus completus: Series graeca, edited by J.-P. Migne
RAC	*Reallexikon für Antike und Christentum*
RivAC	*Rivista di archaeologia cristiana*
SHAW.PH	Sitzungsberichte der Heidelberger Akademie der Wissenschaft, Philosophisch-Historische Klasse
VC	*Vigilae Christianae*

ONE

Visual Art, Portraits, and Idolatry

FOR THE MOST PART, existing examples of Christian visual art come from Rome and date to the beginning of the third century C.E., a time when Roman Christians were enjoying a brief respite from the widespread but sporadic persecutions they had suffered during the reign of Marcus Aurelius (160–180). During the relatively tolerant reign of Emperor Commodus (180–192), the church acquired land outside the city walls, on the Via Appia Antica, for use as a burial ground, allowing them to inter Christian dead in cemeteries separated from their non-Christian neighbors. This cemetery, unlike most necropoli or mausolea from earlier times that were either just at the surface or above-ground, was constructed as an underground network of branching and connecting tunnels on four different levels, containing tiers of narrow horizontal niches for individual bodies (*loculi*) and openings into larger rooms (*cubicula*), which may have held several burials from a single family. The *loculi* were closed with slabs of stone or terra cotta on which were inscribed simple epitaphs and often a figure or a symbol (such as a dove, praying figure, anchor, or fish). The walls and ceilings of the *cubicula* (a word that means "sleeping chambers") were often adorned with traditional decorative motifs as well as some narrative images based on biblical themes.

According to his later rival Hippolytus, the oldest section of the first known Christian cemetery was placed under the supervision of Callistus, a former slave who had been condemned to hard labor in the Sardinian mines as a Christian. After he was released (through an intervention on his behalf by the emperor's mistress Marcia, who seems to have had Christian sympathies), Callistus returned to Rome, where he received a pension as reward for his suffering from Bishop Victor I (189–198 C.E.). Under Victor's successor Zephyrinus, Callistus was put in charge of the

Christian cemetery, and when Zephyrinus died, he became Bishop himself, dying as a martyr in 222.[1] In time, the cemetery Callistus had supervised (although not where he himself was buried) came to be called the

Fig. 1. Wall painting from a hypogeum in the Catacomb of San Sebastiano, Rome (© The International Catacomb Society. Photo: Estelle Brettman).

Catacomb of Saint Callistus.[2] Inscriptional evidence in its oldest area, containing the so-called Crypt of the Popes, was found to indicate the burials of a number of third-century bishops of Rome.

Historians regard this site as especially important because of its many wall paintings, most of which are assumed to be contemporaneous with the first years of its use, making them among the earliest examples of Christian figurative art. No similar body of art works is known from the preceding two centuries of the Christian era. Moreover, given these paintings' location in a site owned and supervised by church officials, we can assume that Callistus and other subsequent ecclesial authorities allowed the production, style, and content of the frescoes. In other words, the images that decorate these burial spaces were officially permitted, even though they appeared in quasi-private space (family tombs) and were presumably commissioned by ordinary individuals to enliven the crypts of their deceased relatives. In time, the decoration became even more "official" as frescoes came to adorn the more public burial chambers of clergy and martyred saints.[3]

Fig. 2. Good Shepherd, Catacomb of Callistus, Rome (© The International Catacomb Society. Photo: Estelle Brettman).

These early images are fairly simple, and many were clearly modified from conventional Roman funerary art and traditional wall painting. They include the purely decorative, customary, and religiously generic iconography of garlands, fruit, flowers, and birds that appears in neighboring pagan burial chambers as well as domestic settings (fig. 1). Some common figures borrowed classical motifs and adapted them to convey specific Christian meanings such as the fish, dove, anchor, shepherd, praying figure (*orant*), boat, and funeral banquet (figs. 2–4). However, we also find a number of distinct, recognizable Christian motifs in the oldest chambers of Callistus's catacomb including the so-called cubicula of the sacraments, where, alongside the figures of the shepherd and the orant, we also see the figures of Jonah, Moses striking the rock, Abraham and Isaac, and some early scenes from the New Testament, including the baptism of Christ and the healing of the paralytic

(figs. 5–7). In time, as this and other Christian catacombs continued to be enhanced with frescoes, the iconographic catalog grew even more complex, adding such figures as Noah, Daniel, and Jesus performing various healings and working wonders. By the late third and into the fourth century, these same images began to appear carved in relief on the front and ends of the large stone coffins (sarcophagi), discovered within the larger chambers of the catacombs or sometimes in above-ground mausolea or nearby basilicas (figs. 8–9).

Fig. 3. Praying figure, Catacomb of Callistus, Rome (© The International Catacomb Society. Photo: Estelle Brettman).

These various Christian motifs and symbols referred to ideas, stories, or events that encapsulated an aspect of the beliefs or hopes of the faithful, in this context particularly referring to the expectations for a blessed afterlife promised by the sacraments of the church, or to the character of the deceased as a person who lived a life of steadfast piety, fidelity to the community, familial affection, and high moral character. Most of the early paintings were of relatively low quality and style when compared to much more beautiful examples of Roman wall painting, although they strike the viewer as expressive and vigorous in their own right. The relief carvings, on the other hand, often were beautifully crafted and well composed. Whether highly crafted or not, these paintings and carvings are necessarily exceptional and groundbreaking as some of the very first examples of Christian art. The visual image was allowed to carry the weight of message and meaning, in the context of the most significant of all life's moments—death and the burial of the body by the relatives and friends of the deceased. Perhaps more generally, these artworks demonstrate that Christians valued and used visual art, at least from the time that we may identify objects and spaces that were openly Christian-owned.

Fig. 4. Funeral banquet, Catacomb of Callistus, Rome (© The International Catacomb Society. Photo: Estelle Brettman).

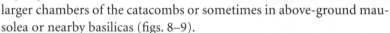

Early Christian Views of Visual Art: Historical Analyses

The very fact that we may study Christian art from the turn of the third century is likely due to the fortuitous survival of certain sites, in particular those that were underground (catacombs) and safe from future

urban renewal or deliberate destruction during earlier eras of persecution or later periods of Christian iconoclasm (especially in the eastern part of the Empire). Because of such vicissitudes of survival, whether the corpus of catacomb art points to a significant change or development in Christian tradition and practice around the turn of the third century may be a debatable point. However, the absence of any significant and definitively Christian artworks prior to this time has often been

Fig. 5. Jonah at rest: Scene from Jonah cycle, Catacomb of Callistus, Rome (© The International Catacomb Society. Photo: Estelle Brettman).

taken as evidence that, for a century and a half, the church had no large body of clearly recognizable visual art of its own. If this is so, the painting of these catacombs signaled a watershed moment, when the church changed its habits, traditions, convictions, or values and created a distinct form of art where there once was none—a form based on a combination of familiar and newly invented motifs.

Fig. 6. Moses striking the rock in the wilderness, Catacomb of Callistus, Rome (© The International Catacomb Society. Photo: Estelle Brettman).

The positing of such a radical shift suggests a possible theological or social transformation within the community—a change of perspective that allowed something to exist that would have been seen as problematic in the previous era. Alternatively, this shift may merely imply a

change in the community's social or economic circumstances. Historians have offered different theories to account for this change of pattern. To some interpreters, earlier generations of Christians consciously decided that visual art was to be rejected because it amounted to idolatry and was tainted with the vanity of pagan decadence. For these interpreters, Christians were acting like law-abiding Jews, taking the prohibition of graven images to heart, thus neither making nor using fig-

Fig. 7. Baptism of Christ, Catacomb of Callistus, Rome (© The International Catacomb Society. Photo: Estelle Brettman).

urative artworks (despite evidence that actually demonstrates a widespread use of figurative art among Jews—see below). The production of visual art at the beginning of the third century consequently indicates a change in attitude toward that prohibition, perhaps capitulating to popular culture, or extending a grudging tolerance to new converts who were less zealous or theologically conscious and wished to continue their traditional pagan practice of embellishing their family tombs (at least) with images.[4]

A different theory takes a more progressive and positive view of the development of recognizably Christian examples of visual art. Instead of seeing the advent of visual art in Christianity as a signal of the loosening of discipline or a mark of decadence, this view argues that the appearance of art was a natural development of an evolving faith, as it came to have its own modes of expression and communication. If one assumes that such new modes require a period of gestation before they emerge on the scene, then it stands to reason that Christians first used those symbols and motifs that were available and generally understood, having come from the iconographic vocabulary of the common culture. Of course, although these "borrowed" images were adapted for Christian use and endowed with meanings that conveyed key aspects of the new religion, they might not be obviously "Christian" to the majority of viewers then or now. Eventually these symbols and motifs would be entirely transformed, and new ones would emerge, about the same time as adherents as well as new converts achieved the necessary social, economic, and intellectual stability necessary to generate a religious material culture of their own.[5]

Both points of view assume that the apparent emergence of Christian art at the turn of the third century indicates that at that time Christianity became engaged with its surrounding culture in a different way than it had been previously. Either Christian practitioners ceased to be so distinct from certain aspects of pagan society and religion (in particular from its rich artistic tradition), or they began to produce a distinctive iconography that would clearly identify them, instead of adapting religiously generic images. The main difference between the two perspectives is whether such cultural engagement and/or artistic development is understood as signifying the erosion or the elaboration of a distinct theological identity. In the first view, Christians became more like their pagan neighbors, and in the second, they became more markedly Christian (at least in their visual art). Both views accept that Christian iconography in the early third century marks a cultural evolution—whether that evolution was a good thing for the religion itself is also the subject of some disagreement.

Other explanations have been offered for the lack of Christian visual art from the first and second centuries. One argument, that the first generations were expecting an immediate end to the world as they knew it, presumes that believers saw no value in (or had no time for) making visual expressions of faith. Only when the *parousia* (Christ's return) was seen to be indefinitely delayed was there widespread effort to establish the kind of cultural permanence that would include tombs, churches, and collections of sacred texts. Another theory, that almost all older artifacts were lost or destroyed owing either to the vicissitudes of persecution (the destruction of Christian objects and buildings) or the consequence of urban renewal (when older and less opulent churches were torn down to make way for new building in the fourth century), is supported by archaeological finds. The Christian building at Dura Europos, for instance, survived because it was deliberately covered over as a defensive move by a Roman garrison. Burial places likewise survived because they were left intact, perhaps out of respect, but also because they were underground and therefore not as subject to destruction. In fact, this latter argument also serves to explain the very limited context and geography of those artifacts that can be dated prior to the Constantinian era, which brought an end to persecution but also marked the beginning of monumental, large-scale, and significantly permanent building projects, many of them adjacent to or incorporating these very burial grounds.

Fig. 8. Jonah sarcophagus, late 3rd cen. C.E., Museo Pio Cristiano, Vatican City (Photo: Author).

Despite these various theories, many historians still assume that the first- and second-century church consistently repudiated the creation of figurative art for theological reasons. As Mary Charles Murray so clearly showed nearly a quarter-century ago, leading historians of Christianity as well as many important art historians often assumed that the religion was, from its origins, characteristically hostile to all kinds of pictorial art. She cites articles and books published from the 1950s to the date of her own article in the late 1970s by such prominent academics as John Beckwith, James Breckenridge, Ernst Kitzinger, and Henry Chadwick, scholars whose work is still very influential.[6] For example, in his now classic study, *Byzantine Art in the Making*, first published in 1977, Kitzinger wrote at the end of his first chapter:

> There is no evidence of any art with a Christian content earlier than the year A.D. 200. In all likelihood this is not merely due to accidental losses. The surviving monuments of Christian pictorial art which can be attributed to the first half of the third century bear the marks of a true beginning. Moreover, one can find in Christian literature of the period reflections of a changing attitude toward images and their role in religious life. That attitude was undoubtedly negative prior to this period.[7]

As evidence of this negative attitude, many of these historians of the past century, like the iconoclasts of the eighth, collected ancient written testimonies that could be interpreted to suggest that the early church was officially anti-image. This historical perspective was examined and refuted by Charles Murray, followed in detail two decades later by Paul Corby Finney. Briefly, however, the sources that historians most often cite as evidence of early opposition to pictorial art are short excerpts from the writings of Tertullian and Clement of Alexandria. For instance, Henry Chadwick, in his widely read *The Early Church* (first published in 1967), wrote: "The second of the Ten Commandments forbade the making of any graven image. Both Tertullian and Clement of Alexandria

Fig. 9. Jesus healing and working wonders, Christian sarcophagus early 4th cen. C.E., Museo Pio Cristiano, Vatican City (Photo: Author).

regarded this prohibition as absolute and binding on Christians. Images and statues belonged to the demonic world of paganism." Actually in reference to a rather polemical aside by Irenaeus, although identifying his informant by name, Chadwick continues, "In fact, the only second-century Christians known to have had images of Christ were radical Gnostics, the followers of the licentious Carpocrates."[8]

In this short quotation, Chadwick claims that the so-called Second Commandment (Exod 20:4-5a; Deut 4:16-19; 5:8-9) was normative for the early church in respect to visual images. Here Chadwick repeats the predilections of earlier scholars and takes early Christian aniconism for granted. Chadwick further cites the writings of Tertullian and Clement to imply that Christian teaching at the time generally forbade "images and statues" of any kind as belonging to the demonic pagan world. However, the actual sources themselves are far less clear about the matter of visual art in general than they were about idolatry, specifically.

For example, an often-cited excerpt from Tertullian's treatise *On Modesty* has been judged to condemn any use of religious pictures (in this case, of a shepherd) on chalices used during the eucharistic meal.[9] The text, however, actually denounces those who favored a laxist approach to forgiveness after baptism, in particular the author of the treatise *The Shepherd of Hermas*. Since Tertullian associated such eucharistic cups with this treatise (because of the shepherd image), he assumes that those who had such implements believed that they could be forgiven transgressions such as drunkenness and adultery. Tertullian's objection to the image on these cups was an objection to what it signified (a lack of moral rigor), not to its mere existence as a piece of art.

Furthermore, Chadwick suggests that the production of visual art occurred first within heretical sects, specifically among Gnostics. His evidence for this association of art and heresy comes mainly from Irenaeus's treatise *Against Heresies*, written in the late second century. Listed among the many undesirable practices and traits of the Carpocratians, such as practicing sorcery and astrology, Irenaeus also accuses them of making and honoring images—according to him, a practice peculiar to this sect. Irenaeus even notes that they had a portrait of Jesus, fashioned by none other than Pilate and honored with garlands and other unnamed traditional pagan offerings (probably lit candles and incense):

> They also possess images, some of them painted, and others formed from different kinds of material; while they maintain that a likeness of Christ was made by Pilate at that time when Jesus lived among them. They crown these images, and set them up along with the images of the philosophers of the world; that is to say, with the images of Pythagoras, and Plato, and Aristotle, and the rest. They also have other modes of honoring these images, after the same manner of the Gentiles.[10]

While this short excerpt demonstrates Irenaeus's assumption that honoring portrait images was a reprehensible characteristic of certain heretics, he offers no general condemnation of visual art, whether secular or religious, narrative or iconic. What he apparently objects to is the inclusion of Jesus with the other philosophers, and the crowning and honoring of their images.

Art and Idolatry in the Early Third-Century Christian Writings

Because Tertullian (ca. 200 c.e.) was deeply concerned about the problem of Christians being ensnared in a polytheistic culture, his treatise *On Idolatry* extends the definition of idolatry far beyond anything to do specifically with pictorial art. For Tertullian, idolatrous practices include preoccupation with the way one dresses, the foods one eats, or the pursuit of sexual pleasures or material wealth—all things that humans mistakenly take for having intrinsic value and that they honor more than God. In regard to visual art, for example, Tertullian worries about the temptations that artisans must face and the fact that both their skills and their tools could be misused: "There are also other species of very many arts which, although they extend not to the making of idols, yet with the same criminality, furnish the ingredients, without which idols have no power. . . . No art exists that is not mother or kinswoman to some allied art; nothing is independent of its neighbor."[11] Tertullian even urges those in his audience who make their living by craft to use their skills to make useful objects that could not possibly serve the purpose of polytheistic worship. Rather than sculptors, these folks should be plasterers, roof menders, or marble masons in the building trades.

However, recognizing that some fine artisans earn their living by making ostentatious and luxurious objects, he allows that it is better to gild slippers than to fashion a statue of Mercury or Serapis. Tertullian may have had Acts 19:23-41 in mind as he wrote this, comparing the predicament of Demetrius and the other Ephesians whose income depended on making and selling images of the goddess Diana. Tertullian, wishing to support artisans in their work and not to reduce them to poverty, suggests that they find other avenues for their craft and merely avoid making images of the pagan gods.

Clement of Alexandria (ca. 160–215 c.e.) approached the problem of figurative art from an angle more characteristically his. Less concerned about Christian engagement with the habits and pleasures of Roman culture than Tertullian was, and not as fundamentally disturbed by the construction of images of the gods as a profession, Clement adapts Platonic teachings to offer a more complex discussion of the inferiority of an image to its likeness, and the potential for the confusion of likeness and prototype on the part of those who view art. Attending to the deceptive power of imitation as well as the attraction of both material and natural objects, Clement sees danger in the human tendency to misunderstand the image—and to fail to distinguish between representation and reality—between the sensible and transcendent realms. And because objects of worship are not always only human-made idols, he extends his concern to include even the mistaken veneration of things found in the natural world. It was in this respect that he reminds his audience of the biblical prohibition:

> What is more, we are expressly forbidden to practice a deceitful art. For the prophet says "Thou shalt not make a likeness of anything that is in heaven above or the earth beneath." . . . But as for you, while you take great pains to discover how a statue may be shaped to the highest possible pitch of beauty, you never give a thought to prevent yourselves turning out like statues owing to want of sense. . . . Here the host of philosophers turn aside, when they admit that humans are beautifully made for the contemplation of heaven, and yet worship the things which appear in heaven and are apprehended by sight. . . . Let none of you worship the sun; rather let him yearn for the maker of the sun.[12]

Clement's objection to images is clearly different from Tertullian's. His concern is not so much the adoption of polytheistic practices or being captive to the alluring aspects of popular culture, but misunderstanding what it is that deserves honor—what the "true image" is. He follows a well-known Platonic axiom that images made by artists (or even things of the natural world) are only reflections of reality and should not be confused with the eternal and ideal Form (or in Clement's case, the Maker) that transcends any earthly creation. However, he also argues that, properly understood, images can serve the useful function of reminding the viewer of a higher truth—which is why, although he generally disapproves of jewelry, he lists the appropriate images for Christian signet rings (a dove, a fish, a ship, a lyre, or an anchor) and urges the faithful to avoid seals with images of the gods, weapons, drinking cups, or scenes of sexual intercourse. The former symbols draw the eye and the mind away from themselves and toward the reality they represent, while the latter indicate a life of idolatry, indulgence, and even licentiousness. On the other hand, modest Christian symbols on everyday objects of some practical necessity did not constitute a form of idolatry.[13]

In the *Stromateis* (or *Miscellanies*), the last of his treatises and the most esoteric of them all, he continues with that same theme and this time credits Moses with the original formulation, later taken up by Pythagoras:

"Don't wear a ring, nor engrave on it the images of the gods," enjoins Pythagoras; as Moses ages before enacted expressly, that neither a graven, nor molten, nor molded, nor painted likeness should be made; so that we may not cleave to things of sense, but pass to intellectually known objects: for familiarity with the sight disparages the reverence of what is divine; and to worship that which is immaterial by matter, is to dishonor it by sense.[14]

Clement's problem with visual art poses a distinct set of issues. In another place in the *Stromateis*, Clement claims that the injunction an artist breaks is not only that against making idols but also that against robbing the divine prerogative in the act of creation.[15] In these passages we see how Clement develops his own version of the doctrine of imitation, asserting that a work of art is deceptive, intended to fool the viewer into mistaking a mere copy for its model, into confusing the imitation with the reality. Perhaps Clement was cognizant of Pliny's critique of artists of old, who prided themselves on work so convincingly lifelike that viewers mistook the image for something real. Zeuxis, for instance, is said to have painted a child carrying grapes that caused birds to fly down to pick at the fruit.[16]

After Tertullian and Clement, the matter of early Christian attitudes toward pictorial or figurative art becomes more complex, perhaps in part because the art itself has begun to be made and owned by the Christian community. Probably the most vehement condemnation of figurative art prior to the iconoclastic period comes from Origen's argument about Christianity with the polytheist Celsus in the early third century. Origen's argument is similar in certain respects to Clement's objections to visual art as setting up false objects of worship, although at first it appears to draw a parallel between faithful Jews and Christians regarding the biblical injunction. In his long and complicated defense of Christianity, Origen argues that Christians are at least as enlightened on the matter of the vanity of images as the philosophers were. He also defends the Jews against what was apparently a fairly vicious attack by Celsus on their culture and religion, which he saw as an earlier form of Christianity. Jews, according to Celsus, were "fugitives from Egypt, who never performed anything worthy of note and never were held in any reputation or account."[17]

Taking exception to this unfair characterization and turning the tables on Celsus by pointing out that he represents a religion that worshiped images of "corruptible human beings, and birds, and four-footed beasts," Origen offers an example of a particularly praiseworthy accomplishment of the Jews, citing their observance of the prohibition as found in Deuteronomy (4:16-18):

> Among [the Jews] God is recognized as nothing else, save the One who is over all things, and that among them no maker of images was permitted to enjoy the rights of citizenship. For neither painter nor image-maker existed in their state, the law expelling all such from it; that there might be no pretext for the construction of images,—and art that attracts the attention of foolish people, and that drags down the eyes of the soul from God to earth. There was, accordingly, among them a law to the following effect: "Do not transgress the law and make to yourselves a graven image, any likeness of male or female; either a likeness of any one of the creatures that are upon the earth, or a likeness of any winged fowl that flies under heaven, or a likeness of any creeping thing that creeps upon the earth, or a likeness of any of the fishes which are in the waters under the earth (Deut 4:16-18)."[18]

Origen also praises the Jews for the associated injunction (a "venerable and grand prohibition") against looking up to heaven lest seeing the sun, moon, and stars one should be led astray to worship them (Deut 4:19). Clearly, Origen worries more about the worshiping of idols than about the making of images but, nevertheless, thought that the Jews should be praised for their intolerance of visual artists, lest such work be a pretext for or temptation to idolatry.

In his homilies on Exodus, Origen turns again to the biblical prohibition, but he offers an important distinction between the terms "idol" (*eidōlon*) and "likeness" (*homoiōma*). According to his reading of the Greek translation, Exod 20:4 prohibits the making of both ("You shall not make for yourself an idol nor any likeness of those things which are in heaven or which are in the earth or which are in the waters under the earth"). To justify this distinction, Origen turns to Paul's first letter to the Corinthians. He notes that the apostle says that "no idol in the world really exists," while at the same time saying that "there may be many so-called gods in heaven or on earth—as in fact there are many gods and many lords" (1 Cor 8:4-5). Since Paul seems to have deliberately omitted any claim that likenesses, like idols, were nonexistent, Origen argues that it is one thing to make an idol and something else to make a likeness. The essential difference between the two is that the likeness shows something that actually can be seen (for example, a bird, fish, sun, or moon), while the idol comes entirely from the human imagination and never occurs in nature (for instance, a ram's head on a human body). This is why Paul can call idols nonexistent. But, as Origen points out, both likenesses and idols were prohibited by the Second Commandment, just as both were forbidden either worship or adoration (Exod 20:5), and the possible excuse that no harm comes from adoring "nonexistent" things is thus invalidated.[19]

In fact, Paul clearly distinguishes between idols and likenesses, as he never uses the word "idol" (*eidōlon*) in any positive sense, in contrast to the term "likeness" (*homoiōma*), which often has a positive meaning. In addition to the above-cited text from 1 Corinthians, Paul speaks of idols, idolatry (*eidōlolatreia*), and idolaters as deceived sinners, led astray by the mute idols (1 Cor 12:2) and given up by God to lust and degradations of various sorts (Rom 1:24-27). Paul does not, apparently, distinguish between idols and likenesses according to their model's occurrence or nonoccurrence in nature. They simply have no life and cannot speak (compare 1 Cor 10:19).

Origen's argument points to a problem, however, in regard to the different ways the New Testament Gospels and Epistles use the terms "likeness" (*homoiōma*) and "image" (*eikōn*). For example, in the story of the coin with the portrait of the emperor (Mark 12:16), the word used for that representation is "image" (*eikōn*), while in Acts 14:11, the crowds mistake Barnabas and Paul for gods in human likeness (*homoiōthentes*). In Rom 8:3, Paul says that God sent his own Son in the likeness of human flesh (*homoiōmati sarkos*), although he later says that those who love God will be conformed to an image (*eikōn*) of his Son. In 1 Cor 11:7, men are the image (*eikōn*) and glory of God, just as humans bear the image (*eikōn*) of the man of dust (1 Cor 15:49) and will someday bear the image (*eikōn*) of the man of heaven (1 Cor 15:49). In 2 Cor 4:4, Christ is the image (*eikōn*) of God. Whereas in Phil 2:7, Christ takes the form (*morphōn*) of a slave and is born in human likeness (*honoiōmati anthrōpōn*), in Colossians he is the image (*eikōn*) of the invisible God (1:15). According to Jas 3:9, humans are made in the likeness of God (*homoiōsin theou*), and in 2 Cor 3:18, Paul writes that humanity will be transformed into the image (*eikōn*) of the glory of the Lord. Apart from the first example (the coin portrait), the general rule seems to be that earthly representations have "likeness" while divine similitude and future transformations are spoken of in terms of "image."

Despite Paul's claim that idols are nonexistent objects, these late second- or early third-century Christian writers worried about the pagan practice of idolatry, and to some extent they associated the making and use of visual art in general with that practice. They realized that certain kinds of artworks could be misunderstood and abused or draw veneration or worship, and, in particular, they warned against making images of the pagan gods or other implements of pagan cult worship. Furthermore, they worried about the temptations of the surrounding pagan culture and its alluring attractions. Most Christian converts were former polytheists, and aspects of that polytheism were ubiquitous. Christians could not enter the home of a non-Christian neighbor without encountering the domestic shrine to the family's tutelary gods and ancestors, nor could they go into the public baths or theater, attend the games, or even enter ordinary public buildings without confronting statues of the gods and portrayals of their myths on doorposts, floors, walls, and ceilings.[20] Because of their high risk of contamination, painters and sculptors, along with actors and even teachers of classical literature, were barred from baptism until they could demonstrate that they had left professions that produced, used, or even brought them into the proximity of these kinds of images.[21]

Resisting idolatry was not easy for Christians who lived in urban settings at that time. Their surroundings were filled with the temptations of luxuries as well as with signs and tokens of polytheistic religions. Greco-Roman cults depended on images, rituals, and public spectacles; they did not draw upon texts of sacred scriptures (apart from those myths found in the writings of Homer and Hesiod) or dogmatic statements of faith. The traditional gods had shrines that were open and reflected civic pride and identity. Almost any aspect of daily life, even just passing through certain neighborhoods, brought early Christians into contact with images of the traditional Greek and Roman gods. Therefore, the earliest Christian writers who have been presented as objecting to pictorial art were actually pointing out inherent dangers that attached to the making or even admiration of things that were made for polytheistic cult. Given the wide distribution of such objects in the everyday world, even the most stalwart Christians might be implicated in a kind of accidental idolatry, even if they tried to steer clear of anything that might tempt or unwittingly taint them.[22]

That Christians were unable always to avoid the images is apparent from the instruction about what they might do if they came into contact with the idols. Apparently some Christians practiced explicitly disrespectful behavior toward images or their altars. Tertullian refers to Christians spitting or blowing on smoking altars as they passed by, and according to the *Octavius* of Minucius Felix, Christians offended pagans by spitting on statues of the gods, perhaps as a way of protecting themselves against inherent and ever-present danger.[23] Tertullian assures martyrs that one of the advantages to their imprisonment is the fact that they no longer have occasion to see strange gods or bump into their images and no longer can be even accidentally involved in some pagan feast or sacrifice.[24] Cyprian also urges Christians to avoid looking at the idols, even declaring that Christians who did not avert their eyes from the images were guilty of a form of apostasy, and their subsequent tears of penitence (a literal cleansing of the eyes) were a way to make satisfaction to God for their sins.[25]

Thus, the typical early Christian theological position on visual art was less an objection to art as such than an attack on *non-Christian* images that invited worship and activities that drew the faithful into the values and practices (both religious and secular) of the surrounding culture. Significantly, these first- and second-century writers said almost nothing about *Christian* art, either because there was very little (or none) in their purview or because if there was, they did not see it as problematic. Clement's recommended motifs for Christian signet rings offer such an example. Furthermore, these writers said very little about art that was basically secular or neutral and without obvious pagan religious associations, such as images of fish, birds, shepherds, or grapevines. Such art may have been like the gilding of slippers, to borrow a phrase from Tertullian, and not especially troubling by itself. Notably, however, these were the very sorts of images first adapted for Christian use and perhaps given specific Christian meaning.

A century or so later, Athanasius wrote a treatise against the "errors of the pagans" that attacked idolatry in language similar to these earlier writers, while hinting at his subsequent construction of an incarnational theology that would elevate material existence by its incorporation into divinity. For Athanasius, the definition of idolatry is based less on actual worship of specific material objects than on the distracted soul turning toward earthly pleasures and away from divine things. Humans who indulge their lusts come to find their gods in material things and, as they fall lower and lower, come to set up idols made of ordinary and lifeless material, deifying the shapes of animals as well as ordinary mortals and mistaking the image for its model, dragging them even further into the mud of their vile passions (cf. Rom 1:22-25).

The true God, on the other hand, is incorruptible and cannot be represented through or in destructible materials, nor can God appear in such exotic diversity of forms. Athanasius, interestingly, also claims that image worship is condemned by Scripture, but he omits a mention of the Decalogue, turning instead to Ps 115:4-8 ("Their idols are silver and gold, the work of human hands") and Isa 44:9-10 ("All who make idols are nothing. . . . Who would fashion a god or cast an image that can do no good?"). In addition, Athanasius makes an argument that worshipers of idols actually dishonor the skill of artists, who should be more highly honored than the products of their craft. However, he would claim the more skillful the artist, the more likely the image will be seen to summon the deity, rather than generate homage for the maker of that image.[26]

Jewish Background for Christian Rejection of Visual Art

We have noted that some historians of Christianity (and of Christian art) cite Christianity's Jewish roots as a reason for its apparent reticence regarding visual art. Such an assumption takes chronologically contemporary Jewish aniconism for granted, as well as a self-conscious Christian acceptance of this heritage as the basis for a similar aniconic position. Although the preceding review of the documentary evidence shows that some second- and third-century Christian condemnations of idolatry cited the repudiation of graven images in the Ten Commandments (which they did not see as specifically Jewish), apart from Origen's argument with Celsus, actual Jewish practice never figured predominantly in their arguments.[27] In fact, scholars have argued that the

Decalogue itself generally played a minor role in Christian theological reflection before the mid-second century and moreover was often misunderstood, abbreviated, or quietly sidelined.[28]

Added to that, the ways that Jews themselves understood the injunction against graven images at this time (or any time) are neither clear nor consistent. The Hebrew Scriptures themselves offer some internal contradictions, if we note that the apparent condemnation of figurative art is shortly followed by vivid descriptions of the cherubim set up in the tabernacle over the mercy seat (Exod 25:17-22). A bronze serpent healed the Israelites in the wilderness from snakebite (Num 21:8-9), and the figurative decorations of Solomon's temple included lions and oxen as well as cherubim (1 Kings 6–8). Enacting the Decalogue's prohibition of graven images may date no earlier than to the religious reforms of images of King Josiah in the seventh century B.C.E.— reforms that may have had political motivations as much as religious purity at heart (2 Kings 23).[29] The iconoclastic destruction of the high places coincided with a centralized juridical and religious power in Jerusalem and its temple. Thus the prohibition came to be understood as prohibiting any sculpted figure that might be taken as an image of a god or otherwise draw the people of Israel into polytheism (the worship of foreign or multiple gods) and idolatry (the worship of divine images) and away from the exclusive worship of their one, invisible God. No one is allowed to paint or sculpt an image of God according to the book of Deuteronomy, because no one actually knows what God looks like (Deut 4:15-18).[30]

Jews in the Greco-Roman period, like Christians, consistently condemned images associated with other religious cults, especially when they were required to tolerate or even worship those images by foreign occupiers or Roman governors. Such repudiation is evident in the polemic against worshiping Baals and Astartes in Judges 2, the humorous description of Bel and Nebo hanging off pack animals in Isaiah 46, or the 1 Maccabees account of Jewish resistance to the desecrations and anti-Jewish practices instituted by Antiochus IV Epiphanes. In the first century C.E., Josephus criticized Solomon for allowing images in the temple, and he records Jewish repudiation of certain kinds of figurative art (including images of living creatures and God), especially their refusal to set up images of the Roman emperor, which, he explains, was an allowance made by the Romans themselves to the Jews.[31] In his history of the Jewish war, Josephus tells about Jewish riots in opposition to Roman imposition of images of the gods or the effigies of the emperor (busts or portraits attached to the standards). Not only did Jewish law generally forbid figurative images, but these portraits were particularly offensive because the Romans wanted to set them up at particular Jewish holy places. Moreover, he insists, the Romans themselves had granted Jews the right to abide by their ancient religious laws. Like the later Christian apologists, Josephus also casts Jewish convictions as parallel to sound philosophical teachings, that images were useless things, worthy neither of humans nor of the divine.[32]

Philo, the Jewish Alexandrian philosopher, objects to figurative art on even more self-conscious philosophical terms. Philo's treatise on the Decalogue asserts that those who worship the sun, moon, or other heavenly bodies are less grievously in error than artisans who fashion images out of wood, stones, or precious metals, "the workmanship of which, either by statuary, or painter, or artisan, has done great injury to the life of man," by undercutting the soul's mainstay—namely, the proper conception of the ever-living God.[33] The poor souls that the artisans have deceived with their work misunderstand not only the nature of God, but also the difference between the creator and the object of creation. Furthermore, they attribute some kind of life or soul to dead and lifeless matter to which the artist gives shape, tossing the remaining material away for a lesser purpose.[34] It would be better, he says, to deify the sculptors rather than their statues, or for the artisans themselves to worship their tools or their hands instead of their products. In another place, Philo describes Moses as a "man as far removed as possible from any invention of fables and who thinks fit only to walk in the paths of truth itself." The outcome of such resistance to pursuits of the imagination is that he "banished from the constitution, which he has established, those celebrated and beautiful arts of statuary and painting, because they, falsely imitating the nature of the truth, contrive deceits and snares, in order, through the medium of the eyes, to beguile the souls which are liable to be easily won over."[35] Here Philo's negative view of art is detached from the prohibition of the Commandments and is based on its ability to deceive and seduce naïve viewers.

Despite Josephus's historical record and Philo's philosophical argumentation, archaeological discoveries of the past century have demonstrated that Jews of the first several centuries of the Common Era held varying and sometimes even positive views of figurative art, even art made for religious contexts. These discoveries have included a variety of media, motifs, and venues: frescoes of various birds, animals, or dolphins found in the Jewish catacombs of Rome and on sarcophagi; figurative motifs (including zodiac figures and representations of the god Helios) found on mosaic floors of synagogues in the Galilee between the fourth and sixth centuries; and, more significant, the mid-third-century monumental frescoes filled with figurative painting in the Dura Europos synagogue.[36] Documents dated to these same centuries suggest that at least some Jewish leaders were (like their Christian counterparts) more concerned with the practice of idolatry than with the making of pictorial art as such. While urging Jews to avoid contact with an idolatrous Gentile culture, they took a variety of stances on visual art, often permitting Jews to make and own images so long as they did not worship them.[37] For example, according to the Jerusalem Talmud, the third-century Rabbi Johanan apparently tolerated images painted on walls, and Rabbi Abun permitted the making of images in mosaic.[38] Other rabbis clearly considered figurative images dangerous and urged Jews to shun them.[39] Even when we find a Christian reference to Jewish aniconism, such as Origen's cited above, we must decide whether this was based on actual observation or only a projection of a useful assumption.

Thus, Jewish aniconism in the second and third centuries c.e. may have been mainly directed against Jewish worship of foreign images, not against visual art in general, or even against enhancing the interiors of synagogues with figurative decoration. It is unlikely, therefore, that Christians emulated their Jewish neighbors' aniconism. Instead, early Christian motivations for resisting figurative art were, like Philo's, shaped by philosophical arguments about the deceptive and distracting qualities inherent in art or were based on concerns that making or using art would eventually draw the faithful into the idolatry associated with the surrounding culture. The early apologists present Christianity as an intellectually and spiritually enlightened faith, and they clearly hoped that their arguments would appeal to the sensibilities of a philosophically sophisticated audience. They could easily have believed themselves on fairly safe ground attacking images as illusory and even dangerous, since the respected Greek sages essentially agreed with them.[40]

In any case, neither concerns for observing the biblical commandment against images nor awareness of the philosophical critique of imitative art seemed to have daunted the individuals who first decorated the walls of the Christian catacombs in the early third century. The artisans and their clients did not understand what they were doing as idolatry, probably because the work was not intended, designed, or executed so as to attract any kind of worship. It was not like the fashioning of images of the pagan gods. The images they created were essentially symbolic, narrative, or didactic and not likely to be mistaken for idols nor invite worship.

Therefore, it seems reasonable to conclude that if Christians began to make and use significant and characteristic visual art of their own around the beginning of the third century, it was not because most first- and second-century Christians were generally iconophobic or unanimous in their views on the matter of images. Once this art began to appear, it became immensely popular and influential, as it was widely dispersed and copied by others, first near and then far. At the same time, we know that church authorities had a continuing concern with the problem of idolatry, not identified with the making of images but perhaps related to it. Art, in particular art made for a religious context, was something that, while permissible, required management and control to ensure that it was understood in its proper sense. In other words, it should include only appropriate images (excluding certain forbidden ones) and be as different from a pagan idol as possible.

The Earliest Examples and Types of Christian Visual Art: Church Regulation

Obviously, such definitions and regulations only make sense for a time when Christian images were being produced in enough quantity to make these policies necessary. As we have seen, Christian writers of the second and early third centuries seem unaware of any significant amount or type of Christian art worthy of condemnation. Their objections were aimed at the art of others, pagans or perhaps Christian heretics, and not at their own coreligionists. The warnings against idolatry were warnings against the cult images of other religions, not against Christian artworks. Based on this lack of awareness, we might reasonably conclude that Christians produced very little religious art, or that what they did produce was so innocuous that it neither attracted attention nor raised concerns.

In the third century, however, the material situation began to change. In addition to the modest domestic objects that may have seemed uncontroversial (small pottery lamps with images of the Good Shepherd, for example), the catacomb frescoes in Rome, relief carvings on sarcophagi and tomb epitaphs, and early evidence for wall paintings in

Fig. 10. Reconstruction of the interior of the Christian baptistery, Dura Europos, mid-3rd cen. C.E. (Photo: Rights and Reproductions Department, Yale University Art Gallery).

churches demonstrate that change. Of these, the most important existing example is the decorated baptistery found in a Christian house church at Dura Europos, with its frescoes depicting biblical scenes (ca. 249 C.E.; fig. 10). Above the font, an image of the Good Shepherd and his flock stand over the smaller figures of Adam and Eve. The side walls contain painted scenes particularly appropriate for a baptismal space: the healing of the paralytic, the stilling of the storm, the walking on the water, and the woman at the well, as well as a somewhat enigmatic painting of three women carrying lamps approaching a tent-like structure (variously identified as the three women arriving at the empty tomb; three of the five wise brides carrying their lamps to the tent of the bridegroom; or virgins escorting Mary to the temple, an illustration of a passage in the *Protoevangelium of James*).[41]

Based on the example from Dura, it seems likely that other early Christian buildings were similarly adorned. We do know that Christian buildings were demolished during the great persecution of the early fourth century, and their walls may well have been enhanced with paintings.[42] Despite certain distinctions in style, the similarity between some of the themes found on the Dura baptistery walls and motifs from the Roman catacombs also suggests some common influence and perhaps even some shared models. Although we have no extant examples, it seems possible that certain influential prototypes (illuminated biblical manuscripts, perhaps) provided patterns or cartoons contained in circulating books of artisans' motifs that could account for some level of consistency.[43] In any case, given the certain fact of an emerging and distinctive Christian iconography, church authorities may well have tried to regulate the trend, especially if they continued to be concerned about the snares of the surrounding pagan religious or even secular culture.

Surprisingly, however, we do not have much evidence of such reaction. The earliest known regulation of Christian visual or figurative art comes from a canon of a local church council held in Elvira, Spain, about 305 C.E. Curiously, the canon's meaning is a bit ambiguous. Two different translations of a key Latin clause in that canon are possible, resulting in two rather different meanings. The Latin reads: *Placuit picturas in ecclesia esse non debere, ne quod colitur et adoratur in parietibus depingatur*. One possible translation is: "There shall be no pictures in churches, lest what is reverenced and adored be depicted on the walls," while a second reverses the verbs and modifiers of the second clause, that is, "lest what is depicted on the walls be reverenced and adored."[44] The first translation, which seems the more grammatically straightforward, prohibits pictures because of the danger that certain sacred or holy things or persons might be inappropriately portrayed (or even exhibited to view).

If one accepts this as a limited prohibition, then perhaps other images might be permissible (perhaps in other places than the walls of a church), or at least not as problematic. The second translation demonstrates a concern that viewers might confuse the image with its model and mistakenly offer the image some kind of adoration or worship, thereby falling into idolatry, in which case the prohibition primarily attends to the potential for misuse, not exactly on the images themselves. Nevertheless, both translations appear to prohibit art on the walls of the church, albeit for somewhat different reasons. Furthermore, the canon offers demonstrable evidence that pictures had arrived in the church before the time of Constantine.

Subsequent documents continue to show that the existence of religious art was less controversial than how it was used or understood by those who viewed it. Authorities felt that they needed to exert some leadership or control over a potentially problematic, but also a potentially useful, resource. Paulinus, the late fourth-century Bishop of Nola, saw visual art as a way to enliven the basilica he founded in honor of Saint Felix. Explaining his motives for adorning a church building with representations of living individuals, which he admits was an unusual custom, he claims that he did it largely to attract the "rustics" who would otherwise spend their time feasting and drinking at the tomb of the martyr, rather than coming inside the church.[45] Thus, in time, pictorial art was acknowledged to have benefits, especially as a didactic or inspirational aid.

Such usefulness was again asserted, two centuries later, in two well-known epistles of Gregory the Great to Bishop Serenus of Marseilles. In these letters, Gregory admonishes his brother bishop for banishing images from churches in his diocese (one of the first known instances of iconoclasm directed at Christian images), yet praises him for his firm stance against idols. Gregory acknowledges that even though images have their dangers, they should have not been destroyed, for art also has its positive uses:

> For pictorial representation is made use of in churches for this reason; that such as are ignorant of letters may at least read by looking at the walls what they cannot read in books. Your fraternity therefore should have both preserved the images and prohibited the people from adoration of them, so that persons ignorant of letters may have something so that they may gather knowledge of the story and the people might not sin through adoration of a picture.[46]

A year or so later, Gregory discovered that Serenus had disregarded his exhortation (using the excuse that he thought Gregory's letter had been forged), and he fired off an even stronger statement: "For it has been reported to us that, inflamed with inconsiderate zeal, you have broken images of saints as though under the plea that they should not be adored. And indeed, in that you forbade them to be adored we praise you; but we blame you for having broken them."[47] And, reiterating his point about the value of pictures for the illiterate (especially for the "nations," that is, the local non-Latin readers or speakers), Gregory furthermore noted that such pictures "of saints' stories" had a venerable and ancient precedent. He concludes his argument by claiming that such images also raised the viewer's sensibility beyond the sensible objects and toward the Divine through an awakening of love for that which they portrayed. Leaving aside the problem of what image Gregory might have meant when he referred to reading by "looking at the walls," it is clear that he considered certain "appropriate" images of things deserving of devotion when he made his case for the value of visual images. Since Gregory speaks of saints' stories, we may assume that what he refers to are representations of biblical stories or episodes from the lives of saints.

The issue, then, was about how images were actually regarded, not about their existence per se or even their placement in churches. Given that the ecclesial authorities (at least initially) supervised the construction and decoration of the earliest Christian catacombs in Rome—it seems logical to assume that someone officially approved the decoration of the Christian building at Dura—we may conclude that the kinds of images produced for and placed in these spaces were judged acceptable by local church authorities at the time. The elaboration of Christian buildings gained enormous momentum in the fourth century, initially fueled by the patronage of Emperor Constantine. By Gregory's time, the view that the images had no place in the church would likely have been regarded as out of step as well as unpopular, which is perhaps why a significant part of Serenus's congregation went into schism against their bishop.

In the mid-fourth century, however, the motifs and themes of Christian art had just begun to change, deemphasizing the symbolic and narrative art of the third and early fourth centuries in favor of the more dogmatically derived representations of Christ's passion, enthronement, and triumph. The visual art was still edifying, but those previously popular biblical narratives that showed the Old Testament heroes or the works of Jesus (for example, his healing or wonderworking) were gradually supplanted by images of Jesus handing over the law to his apostles or being judged by Pilate. The depiction of Jesus' mission or divinity was thereby changed from an emphasis on the deeds of his earthly ministry to an emphasis on the events of his passion, ascension, and judgment. By the end of the fourth century, this development went another step further, when explicitly devotional images of Christ and portraits of the saints also began to appear. These images had a role in the developing cult of martyrs and saints, not only by honoring a holy person with a portrait, but also by playing a part in the cult itself, in parallel development with the cult of relics, which started to appear at the shrines of martyrs.

As we have noted, the earlier symbolic and narrative images, perhaps even the dogmatic images of the later fourth century, were not intended to attract prayer or veneration. Their purpose was to symbolize or illustrate a key aspect of Christian belief (such as the love of God or Christ for the individual believer, the resurrection of the dead to Paradise) or to offer a visual reference to a biblical story that might convey central Christian beliefs or values, or to serve as christological or sacramental types. Even the later visual representations of Christ's passion, resurrection, or enthronement were more edifying than iconic. They were meant as visual presentations of Christian teachings, and they paralleled certain verbal modes including homilies, hymns, and catechetical instruction. They were meant to instruct viewers in the fundamentals of the faith or to inspire them to offer praise and thanksgiving. The images narrated certain actions in the past that one could, in a sense, "watch" rather than mediating a living holy presence that one could engage in the present. These narrative images were Scripture presented in pictures rather than words; they pointed to God's salvific acts of history as a sign of hope and promise for the future.[48]

By contrast, the new images that began to appear in the late fourth century offered encounter more than edification. These were the portraits of Christ or the saints that omitted specific narrative context or background and instead presented a likeness of their subject for its own sake.[49] Portrayals existed of the deceased, made for their own tombs and sometimes set into scallop shells or medallions, but these were not "holy images."[50] And although often described as a representation of Christ, the figure of the Good Shepherd was not a portrait of Christ but a metaphor expressing the qualities of Jesus as a loving caretaker of souls. Scenes of Jesus or the apostles show them as characters in specific stories or settings performing or witnessing certain acts or works. These are not portraits as such.

This lack of early Christian portraiture cannot be explained as an accident, but rather as the result of a conscious effort to resist idolatry by producing art that primarily served a didactic function. Early Christians seem to have known that the simple representation of Christ's or a saint's face, without any narrative context, had the potential to attract devotion or worship. In the first three or four centuries, this was dangerously similar to the ways that images of the traditional Roman gods might be treated. Thus, by limiting the kinds of visual art forms that could be deemed acceptable, idolatry was avoided, even while symbolic or narrative art was permitted. Christians differed from their pagan neighbors by avoiding a certain *kind* of image, not by avoiding images in general. At a later time, when a different kind of danger or need was perceived, a new kind of image could emerge and find its place in Christian practice and theology—the holy portrait.

Portraits: A Particular Kind of Problematic Image

Perhaps the most often-cited patristic condemnation of holy portraits is found in a famous letter purported to be from Eusebius of Caesarea to Emperor Constantine's sister, the Augusta Constantia (married to his rival in the east, Licinius), in which he refuses her petition for a painted portrait of Christ and reproaches her for her theological naïveté:

> Since you have written referring also to a certain image [icon] of Christ that you wanted us to send you, which image of Christ do you mean? . . . that which is true and unchangeable and which bears the characteristics of his nature, or that which he assumed for us, the figure, that is, that he took in the form of a servant? . . . But certainly you are asking for an icon of the form of the servant and that of a bit of flesh, which he put on for us. . . . Who would, then, be able to draw with dead and inanimate colors, or in sketches, the glittering and sparkling scintillations which are so very precious and glorious? The divine Apostles on the mountain could not even endure to look at him, and they fell on their faces confessing that they could not bear the sight.[51]

In a longer version of the letter (found in a different document collection), Eusebius adds: "But if you mean to ask of me the image, not of his form transformed into that of God, but that of the mortal flesh before its transformation, can it be that you have forgotten that passage in which God lays down the law that no likeness should be made either of what is in heaven, or what is in the earth beneath?"[52] According to this letter, the bishop's objection to the empress's request emerged out of a dual concern. On one hand, he believes that it was impossible to present a true image of the incarnate Divine Son without denying the reality of both his human and divine natures, since each is so inextricably bound up with the other that it is impossible to represent the union itself in a visual form. On the other, he points to the Second Commandment, which he interpreted to be against likenesses in general. Significantly, both arguments anticipate the objections of the Byzantine iconoclasts.

Finally, Eusebius asserts that, because such images simply did not exist, he could not honor the empress's request in any case: "Have you ever heard anything of the kind either yourself in church or from another person? Are not such things banished and excluded from churches all over the world, and is it not common knowledge that such practices are not permitted to us alone?" By way of illustration, he offers a personal anecdote, telling of a time when another woman brought to him a picture of two men in the guise of philosophers, claiming that they were Paul and Christ. Because the object offended him, Eusebius confiscated it. Eusebius also refers to images of Simon Magus and Mani to demonstrate the association of painted portraits with, in his opinion, the worst sort of heretic.[53]

Drawing conclusions from this document about an early Christian repudiation of visual art (specifically portraits of Christ) is difficult because the text contains several troubling inconsistencies when compared to other writings of Eusebius. The last argument directly contradicts mentions he makes elsewhere of figurative images, for instance of a (now lost) bronze statue group in Caesarea Philippi that showed a kneeling woman with her arms outstretched in supplication to the upright figure of a well-dressed man. The locals held this to be a representation of Christ healing the woman suffering from hemorrhages, an event reported to have taken place at this very site. Eusebius neither denies its identity nor denounces its existence. He even commends the Gentiles who set up the statue as a sign of their thankfulness and notes that the locals believed the statue bore the likeness of Jesus, which was easily recognizable from other painted images that he had himself seen, and he also mentions other portrait likenesses of Peter and Paul:

> Nor is it strange that those of the Gentiles who, of old, were benefited by our Savior, should have done such things since we have learned also that the likenesses of his apostles Paul and Peter, and of Christ himself, are preserved in paintings [*graphais chromaton*], the ancients being accustomed, as it is likely, according to a habit of the Gentiles, to pay this kind of honor indiscriminately to those regarded by them as deliverers.[54]

Eusebius's comment here has strong parallels with the much earlier critique that Irenaeus launches against the Carpocratians, who honored portraits of Jesus with garlands and probably with prayers, and, in particular, one reported to have been made by Pontius Pilate. Irenaeus further claims that these images of Christ were set up on a par with images of Pythagoras, Plato, and Aristotle, which to him was typical of the behavior of a certain kind of Gnostic.[55] If we take these two testimonies together, even though widely separated in chronological time, we might conclude that the making and honoring of religious portraits were typically associated with heretical groups, pagans, or well-meaning but misguided recent converts who continued to practice what these Christian leaders considered to be "old idolatrous customs."

The authenticity of Eusebius's letter has been challenged on other grounds as well. One leading theory suggests that it may be a forgery from a much later period, incorporated into the *florilegia* of the iconoclasts in the mid-eighth century and refuted in the acts of the Seventh Ecumenical Council (787 C.E.).[56] As we have noted, Eusebius's theological arguments seem to be more characteristic of the disputes from the era of iconoclasm than from the theological polemics of the mid-fourth century. The difficulty of showing the dual natures of Christ in a single portrait image could arguably have been understood only after the terms had been set in the christological controversies of the next century.

Whether or not we accept Eusebius's letter as authentic, additional and somewhat more reliably authentic testimony to the resistance to Christian portraiture in the late fourth century can be cited in this regard. Several fragments of the writings of Epiphanius of Salamis, otherwise known for his condemnation of a variety of heresies, attack the practice of making and honoring images of the saints, particularly those he has seen painted on walls or woven into curtains. His writings also seem to indicate that, in his view, this is a somewhat new practice, and he urges his readers (in one case the Emperor Theodosius and in another Bishop John of Jerusalem) to stop the practice outright. Refuting the defense of images that must already have been circulating, he declares:

> You may tell me that the Fathers abominated the idols of the gentiles, whereas we make images of saints as a memorial to them and worship these in their honor. It is surely on this assumption that some of you have dared to plaster the walls inside the house of God and by means of different colors to represent pictures of Peter and John and Paul, as I see by the inscription of each of these false images, set down through the stupidity of the painter and according to his own inclination.[57]

Epiphanius goes on to point out that a portrait of an exterior appearance is merely a representation of something that is dead and useless, especially since these saints are now deceased. When we next see them, he says, these saints will be conformed to the image of Christ and "adorned with glory."[58]

Visual portraits, as we have defined them, are different from narrative or symbolic images, in that their primary purpose is to present an individual human (or divine) countenance to viewers for contemplation. They usually are presented frontally, sometimes as full figures, but often only the bust or face. Contemplation, of course, can lead to rapt attraction and then all too easily to veneration, which is the point at which the portrait is especially vulnerable to misunderstanding or misuse, and why most third- and fourth-century Christians may have deliberately avoided them. Artworks whose primary purpose is to portray the face and general character or personality of a subject claim to achieve some kind of "likeness"—either realistic or expressive, and internal as well as external—rather than presenting that subject as an actor (whether incidental or central) in a larger composition. As we have seen, based on available evidence, such early Christian resistance to portraits implied no general resistance to figurative art that occurred within a larger narrative frame and made no claim to present a "real likeness."

The absence of early Christian portraits is even more striking when we consider that the art of portraiture was well established in the Roman world and was, in fact, extremely popular among the upper classes at the time when Christians were beginning to produce plastic and graphic art.[59] We cannot credit a lack of cultural prototypes, then, for the absence of portraiture in early Christianity. An alternative explanation—that this particular kind of art emerges only in segments of the population (the wealthy upper classes) who had the resources to commission such things—fails to note that other artworks would also have depended on this kind of patronage. Artwork is more or less costly depending on the quality of the work, not on its subject matter. We must conclude that something in particular about portraits made them off-limits for early Christian visual art, and, as we have seen, it was not the prohibition of figurative art per se. What made portraits different in early Christian thought was their similarity to the idols of the polytheists. Furthermore, as representing a "likeness," portraits were deceitful. They falsely pretended to be something they were not. To some extent, the supposed letter of Eusebius to Constantia or the arguments of Epiphanius made a point not totally out of sync with sentiments expressed by the philosophers. The images of the saints were arguably "invented" by the artists out of their imagination. The image could not contain the total reality of who Christ was, even in his human incarnation.

Thus, the objection to portrait images, as with earlier objections to visual art in general, drew as much upon the classical philosophical tradition as upon any ancient Jewish precedents. In other words, one might say that for some early Christian teachers, Plato was as significant a source as Moses for the Christian perception that all portraits, and especially divine images, should be avoided (even though they may have argued that Moses was the original source for such teaching). From a philosophical point of view, a portrait's danger stems from its deceptive or mistaken claims to present something beyond surface reality and from its potential for confusing viewers' identification of the external and finite with the spiritual and infinite. In Christian terms, such confusion could only lead to apostasy or idolatry, and, as such, it was associated either with polytheistic practices or with heterodox theology (for example, the Carpocratians).[60]

However, several excerpts from second- and third-century writings reveal a particular reservation about portraits, even among certain Gnostics. First, a short section in the second- or third-century (probably Valentinian) *Acts of John* relates the story of a certain wealthy man, Lycomedes, praetor of the Ephesians, whose wife, Cleopatra, was miraculously healed by John. The grateful Lycomedes, wishing to have a portrait of John so that he might venerate his image, commissioned a painter to make the likeness in secret, without John's knowledge. Lycomedes, overjoyed to have the portrait, put it in his bedroom, hung garlands on it, and set lamps and an altar before it. When John discovered what Lycomedes had done, he was severely critical, accusing him of continuing to live as a pagan. Lycomedes responded: "He alone is my God who raised me up from death with my wife. But if besides that God we may call our earthly benefactors gods, it is you, my father, whose portrait I possess, whom I crown and love and reverence, as having become a good guide to me."[61] John took a look at the image and was startled to see his own face for the first time (as well as flattered by its beauty).

Nevertheless, he repudiated Lycomedes, neatly summing up the problem of image and likeness, reiterated the classical argument, and, in words that Epiphanius would later echo, declared:

> As the Lord Jesus Christ lives, the portrait is like me; yet not like me, my child, but like my image in the flesh; for if the painter who has copied my face here wants to put me in a portrait, then he needs the colors that were given you, and boards, and the shape of my figure, and age and youth and all such visible things. But do you be a good painter for me, Lycomedes. You have colors which he gives you through me, that is, Jesus, who paints us all from life for himself, who knows the shapes and forms and colors which I tell you to paint with: faith in God, knowledge, reverence, kindness, fellowship, mildness, goodness, brotherly love, purity, sincerity, tranquility, fearlessness, cheerfulness, dignity, and the whole band of colors which portray your soul and already raise up your members that were cast down and level those which were lifted up, which cure your bruises and heal your wounds. . . . In brief, when a full set and mixture of such colors has come together into your soul it will present it to our Lord Jesus Christ undismayed and undamaged and rounded in form. But what you have now done is childish and imperfect; you have drawn a dead likeness of what is dead.[62]

This brief account parallels a somewhat unreliable record regarding the (polytheistic) Emperor Alexander Severus (ca. 208–235 C.E.), who is said to have set up a pantheon of gods, heroes, and philosophers in his private chapel, including images of Jesus, Apollonius of Tyana, Abraham, Alexander the Great, and Orpheus. The emperor's mother, Julia Mammea, had summoned the theologian Origen for a conversation, so the story may have been based on some factual detail.[63] Again, we are reminded of Irenaeus's claim that the Carpocratians set up images of philosophers (such as Plato, Pythagoras, and Aristotle) as well as of Jesus and offered them crowns and other signs of veneration ("like the Gentiles"). Of course, in each case, portrait images of Christ are associated with the opposition—heretics or pagans.

In summary, the problem of portraits was at least twofold: they were likely to be misused—set up and covered with garlands, scented with smoking incense, illumined with votive candles, and offered worship or prayer like the idols of the polytheists—and they were false and imitative copies of something that was absolutely beyond their ability to represent. The distance between model and image was unbridgeable, in the prevailing worldview, which regarded the making of images as one of the lowest levels of participation in reality or truth. The truth was understood to be beyond containment in physical or material creation, and the work of human hands was perceived as imitative at best. The usefulness of art was in the realms of the symbolic and didactic, where it referred directly to the intellectual and cognitive realm of ideas and arguments, stories and lessons. And visual representations of stories and lessons are unlikely to attract offerings of flowers, incense, or even prayers.

As we have seen, the criticism of portraits as essentially fraudulent did not emerge first within Christian theology but was a standard philosophical truism that can be traced all the way back to Plato's doctrine of mimesis, in which the earthly "copy" is many steps removed from the reality of the eternal "model."[64] This standard philosophical adage was carried forward into the Christian period in the thinking of the middle and neo-Platonists, but most notably Plotinus (ca. 205–270 C.E.), who was said to refuse any attempt to have his portrait made. His rebuff incorporated the standard Platonic objection: "Is it not enough to carry about this image in which nature has enclosed us? Do you really think that I must also consent to leave, as a desirable spectacle to posterity, an image of the image?"[65] His disciple and biographer, Porphyry (ca. 232–305 C.E.), began his *Life of Plotinus* by recounting how the foremost portrait artist of the day, a certain Carterius, attended Plotinus's public lectures so that he could observe the philosopher and catch his "most telling personal traits" in order to produce from memory (and clandestinely) a sketch that could then be circulated among friends for their critique and suggestions until a lifelike portrait had emerged. Such a portrait would have been a sort of hybrid of "from life" and "from memory"—an attempt not simply to capture an external likeness but also to represent the character of the model.[66]

Since the Christian church emerged in this cultural milieu, we must assume that converts not only were familiar with the practice of making and using portraits but were possibly also aware of the criticism of that practice. If so, they may have adapted this criticism to reflect their own theological issues—asserting, with Plotinus, that portraits mistook the external world for the true (invisible and ideal) one or that they were products of a materialistic and idolatrous culture that adherents to the new faith ought to reject on general principle. If such objections were taken from the philosophical sphere into the Christian theological one, we may also assume that concern with the dishonesty and even danger of portraits could run deep within the intellectual tradition, affecting the everyday practice of Christians, including the art they created to express their faith.

Evidence for Christian adoption of Platonist objections to art may be found within the wider Christian intellectual circles including the writings of Valentinus (ca. 120–160 C.E.), who offers a criticism very similar to Plotinus's, but from a century earlier:

> However much a portrait is inferior to an actual face, just so is the world worse than the living realm. Now, what is the cause of the [effectiveness of the] portrait? It is the majesty of the face that has furnished to the painter a prototype so that the portrait might be honored by his name [either of the model or the painter]. For the form was not reproduced with perfect fidelity, yet the name completed the lack within the act of modeling. And also God's invisible [nature] cooperates with what has been modeled [Adam] to lend it credence.[67]

In this short fragment of Valentinus's teaching, as reported by Clement of Alexandria, the Gnostic Christian philosopher raises his concerns about the problem of visual representation between general statements about artistic verisimilitude and the impossibility of producing a true likeness comparing the inadequacies of human art with God's creation of Adam in the image and likeness, thus making a "credible portrait" of a certain kind.

In conclusion, we see that the early church struggled with the problem of artistic representation at all kinds of levels, a struggle that no doubt hampered the artists and worried the theologians. The Mosaic prohibition of image was perhaps only one of their considerations. The desire to be distinct from the surrounding culture, with its almost inherent idolatry, to avoid any visual representations of the Divine nature, and to encourage images that were essentially didactic is evident both in the literary sources and in the extant material evidence. Yet the portrait image did finally appear toward the end of the fourth century and throughout the fifth and sixth, rapidly becoming an essential form of Christian visual art, at least on a par with narrative imagery. We must ask what theological, cultural, or artistic forces were responsible for this important transition in the composition of Christian iconography.

The First Portraits

Of course, much of this transition took place in tandem with radical changes in the church's status and support. After Constantine's conversion to Christianity in 314 C.E., the circumstances of the church changed abruptly from persecuted cult to state-supported religion. The practice of decorating burial chambers with biblical narrative scenes was soon expanded to include portraits of the saints. Churches were built and decorated as well, stimulated at first by imperial patronage and money, but also by a gradually emerging argument for the value of visual art for the church.[68] In addition to the statue of Christ and the woman in Caesarea Philippi (which causes him to note that he has also seen portraits of the saints Peter and Paul), Eusebius reports that Constantine commissioned sculptural figures of the Good Shepherd and Daniel for public fountains in Constantinople.[69] According to the *Liber Pontificalis*, that same emperor donated nearly life-sized figures of John the Baptist and Christ in cast silver to the Lateran Baptistery while the Lateran Basilica was supplied with silver statues of Jesus and his twelve apostles (none of these are known to exist today).[70]

By the late fourth century, portraits of Peter and Paul began to be included in the iconographic programs of the catacombs and appeared on other media, such as gold-glass and gems. In the fifth and sixth centuries, portraits of the saints and Christian heroes (apostles, martyrs, and bishops) were added to the frescoes of the Roman catacombs long after burials ceased in these places, particularly at the sites where their remains were interred. The emerging cult of the saints in the fourth and fifth centuries brought pilgrims to these places, where they might share a commemorative banquet to honor the holy persons near their mortal remains. Jerome, for example, mentions regular Sunday visits to the catacombs when he was a boy in Rome "to pay homage to the sepulchers of the apostles and martyrs."[71] The art of the catacombs changed from symbolic and narrative images to representations of the saints buried therein, or portraits of the martyrs, apostles, or Mary in company with the deceased.[72]

Just prior to the emergence of saints' portraits, however, the first examples of portraits of Christ appear, including one in the vault of a burial chamber in the Catacomb of Commodilla, showing the head and shoulders of Jesus featuring a full dark beard and long wavy hair (fig. 11). Dated to the late fourth century, his head is framed by a halo and on either side we see the letters *alpha* and *omega*. Christ's face seems to float on a patterned background of squares and rosettes, perhaps meant to represent a coffered ceiling. Elsewhere in this catacomb are images of the denial of Peter and of Christ shown between two martyrs (or

Fig. 11. Bust of Christ, Catacomb of Commodilla, Rome, mid- to late 4th cen. C.E. (Photo: Italy/Held Collection, Bridgeman Art Library).

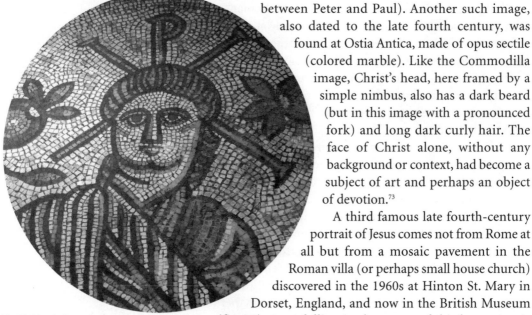

Fig. 12. Mosaic Portrait of Christ from Roman Villa at Hinton St. Mary, Dorset, late 4th cen. C.E., London, British Museum (Photo: Author).

between Peter and Paul). Another such image, also dated to the late fourth century, was found at Ostia Antica, made of opus sectile (colored marble). Like the Commodilla image, Christ's head, here framed by a simple nimbus, also has a dark beard (but in this image with a pronounced fork) and long dark curly hair. The face of Christ alone, without any background or context, had become a subject of art and perhaps an object of devotion.[73]

A third famous late fourth-century portrait of Jesus comes not from Rome at all but from a mosaic pavement in the Roman villa (or perhaps small house church) discovered in the 1960s at Hinton St. Mary in Dorset, England, and now in the British Museum (fig. 12). A medallion in the center of this large mosaic shows Jesus with quite a different facial type than that of the Commodilla or Ostia images. This portrait of Jesus, which may have been placed originally in the domed ceiling, shows him beardless and wearing a rather mild expression. His hair is light in color and pulled back from his face. Instead of a nimbus, he has only a chi-rho monogram behind his head; on either side are pomegranates, the symbolism of which is somewhat unclear—perhaps of his passion or of abundance in the resurrection. At the corners of the mosaic are personifications of the four seasons—a popular secular theme in Roman art, especially pavement mosaics. Adjacent to this composition is another, smaller mosaic portraying the mythological figure Bellerophon slaying the Chimera (or perhaps a Christianized version—Christ slaying the Chimera).[74]

A statuette, now assumed to be a portrait of Christ seated and holding a scroll, was discovered in Asia Minor and is now housed in Rome's Museo Nazionale (fig. 13). The work generally has been dated to the late fourth century, although both its date and its identification as an image of Christ have been questioned.[75] The beardless, youthful, and almost feminine appearance of the figure has recently been discussed in some detail and certainly offers contrast with the images from Commodilla and Ostia in particular.[76] The figure in this case bears more resemblance to the figure of Christ on mid-fourth century sarcophagi, including the tomb of Junius Bassus, now in the Vatican (fig. 14). Although the original context of this statuette is unknown, it appears to have been designed to be an independent work of art, not a part of a group or larger composition.

Concurrent with the development of visual art for the church, along with explanations of its potential value, was a fading concern about idolatry in the late third and early fourth centuries. This may have been because the surrounding culture was gradually becoming Christian (and thus less threatening), or because the traditional gods were steadily disappearing from the scene, or perhaps, even more significant, because the focus of theological condemnation moved from the dangers of idolatry to the controversies about the person and nature(s) of the savior. The demons that entrapped the people into worshiping the vain and empty creations of human hands now had another way to drag the unwary into perdition, through false teachings rather than through the worship of false gods or the veneration of idols. Pagan gods were no longer the competition and threat that they were in the first centuries, and the secular world was something to be accommodated rather than avoided. Until the beginning of the eighth century and the outbreak of iconoclasm, portraits of the saints, Mary, and even Christ were hardly a matter for concern.

Instead, images of saints as well as scenes taken from the Bible became more and more popular for church decoration. Intended to inspire awe as well as to teach, the artwork in church was as much a mode of theology as the writing of treatises or delivering of homilies, and it was as effective a means of nurturing devotion or pious emotion as any of the rhetorical arts. However, even though the material evidence certainly demonstrates

Fig. 13. Statuette of seated Christ as teacher, early to mid-4th cen. C.E., Museo Nazionale (Palazzo Massimo alle Terme), Rome (Photo: Author).

that portraits of the saints, Mary, or Christ had arrived, at least one provincial but famous bishop at the turn of the fifth century was worried about how the existence and popularity of such images still might lead his congregation astray. Noting that some of the better educated pagans in his city had turned the tables and actually were chiding Christians for being "adorers of columns, and sometimes even of pictures," Augustine grants that such things are taking place ("would to God that we didn't have them") and notes that the practice is defended by what will become the standard Christian agument: "'We,' they say, 'don't adore images, but what is signified by the image.'"[77] Augustine objects to such an argument by pointing out that it would be wiser to pray directly to the saint rather than to the image of that saint, an argument that might seem eminently sensible if posed to a congregation that was unattached to such visual and material aids to prayer. Whether his congregation was persuaded or not (we have no surviving icons from Hippo) is ultimately less interesting, however, than the fact that, according to Augustine, Christians are being accused of the very acts their authorities had formerly ridiculed in others.

Fig. 14. Sarcophagus of Junius Bassus, 357 C.E., Treasury of St. Peter's Basilica, Rome (Photo: Scala/Art Resource, NY).

TWO

Image and Portrait in Roman Culture and Religion

PLOTINUS objected to having his portrait painted because he distinguished between an individual's character and mere external appearance. The outward form and, even more, the representation of that form made by an artist using pigments on wood was, to his mind, an illusion. A painted portrait had no life, depth, or meaning beyond recording the transitory and superficial aspect of the model, and, if it pretended to show any more than that, it was a fraud. Plotinus, like Plato, not only regarded artistic images as inferior copies but also as deceptive snares that would lure the eye and turn the mind away from contemplation of reality. Plotinus was wary of the material world and of seductive physical delights that entrapped the soul in base pursuits and pleasures, keeping it from ascending to more lofty truth.

Whether or not this philosophical critique was heeded, the ancient monuments that fill today's museums show that the production of portrait images was widespread in the ancient world and no less in the Roman Empire in Late Antiquity. The disapproval of intellectuals does not appear to have affected the population's desire for artistic representations of family members, great heroes, rulers, statesmen, and the gods. However, the question of what constituted a worthy portrait—or likeness—is complex. Although the ancient Egyptians may have been the first to have fashioned portrait-like art works, art historians (like many ancient philosophers) generally credit Greek sculptors with the first recognizable artistic likenesses, a development that characterized the transition from the archaic to the classical period, reflecting an increased emphasis on individuality and naturalism over standardized types or forms. From that time on, classical portrait images ranged back and forth on a spectrum between realistic and idealized representation—the matter of what constituted a portrait dependent on how the concept itself was understood.

For example, Pliny the Elder (ca. 24–79 C.E.) devoted nearly an entire volume of his *Natural History* to the painting of portraits. Here he laments the lack of taste motivated by the scramble for status symbols among the upwardly mobile middle classes of his time. In his view, a portrait's most important function was to foster memory and respect for family and tradition. However, Pliny complains, the defining characteristic of a portrait (its physical likeness to its model) was less valued than the costliness of the object, the quantity of items in a collection deemed more important than their quality, and the quality rated on the pretentiousness of the workmanship. Sounding very much like an old-fashioned member of the older generation lamenting the crass values of the younger, he decries the deterioration of tradition and style, the loss of respect for time-honored customs, and the deplorable habit of popping a new portrait head upon an older torso just to save money or time. Finally, he contends that, since the individual's mind cannot be visually portrayed, at least a decent likeness should be sought:

> The painting of portraits, used to transmit through the ages extremely correct likeness of persons, has entirely gone out. Bronze shields are now set up as monuments with a design in silver, with only a faint difference between the figures; heads of statues are exchanged for others, about which before now actually sarcastic epigrams have been current; so universally is a display of material preferred to a recognizable likeness of one's own self. And in the midst of all this, people tapestry the walls of their picture-galleries with old pictures, and they prize likenesses of strangers, while as for themselves they imagine that the honor only consists in the price. . . . Consequently, nobody's likeness lives, and they leave behind them portraits that represent only their money not themselves. . . . That is exactly how they are; indolence has destroyed the arts, and since our minds cannot be portrayed, our bodily features are also neglected. In the halls of our ancestors it was otherwise; portraits were the objects displayed to be looked at . . . wax models were set out, each on a separate side board, to furnish likenesses to be carried in procession at a funeral in the clan, and always when some member of it passed away the entire company of his house that had ever existed was present.[1]

However, the question of what constituted a true likeness, even a physical likeness, was debatable. Despite Pliny's assertion that "minds" could not be portrayed, he also recognized that the elements that made an external portrait true or false were deeper than mere outward appearance. The expression of some element of the soul, or at least the character, of the model was necessary. Pliny criticized the custom of placing portrait busts of great poets and authors in libraries where their works were kept, and he commented that many of these images were wholly invented, since no one knew what certain individuals looked like (such as Homer or Socrates). For Pliny, the creators of true portraits were actually the biographers who recounted the qualities of an individual character, or even bibliophiles (like himself) who preserved and edited the works of others—creating libraries to house the thoughts and writings of great thinkers, rather than merely showcasing their imaginary and ephemeral exterior likenesses.[2]

By Pliny's criteria, Plutarch (ca. 50–120 C.E.), the writer of biographies, was a true portrait painter. As Plutarch himself explains, genuine biographers care less about the great deeds of their subjects than they do about the content of their character or the state of their soul. However, he too believed that a gifted visual artist should be less concerned with external appearance and more with conveying the intangible aspects of the personality, perhaps through the expression of the face and the eyes. In describing his life's work, writing the lives of famous men, Plutarch asserts that an individual's great deeds or acts are far less revealing of character than the subtler ways that a person's nature may be delineated:

> For it is not histories that I am writing, but Lives; and in the most illustrious deeds there is not always a manifestation of virtue or vice, nay a slight thing like a phrase of a jest often makes a greater revelation of character than battles where thousands fall, or the greatest armaments, or sieges of cities. Accordingly, just as painters get the likenesses in their portraits from the face and the expression of the eyes, wherein the character shows itself, but make very little account of the other parts of the body, so I must be permitted to devote myself to the signs of the soul in men, and by means of these to portray the life of each, leaving to others the description of their great contests.[3]

Plutarch's protest only highlights one of the main functions of visual commemorative portraits, however. Visual images, like rhetorical or documentary portraits, were intended to honor an individual because of his or her deeds or actions. Although countless portraits of now nameless individuals have been found whose accomplishments we cannot know, nevertheless, having been the subject of a portrait suggests achievement, even perhaps fame. At least it warded off oblivion and fostered some posthumous respect. Naturally, portraits that merited prominent and public locations within the city, or that were of the highest quality work, signaled the political status, wealth, success, or even vanity of the model, then as well as now.

Idealization versus Realism in Roman Portraiture

When Pliny remonstrated about the lost values of earlier generations, he may have had in mind the lifelike Roman portraits made from living models (neither posthumous images nor death masks) that were popular during the Republican era, particularly around the mid-first century B.C.E.[4] Art historians have found that this period provided some of the best examples of "realistic" portraits, many of them copied in early

Fig. 15. Bust of Lucius Cecilius
Iocundus, Pompeiian banker,
1st cen. C.E. from Pompeii,
Museo Nazionale di
Capodimonte, Naples (Photo:
Alinari/Art Resource, NY).

imperial times. Although this era was known for its emphasis on realism, there was also a continued tradition of idealized heroic representations based on earlier Hellenistic models. Scholars have noted that late Republican-era realistic portraits focused more on the expression of individual personality through certain unique facial features, depicting their subjects "warts and all." Possibly based on the practice of making death masks for funerary purposes (see discussion below), this shift also seemed to capture the Republican values of practicality, frankness, and unsentimentality. One particularly vivid example of this, now in the National Museum of Naples but originally from Pompeii, is the bust of the Augustan-era banker and businessman Lucius Cecilius Iocundus (fig. 15).[5] The literalism of this portrayal, with its wart and protruding ears, suggests that the aim was to create a particularly detailed and recognizable (and not noticeably beautified) likeness of its model.

During the early imperial era, the classical heroic or idealized portrayal became more popular, although somewhat influenced by the earlier tendency toward realism.[6] The tendency to vacillate between the classicist or idealizing mode and the realistic one sometimes produced odd combinations of realistically executed heads on heroically posed bodies (see fig. 18). Good examples of idealized portraits are the representations of Augustus, who is usually shown as a youthful and heroic figure (fig. 16). The next generations of the Julio-Claudian family generally kept up the idealizing tradition, especially in posthumous portraits of the deified ruler, although occasional reappearances of older Roman realism sometimes reappear in certain instances, such as the almost comical portrait of Claudius in the guise of Jupiter, now in the Vatican Museum (fig. 17). At the end of the first century, the portraits of Vespasian (69–79 C.E.) are also quite realistic, perhaps meant to associate this middle-class emperor with old Republican values. But even Vespasian could be represented as having a realistic visage on an idealized body (fig. 18). Although we

Fig. 16. Augustus from Primaporta, 14–29 C.E., Vatican Museum, Rome (Photo: Author)

Fig. 17 (left). Claudius as Jupiter ca. 50 C.E., Vatican Museum, Rome (Photo: Author)

Fig. 18 (right). Vespasian, mid 1st cen. C.E., from the Shrine of the Augustales, Misenum, Castello di Baia (Photo: Author).

Fig. 19 (below). Portrait of a woman, Imperial Roman Period, Trajanic or Hadrianic, 100–125 C.E. Place of manufacture: Greece (possibly). Museum of Fine Arts, Boston (Photograph ©2004 Museum of Fine Arts, Boston).

cannot make clear judgments about exact likeness, the works suggest an apparent effort on the part of artisans to achieve realism while still flattering their subjects and showing them at their best. The women of the Flavian court, for example, affected elaborate hairstyles on their official portraits and sometimes had themselves appear with the figure and posture of Venus. At the same time, women of this and the next dynasty were also shown as aging, with wrinkled foreheads, bags under their eyes, and sagging cheeks (fig. 19).[7]

Art historians note a pronounced return to ideal types during the era of Emperor Hadrian, when certain facial features clearly were intended to suggest aspects of the model's character or virtues. Hadrian, however, was the first emperor to show himself with a full beard, in the style of the Greek philosophers, a trend that caught on for male portraiture, since it seemed to emphasize the gravitas of the model. Hadrian's lover Antinous, on the other hand, was shown in the form of a young Greek god, with a beardless face, curling hair, and a sensuous, even feminine body type. The bearded emperor types (with luxuriant and curly hair) were still in vogue toward the end of the second century, especially for the portraits of Antoninus Pius and his successors Marcus Aurelius and Lucius Verus, who wished to be regarded as intellectual rulers (fig. 20). Marcus Aurelius's portraits are especially

Fig. 20. Bust of Antinoninus Pius, ca. 138–40 C.E., Museo Palatino, Rome (Photo: Author).

Fig. 21. Septimius Severus, ca. 200–210 C.E., Louvre Museum, Paris (Photo: Author).

Fig. 22. Bust of Caracalla, ca. 214 C.E., Museo Nazionale Romano (Palazzo Massimo all Terme), Rome (Photo: Author).

interesting, however, since they show a progression from attractive youth (beardless), through vigorous middle age (bearded), and finally to a wise and somewhat world-weary old man. The same pattern describes the portraits of his wife, Faustina, who also moved from youthful beauty to middle-aged matron and finally showed the dignity and wisdom of age.[8]

At the beginning of the third century, the Severan emperors were likewise portrayed with long curly hair and forked beards (fig. 21). Caracalla however, favored a more clipped beard and hairstyle (fig. 22).[9] Verisimilitude came back into style beginning in the 230s for portraits of the soldier-emperors Maximinus Thrax and Balbinus. In order to express the personality of the model and to achieve a realistic likeness, artists employed rough and even impressionistic modeling. The results produced an appearance of severity and implied strength of character. H. P. L'Orange has analyzed this shift in style as the attainment of "psychological" imagery. Musing on one example of this type, the bust of Emperor Philip the Arab (244–249 C.E.), L'Orange writes:

> With a great simplifying touch the artist has managed to concentrate physiognomic life in one characteristic sweep. The central motif is the threatening lowering of the brows, corresponding to convulsions of the forehead muscles and responding to nervous contractions of the muscles of the mouth. The psychological picture achieves an almost uncanny intensity. Behind the nervous quivering features the expression itself seems to change and move, flashing like a glimmering flame over the face.[10]

The "man of action" type disappeared again as portraits of Gallienus (253–268) returned to the idealized types. Shown with a short beard, this ruler's smoothly modeled and almost delicately rendered portraits present him as a sensitive person, and his upturned eyes give him the look of spiritual or intellectual aspirations, even though he was an active soldier-emperor in the style of his father, Valerian. Possibly intended to remind the viewer of youthful depictions of Augustus, Gallienus's image also bears some resemblance to a contemporary portrait found in Ostia and identified by some art historians as a portrait (finally achieved) of the philosopher Plotinus.[11]

The intellectual image was dislodged again, however, at the end of the third century, as the Tetrarchs (Diocletian, Maximian, Constantius, and Galerius) wished to have themselves portrayed as strong and decisive types, like the soldier-emperors of the mid-third century. The style was more abstract than realistic, however, and likeness appears to have been less important than a kind of conventional frontality and symmetry. In place of smooth modeling, sharp lines and geometric shapes predominate. Facial features are stylized, with the wide-open and staring eyes that make these subjects look, in Diana Kleiner's phrase, like "bearded blockheads" (fig. 23).[12] However, they also lend the portraits a kind of hieratic quality that foreshadows the portraits of the early Byzantine period, especially their emphasis on the eyes as the most striking facial feature (fig. 24).[13]

Fig. 23. Porphyry group portrait of the Tetrarchs, ca. 300 C.E., originally from Constantinople, now in St. Mark's Square, Venice (Photo: Author).

These stylized or abstract types were adapted once again with the portraits of Constantine. Earlier images of Constantine followed those of the tetrarchs, showing him with a short beard and soldier haircut. After the battle of the Milvian Bridge, however, Constantine's portraiture underwent a dramatic reinvention. He began to be shown as beardless and youthful, with longer hair in curls over his forehead, somewhat like the portraits of the first Augustus, or possibly Trajan.[14] One of the best-known portraits of Constantine, the head from the colossal statue from the Basilica Nova (now in the Museo del Palazzo dei Conservatori; fig. 25), shows some similarities to the earlier tetrarch portraits, with its wide-staring eyes, geometric shapes, and sharp angles. But it also shows the emperor as beardless, looking slightly upward—giving him a kind of spiritualized appearance possibly intended to associate him with his patron gods (Sol and/or the Christian God). Portraits of the sons of Constantine are often difficult to distinguish from those of Constantine himself, as once more the portrait type became conventionalized, now having a more idealized appearance and what Kleiner calls "the bland classicism of Augustan times which also subsumed individuality."[15]

Fig. 24. Theodosius I, ca. 380–90 C.E., Louvre Museum, Paris (Photo: Author).

All these changes in the way that imperial portraits were produced show the difficulty in trying to establish the parameters of a "likeness." Roman portraits, especially portraits of rulers, were carefully constructed images, revealing more than the mere physical appearance of the model. Character and particular virtues were projected through

Fig. 25. Constantine I, from the Basilica Nova, ca. 315–30, Museo del Palazzo dei Conservatori, Rome (Photo: Author).

these objects, and a portrait was often intended to impart a political message. An emperor or other noble who wanted to emphasize his military might and prowess, for example ("a man of action"), might be shown with a kind of rugged mien, having short-cropped military hairstyle and trimmed beard, squared jaw, knitted brow, and penetrating stare. If, on the other hand, the portrait was intended to suggest an individual's piety or devotion to the gods, features could be idealized and an otherworldly gaze achieved by showing eyes upraised and the expression of the face more sensitive than determined. An individual who wished to be perceived as an intellectual might be represented in the guise of a philosopher with untrimmed beard and an introspective gaze.[16] Yet, whatever the message sent by the image, some degree of recognizability was crucial, or the portrait would cease to function at the most basic level. As we will see, these same concerns and patterns are also relevant to the construction of early Christian portraits of Christ and the saints.

This aspect of recognizability, however stylized the portrait, is the mystery and the relativism of "likeness." A face may appear in three different versions, each quite distinct from one another, yet all three may reveal enough recognizable characteristics in common to be acknowledged as likenesses of an identifiable individual. Even if a portrait is idealized, viewers may still recognize the model, if only because of certain recurring aspects, attributes, or features. The image "works" so long as the viewer knows who its model is and so long as it shapes, reinforces, or even transforms the reputation of that model according to the intentions of the client, thanks to the ability of the artisan. In some cases, the portrait works so well that the model must then try to conform to his or her portrait. This is the case with apparitions of saints in later Christian tradition, who are recognizable largely because they "look like" their traditional portraits. Thus the question of realism and verisimilitude of a portrait become complicated by the production and dissemination of the image itself.

The Savior-Type and the Philosopher

Plutarch's reflection on capturing the soul rather than the deeds of illustrious persons through his writing of their "lives" occurs at the beginning of his biography of Alexander. This context seems particularly apt, for Alexander was the prototypical savior-ruler, both in his legend and in his visual portrayals. His portraits, well-known even to beginning students of art history, show him as a classically beautiful and heroic youth, his face passionately expressive, and his eyes turned upward to heaven as if seeking divine inspiration.[17] Eventually, some time after his death, portraits of Alexander went from the heavenward-gazing to actually heaven-bound or apotheosized, as he was transformed into a special kind of transitional deity, a god-man-hero savior figure along the lines of Dionysus, Orpheus, or Hercules.[18]

As art historians have noted, the pattern of Alexander's elevation was borrowed for subsequent rulers, in particular certain Roman emperors who, like the heroes of mythology, were seen as acting with divine guidance in life and undergoing apotheosis or deification after death (Julius Caesar or Domitian, for example). And as these mortals were elevated to the level of the semidivine or divine, they acquired a particular type of portrait image that transfigured even the plainest visage into one of striking beauty. The coin portraits of Julius Caesar before and after his death are a case in point. While the realism of the Republican style guided his portraits in life, after death he was granted a youthful beardless face and an abundance of long, curling hair, often held back with a fillet or a diadem surmounted by a comet—the sign of his elevation to the rank of a god.[19] This affiliation with a Hellenistic prototype (Alexander) also drew upon an actual divine image, the portrayal of Apollo or the sun god, Sol, who served as a model for many of the coin por-

traits of later emperors, including Constantine I (see fig. 41, p. 68). The heavenward turn of the eyes suggested both pious affiliation with the upper world and transcendence of mundane or earthly matters.

As discussed above, emperors such as Antinoninus Pius and Marcus Aurelius, however, dropped Apollo in favor of a different model—the facial features of Jupiter or Serapis with full beard and abundant hair (fig. 26).[20] According to scholars, these emperors chose to project the maturity of age and to appear more majestic and wise than beautiful and heroic. In his book *The Mask of Socrates*, Paul Zanker writes that the male population of the Empire adopted a new style during the second century (a "classical face") and that it was Hadrian's appearance with a beard that marked the turning point.[21] Imperial portraits that reflect this

Fig. 26. Serapis, 2nd cen. C.E., British Museum, London (Photo: Author).

type include the busts of Lucius Verus and Septimius Severus (compare fig. 21).[22] Facial features associated with the "senior" gods (especially Jupiter) emphasize the characteristics these emperors valued—sagacity, gravitas, and ruling authority.

In Zanker's view, this shift of portrait type was driven by a "profound transformation" of Roman society and signaled an emerging "cult of learning." Prior to this time Roman men had been depicted as clean-shaven. This transition to the bearded type reflected an interest in being portrayed as intellectuals, even in the guise of philosophers or poets, with longer beards and hair. They carried scrolls in their hands or had them in baskets at their feet. One popular figure in Roman art was a reader shown in profile, holding a partially unrolled scroll and wearing the traditional philosopher's garb of the *pallium* (an outer mantle wrapped somewhat like the larger and more formal toga, and much like

Fig. 27. Rams Head Sarcophagus, late 3rd cen. C.E., Museo Pio Cristiano, Vatican City (Photo: Author).

the Greek *himation*), often without the undertunic, thus leaving a partially bare chest (fig. 27). Such a physical presentation suggested indifference to worldly beauty and a preference to cultivate the mind and to develop a disciplined or spiritual outlook on life.[23] Many such portraits, shown in half or three-quarter profile, appear on second- and third-century sarcophagi, all with the apparent aim of portraying the deceased as a learned and reflective man.

Funerary Portraits

As we have seen, portraits of living people, from Roman emperors to more ordinary persons, usually had a practical as well as an aesthetic function. They honored, enhanced, and even shaped the character and reputations of their models while preserving evidence of their existence. The funerary portrait, by contrast, was a special kind of image, usually produced after death but also occasionally made while the subject was still alive, meant only as a record of the deceased's physical appearance for posterity. These funerary portraits had a particular ceremonial function and role in the domestic cult. They represented the deceased's presence at anniversary commemorations of death (funeral banquets) or important family or state occasions (while offering a reminder of the deceased in the happy afterlife). More than a mere record of appearance, funeral portraiture served social, genealogical, and even religious functions. Pliny the Elder writes, with particular reference to the high ranking or elite families prior to his era:

> In the halls of our ancestors it was otherwise; portraits were wax models of faces that were set out each on a separate sideboard, to furnish likenesses to be carried in procession at a funeral in the clan, and always when some member of it passed away the entire company of his house that had ever existed was present. The pedigrees too were traced in a spread of lines running near the several painted portraits. . . . Outside the houses and round the doorways there were other presentations of those mighty spirits, with spoils taken from the enemy fastened to them, which even one who bought the house was not permitted to unfasten, and the mansions eternally celebrated a triumph even though they had changed their masters . . . but even to lay a false claim to the portraits of famous men showed some love for their virtues, and was much more honorable than to entail by one's conduct that nobody should seek to obtain one's own portraits![24]

Roughly two centuries earlier, Polybius had offered a still more detailed picture of the tradition of funerary portraits in the Roman tradition. According to him, when an illustrious man died, his body was carried—sometimes in an upright posture and sometimes reclining—to the Forum, where the funeral orations were delivered. Then, following the interment and the "usual ceremonies," the image of the departed one was placed in the most important part of the house, enclosed in a wooden shrine: "This image was a mask, reproducing with remarkable fidelity both the features and the complexion of the deceased. On the occasion of public sacrifices they display these images, and decorate them with much care, and they take them to the funeral, putting them on men who seem to them to bear the closest resemblance to the original in stature and carriage."[25] This spectacle of a company of illustrious (but now dead) men arriving in the Forum in chariots and seated on ivory chairs around the rostra was supposed to inspire all the youth who saw it to similar fame and virtue.

Studies have shown that wax funerary masks of the Republican era continued to be produced into the early imperial era. As ancestral portraits (*imagines*), they clearly played an important part in the domestic cult and helped to establish a family's ancestry, social status, or rank (or their aspirations for such). They also served to keep an individual's physical features alive in the memory of descendents; indeed, they may have been made directly from the face immediately after death. Kept in cupboards, like shrines, usually near the central atrium, and venerated by all members of the household, including clients and slaves, they were carried out or even worn as masks (perhaps by actors hired for this function) during the funeral processions of succeeding members of the clan. Unfortunately, given the fragility of the wax, no examples of such funerary masks have survived. Archaeologists discovered a number of terra-cotta heads in south and central Italy, which may have served a similar funerary purpose. Much finer examples of portrait busts have also been found, for example in the columbarium of Vigna Codini in Rome, in some of the niches originally intended for cinerary urns, which suggests that many traditional bust portraits made from life may have served this secondary (funereal) purpose.[26] Also common were carved or portrait shields (*imagine clipaetae*), which were set up in temples or public places.[27]

Most funerary portraits however, were associated directly with the remains of the deceased, either as part of the coffin or as separate objects sculpted or painted and placed near the grave as an identifying marker. The portrait's proximity to the deceased's remains served the rituals associated with the commemoration of the dead, including the celebrations of birthdays or general festivals of the dead, when family and friends would gather at the tomb for a banquet. The spirits of the deceased were assumed to partake of the meal; their representative presence was guaranteed by the nearness of their physical remains.[28] Some graves were equipped with holes or pipes for pouring food and drink down to their bones or ashes. Others had tables with dishes and bowls carved into them for food offerings. These traditions were carried into Christian ritual, although some church officials objected. Augustine, for example, notes that some "ignorant" Christians worship tombs and honor portraits of the deceased that were placed nearby, holding feasts and drinking to excess over dead bodies.[29] Nevertheless, in time, images of the saints came to be associated particularly with saints' feasts: they were carried in processions; they were evident in the later association of the eucharistic table with the relics; and then, finally, they became the venerated icon of a saint or martyr.

These funerary traditions continued for the first four hundred years of the Common Era. As Richard Brilliant has stated: "Standing between the still-living and the already-dead, Roman tomb monuments testify to the great effort and expenditure of treasure dedicated to the perpetuation of the deceased's memory in the face of death's oblivion. . . . For Romans, in particular, whose culture already acknowledged the dire penalty of non-remembrance implicit in the *damnatio memoriae*, the notion of survival in whatever form seemed to have a special urgency, given the extraordinary abundance of monuments dedicated to the preservation of the tokens of prior existence."[30] The importance of funerary portraits for burial practice at every level of Roman society is evident by the thousands of surviving tomb monuments, grave markers (*stelai*), private altars, and imposing stone sarcophagi that can be found from the second century onward, in which distinctive portraits of the deceased were carved into an overall iconographic program.[31]

These stone sarcophagi probably were usually purchased partially finished, then were customized with likenesses of the deceased, either on the front of the sarcophagus or on the top of the lid, which would be turned into a kind of funeral couch with deceased (often both husband and wife) portrayed as if alive.[32] Modeled on earlier Greek and Roman (as well as Etruscan) monuments, these sarcophagi might display certain standard funerary motifs such as the deceased reclining and sharing a funeral banquet with family and friends often shown in the dress and posture of mourning.[33] Some particularly affecting compositions emphasize the happiness of a marriage by portraying both spouses, sometimes in the guise of Admetus and Alcestis (the quintessential devoted wife), sometimes showing the traditional gesture of marriage (right hands clasped—fig. 28), or a gesture of farewell.[34]

Fig. 28. Marriage scene from Roman sarcophagus fragment, probably early to mid-Antonine (mid-2nd cen. C.E.), British Museum, London (Photo: Author).

Scenes from daily life also appear. Women may be shown with servants and children, even pets; men and sometimes women are depicted with the symbols of their profession or as being philosophically inclined—seated with a scroll on the lap. Not all the funeral iconography is affectingly personal, however. Some sarcophagi have monumental narrative images drawn from mythology or from famous battles, often with the faces of the deceased imposed on those of particular characters— transporting them to the realm of heroes and thus according them both status and honor. Some overtly religious references to certain cults (such as that of Dionysus) may have expressed special beliefs or expectations about the afterlife and triumph over death.[35]

Christian sarcophagi dated to the late third and fourth century also often feature likenesses of their occupants in sculptural relief, sometimes as part of the general composition in which women, veiled, may be represented as praying (hands extended from their sides) or seated with attendants, while the men are shown in philosophical guise, with the scroll, tunic, and mantle (and sometimes bare chest) of the intellectual type (fig. 29; but note the unfinished portrait faces on the figures on this sarcophagus). Some of these images were biographical, intended to reflect a particular aspect of the deceased's life or profession. Beginning in the third century, portraits of the deceased were often set into a medallion or scallop shell recalling the military shield portrait (*clipeata imago*, mentioned above), placed in the center of a

Fig. 29. Sarcophagus from Church of Santa Maria Antiqua, late 3rd cen. C.E., Foro Romano (Photo: Author).

double-registered sarcophagus amid a complex composition of biblical scenes. In many cases we see a husband and wife, but, in one famous example, we see two men within the prominent central portrait (fig. 30). We may assume that in at least some cases the choice of iconography elsewhere on the sarcophagus reflected upon the piety, faith, and hopes of the now deceased. Rare examples of funerary busts have also been found, like the set of six (three pairs of the same husband and wife) now in the Cleveland Museum of Art, which were found along with small-scale sculptures of Jonah and the Good Shepherd and which are usually assumed to be from a tomb somewhere in Asia Minor.

Third- and fourth-century Christian funerary frescoes in the Roman catacombs include a number of praying (*orant*) figures with such individual facial expression and features as to be identified as actual portraits of the deceased—usually women (fig. 31).[36] Here the emphasis is on the religious devotion (*pietas*) of the person portrayed. Occasionally a family group appears (fig. 31), which was sometimes mistaken by early viewers as an image of the Holy Family (Mary, Joseph, and the child Jesus). Some of these funerary portraits are strikingly realistic, showing particular facial characteristics and expressions that suggest a great degree of likeness to the model. The portraits that appear on stone sarcophagi could have been inserted at a late stage of their completion, the personalized details added after the client had selected from among a number of partially finished monuments.

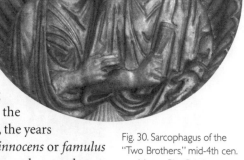

The funerary pavement mosaics typical of Roman Africa were placed directly over the tomb of the deceased and, in the case of the Christian examples, into church floors, either in the nave or in the aisles (although we also have examples of mosaics from open-air cemeteries). These highly stylized mosaic portraits are usually full length and appear to make only a passing attempt at actual likeness. Still, the inclusion of the name (and sometimes ecclesial title) of the deceased, the years of life or date of burial, and simple epithets such as *innocens* or *famulus dei* assist identification. Like the catacomb frescoes and sarcophagus reliefs of praying figures, these individuals also are shown with their hands stretched out from their sides and their eyes often upraised. Figures are surrounded by the birds, flowers (roses), and candles typical of funerary iconography elsewhere (fig. 32).

Fig. 30. Sarcophagus of the "Two Brothers," mid-4th cen. C.E., Museo Pio Cristiano, Vatican City (Photo: Author).

As the burial sites of special individuals became pilgrimage sites, portraits of those saints were often added, either in or near the

Fig. 31. Family group from the Catacomb of Priscilla, Rome (© The International Catacomb Society. Photo: Estelle Brettman).

Fig. 32. Christian funerary mosaic from Tarbarka, 4th cen. C.E., Bardo Museum, Tunis (Photo: Author).

supposed tomb or elsewhere in the church.[37] The emergence and development of the cult of saints in Christianity spurred this increase in funerary portraiture, including detailed frescoes of the saints shown in heaven with Mary or Christ, or more simple objects such as the gold-glass portraits, probably brought from a collection of small domestic objects and left behind as grave gifts or taken home as pilgrimage souvenirs.[38] The importance of these portraits lay partly in their proximity to the relics of the saints. In a real sense, the image participated in the actuality of the physical presence of the saint's mortal remains and drew some of its significance from it. Just as on the African tomb mosaics, names of the departed saints were often added to their images, both as a means of identification (lest someone forget who was buried within) and as a means of associating external appearance with personal character. Placing the name together with the face also signaled a certain quality of presence, allowing the image itself to become a virtual relic in the absence of actual remains. Candles could be lit and

Fig. 33. St. Januarius (with crucifixion halo) from the Catacomb of San Gennaro, Naples (© The International Catacomb Society. Photo: Estelle Brettman).

placed on either side of the image when prayers were offered to the depicted saint. One such scene is illustrated in the fifth-century fresco from a tomb in the Catacomb of San Gennaro in Naples (fig. 33). Another fresco in this catacomb shows the bust of a man in prayer, flanked by two lit candles and standing under a garland. On either side of his head is the legend: "Here lies Proculus." This particular image demonstrates the way a funerary portrait could take on the aspect of a holy (or votive) image, since in this case it already existed on a kind of altar, augmented by the (painted) accessories needed to signal the sacred nature of the representation.[39]

Portraits and Presence—The Image of the Emperor

As we have seen, the strong connection between physical appearance and presence had been a central aspect of the Roman imperial cult long before Christians started making portraits of their saints. The general patterns of the emperor cult in Rome were similar to earlier models from the Hellenistic empire and so were particularly well established in the eastern regions of the Empire.[40] In Asia Minor, in particular, art and architecture of this cult were extensive, commencing early in the reign of Augustus and including temples, altars, and statuary. Processions, games, and public sacrifices (often *for* the emperor, rather than *to* him) were among the rituals associated with the cult. Depending upon the date, region, and ruler (the West was later than the East to take up the cult), the emperor was perceived more or less as equal to the gods, especially while still living. Octavian, for instance, initially kept up the traditional Roman insistence on being revered not as a god himself but as the son of a god (*divi filius*), that is, of the Divine Julius, whose apotheosis was generally acknowledged after his death.[41] This stance changed once Octavian officially became Augustus (or Sebastos in the East), permitted a cult to his guiding spirit (*genius*), and allowed the provincial assemblies in Asia Minor to offer him worship in conjunction with the goddess Roma. Even so, depending on the place and time, the emperor might limit his cult or even refuse to be received as a god while he was still alive, especially in Italy and some of the western provinces.

Historians have disagreed about the extent of actual devotion to the imperial cult. The cult itself has tended to be viewed as crassly political and opportunistic—less a "true religion" than a way of holding power, manipulating loyalty and patriotism, and advancing civic pride. Clearly, the ruler cult, however defined, was an important tool for consolidating authority and enforcing Roman rule, even in areas that were vast and difficult to govern. But drawing clear boundaries between culture and politics or between politics and religious affiliation is tricky, at an historical distance. The portrayal of Augustus as Jupiter or the representation of his descendent Claudius in that same guise (fig. 17) should probably not be taken as an assertion that Augustus or Claudius was transformed into a Supreme Deity, but rather that the position and authority of the emperor was parallel to that of the chief of the gods. However later historians perceive political function, the honor or worship given to the Roman emperor, his ancestors, his wife, and his children was a significant aspect of everyday life in the first four centuries of the Common Era.[42]

As a key material aspect of this cult, the emperor's portrait played a special role in addition to establishing his personal character and general appearance. It could represent the absent ruler and receive the honor and respect due him. The system worked entirely through the connection of image and presence, the actual likeness of the imperial visage being enough to establish a kind of proxy presence. That presence was not, of course, actually of the living emperor himself, because he was bodily elsewhere. What was present was the emperor's *genius* or *numen*, his sacred and guiding spirit that was attached to any image of him. This genius could be simultaneously in several places at once and could be the focus of a cult without a too overt or unseemly show of imperial hubris. Naturally, this spirit became more powerful and omnipresent as the emperor himself was elevated to the rank of divinity while yet living, as in the case of Nero, Caligula, or Domitian. But such a claim, if overstated (at least in Rome), could lead to the downfall of the claimant. The distinction between *divus* (as in *Divus* Julius) and *deus* (generally reserved to the gods themselves) was important and politically sensitive, and titles or honors bestowed in Asia Minor or Egypt were often not acceptable in more traditionally minded Rome itself.[43]

Whatever the divine status granted to the emperor as mediator or vicar between the Romans and their gods, his image mediated presence and allowed access to power—mostly for the purpose of receiving honor, homage, or adoration, but also to establish his authority over political and legal matters. The imperial image was a vital presence that commanded fear and obedience, receiving and dispensing all that was due the emperor himself. It witnessed official acts, presided over judicial hearings, enforced laws, guaranteed oaths, dispensed clemency, and accepted gifts and sacrifices. An illustration of just such a tribunal can be found as late as the sixth century in an illumination from the Rossano Gospels depicting the trial of Jesus before Pilate. Given the image's role as proxy for the emperor, disrespect shown to it was equivalent to treason and was met with the harshest possible consequences.[44]

One well-known description of how the emperor's image functioned (and how it might have been both similar to and different from those of the gods) is included in the correspondence between Pliny the Younger, then Governor of Bithynia, and Emperor Trajan. Pliny had received anonymous accusations concerning certain "Christians," whom he subsequently arrested. He released them, he wrote in his letter to the emperor, so long as they denied the charge, recited a prayer to the gods dictated by himself, and made an offering of wine and incense to the statue of the emperor, which Pliny had brought into the court for this purpose "together with images of the gods." Those arrested also had to curse Christ, something the governor had discovered that those who really were Christians could not be made to do.[45] Pliny may have deliberately distinguished between statues (*simalcra*) of the gods and an image (*imago*) of the emperor, although he does indicate that both types of images were worshiped (*venerati*) on this occasion.

This power by the proxy of image remained entrenched well into the era of Christian emperors, when the claims of divine status were (understandably) moderated. As Severian of Galaba wrote around the year 400:

> Since an emperor cannot be present to all persons, it is necessary to set up the statue of the emperor in law courts, market places, public assemblies, and theaters. In every place, in fact, in which an official acts, the imperial effigy must be present, so that the emperor may thus confirm what takes place. For the emperor is only a human being, and he cannot be present everywhere.[46]

This statement shows that even when the emperor's divinity was no longer asserted, the image was still understood to communicate his practical and potent presence. Indeed, the very need for the image is now explained by of the emperor's *humanity*, not his divinity.

Images of the emperor were of several kinds, from the monumental to the miniature. Permanent statues were set up in the central forum and amphitheater of cities across the empire. A portable painting on a wooden panel or a portrait attached to imperial insignia or a military shield (*clipeus*) could transform any ordinary space into one overseen by the emperor's presiding spirit. A military loss of the imperial standards was a terrible disgrace and was even perceived as a kind of religious sacrilege.[47] Most widespread and accessible of all, of course, were images stamped onto coins (see figs. 40–41, pp. 67–68). The representative presence of the emperor was thus widely and easily available to all subjects in the empire. It may, in fact, have been hard to avoid.[48] Lawbreakers might even gain at least temporary asylum by grasping an imperial image.[49] The popularity of imperial portrait likenesses was one of the subjects of a letter sent some time between the years 145 and 147 C.E. to the young heir to the imperial throne, the Caesar Marcus Aurelius, from his tutor Marcus Cornelius Fronto:

> You know how, in all the money-changers' bureaus, booths, bookstalls, eaves, porches, windows, anywhere and everywhere there are likenesses of you exposed to view, badly enough painted most of them to be sure, and modeled

or carved in a plain, not to say sorry style of art, yet at the same time your likeness, however much of a caricature, never when I go out meets my eyes without making me part my lips for a smile and dream of you.[50]

Whether well or badly executed, the image had to possess at least a conventional recognizability. The achievement of an identifiable likeness was managed by the transport of models, probably originating in Rome and carried to workshops around the empire. While consistency in appearance was necessary in order to allow the image to be recognized, variations often appeared, depending on the prevailing style, regional taste, or desire to emphasize a particular aspect of character such as piety, power, or intelligence. Images might also disappear—intentionally. Images of emperors who were assassinated or disgraced, as well as inscriptions that referred to them, were destroyed or obliterated (*damnatio memoriae*).[51]

Christian attitudes toward imperial images varied, to some degree according to the ways different writers or church officials actually viewed these objects. A great deal of misunderstanding surrounds the role these images played, especially in the persecution of Christians. The apologetic literature of the early period provides some interesting variations on how the imperial images were understood to function and the dangers they posed to Christians who wished to resist idolatry. Justin Martyr referred to imperial images indirectly by citing the Gospel story in which Jesus used the figure of Caesar on a coin to explain what was due to the emperor and what to God (Mark 12:13-17). Justin used this episode to reassure the loyal Romans in his audience that Christians were taxpayers, since they had been taught by their Lord to "render tribute to Caesar." But he then pointed to Jesus' next line—"render worship to God alone"—in order to defend Christian willingness to pray *for* but not *to* the emperor: "Thus to God alone we render worship, but in other things we gladly serve you, acknowledging you as kings and rulers, and praying that with your kingly power you be found to possess also sound judgment."[52]

Tertullian was more direct about the distinction between praying for the safety, health, welfare, and wisdom of rulers and swearing by the tutelary spirit of the Caesars (presumably including those attached to their portraits). Christians, after all were enjoined to pray for earthly rulers (1 Tim 2:2) but not for or to demons, which they were more likely to exorcise than swear by, nor, he says, are Christians able to confer divine honor on the spirit of the emperor.[53] Tertullian thereby tried to portray Christians as patriotic in their own way and, in fact, even protective of the emperor by refusing to grant him divine status or his images the kind of honor only due God. After all, he says, if the emperor were not a human being, he could not be emperor.[54] In a similar way, Minucius Felix argued that kings and emperors are not served by being flattered and fawned upon as gods or by having oaths sworn before their effigies, but they are honored in being offered tribute as actual men of outstanding quality.[55] Both these writers presented Christians as respectful of and even concerned for the welfare of the rulers, perhaps more like old-fashioned Romans than dangerous subversives in their attitudes toward the deification of human rulers. To the extent that patriotism demanded, they could represent themselves as quite respectful of the office or *auctoritas* of the emperor. This was the same position taken by Jews, as described by Josephus, who were quite willing to pay homage to the emperor, including offering daily victimless sacrifices—a "special honor" accorded to no other person.[56]

But while second-century Christian writers kept a discreet silence about the problem of the cult and cultic images of the emperor, the first-century Jewish community did not, once they felt that the Romans had ceased to respect their understanding about not requiring them to erect statues of the emperors or of the pagan gods in their nation. Reports of clashes over such images provide an important source of information about the role of imperial portraits in the religion and politics of the Empire. Josephus recounts a demonstration of outrage that took place among certain pious Jews when Pilate brought military standards with effigies of Emperor Tiberius into Jerusalem. Seeing that they were willing to die as martyrs in a nonviolent protest to uphold Jewish law, Pilate relented and removed the standards.[57] Josephus recounts another incident, in which Caligula sent a deputy by the name of Petronius to Jerusalem to install Caligula's statue in the temple, demanding that he be hailed as a god. Resisters were to be put to death. Faced with a full-scale war, Petronius backed down and was saved from his own execution only by the assassination of Caligula. Apparently, both of these Roman leaders had seriously underestimated Jewish feelings about images of foreign gods (or of occupying rulers) in their holy places.[58]

Nevertheless, like Justin and Tertullian, Josephus took a conciliatory approach, arguing that the Jewish refusal to erect or honor statues of the emperors was not based on hatred—or even disrespect—for Rome and its rulers, but on an understanding that they be officially granted the freedom to abide by their own religious laws. He explains that although pious Jews eschewed the making or veneration of images, they nevertheless were willing to offer sacrifice and prayers for the emperor and his family. Furthermore, although pious Jews had "contempt for a practice profitable to neither God nor mortal [the making of images of living creatures]," they nonetheless offered perpetual sacrifices and prayers for the emperor and his family.[59] The Talmud tells a story of one particularly holy man, Rabbi Nahum bar Simai, who never in his life even looked upon a coin, because it "bore the image" (of the emperor).[60] The Christian polemicist Hippolytus offered similar testimony to Jewish sensitivity about imperial images, particularly on coins.[61]

Fig. 34. Daniel, three youths, and Nebuchadnezzar, 4th cen. C.E. Christian sarcophagus (with detail insert), Musée de l'Arles Antique (Photo: Author).

The story of Shadrach, Meshach, and Abednego in the Book of Daniel provided a model for Jewish resistance to imperial images, and we have abundant textual evidence that Christians saw it as a type for their own resistance to religious persecution in the first three centuries C.E. According to the story, when King Nebuchadnezzar of Babylon set up a gold statue and ordered that it be worshiped, these three refused and were thrown into the fiery furnace. Their miraculous survival demonstrated the power of their God and their own heroism in being willing to die rather than worship a vain idol. Christian interpreters made much of this story, seeing the three as figures of martyrdom—forced by imperial edicts, like many Christians, to choose between performing idolatrous acts or suffering torture and imprisonment. Cyprian praises the confessors (those who survived martyrdom) by comparing them to these biblical heroes: "For we can see that in your own case there have been put into action the words which these courageous and celebrated youths proclaimed before the king. They declared that for their part they were prepared to burn in the flames rather than to serve his gods or adore the idol that he had made; yet, they asserted, the God whom they worshiped (and whom we also worship) had the power to

Detail of Fig. 34.

release them from the fiery furnace, and to rescue them from the hands of the king."[62] Thus the martyrs of Carthage were likened to the youths of Babylon and were accorded highest honors.

A number of scenes found in early Christian art illustrate this story, making it a visual exhortation to resist idolatry. A fourth-century fresco in the Roman Catacomb of Marcus and Marcellinus depicts the three youths standing with the king who points to a bust set upon a column. Another fourth-century work, a relief carved on the lid of a sarcophagus now in Arles, shows the three youths turning their backs on a similar bust atop a rather more ornate column. Daniel appears just to the right of this scene, a heroic nude with his rather tame lions on either side (fig. 34). Neither of these works of art accurately illustrates the details of the biblical story. The statues are not made to look as if they are forty cubits high and made of gold as described in the Bible. Instead, these tableaux appear to interpret the statue as an image of Nebuchadnezzar himself, looking very much like a portrait of a Roman emperor, set up for honor or sacrifice in the public square. The art has already incorporated the current (or just recently past) situation of Christians, who resisted paying honors to images of the emperor along with those of the traditional Roman gods.

The change of Christianity's status under Constantine affected the character of the imperial cult only superficially. Constantine, like his predecessors, was proclaimed a *divus* after his death, and coins and medals were minted showing him ascending into heaven in a chariot, being received by the hand of God. His Christian subjects granted this distinction, interpreting it as a claim that Constantine was especially guided by, and in a privileged relation to, their God. In life, Constantine had fashioned himself as the thirteenth apostle, convening and presiding over the first ecumenical council at Nicaea in 325 C.E.; after his death, he was honored as a saint and buried in the Church of the Apostles. His portraits, whether on coins or statues, visually expressed his saintly character.[63] According to his not-unbiased biographer Eusebius:

> How deeply his soul was impressed by the power of divine faith may be understood from the circumstance that he directed his likeness to be stamped on the golden coin of the empire with the eyes uplifted as in the posture of prayer to God; and this money became current throughout the Roman world. His portrait also at full length was placed over the entrance gates of the palaces in some cities, the eyes upraised to heaven, and the hands outspread as if in prayer.[64]

In this way, Constantine's biographer flatteringly portrays the emperor not only as pious, but also as a heavenly inspired and divinely legitimated ruler.

Although Constantine ordered sacrifices to the imperial images to cease, in other respects the role of imperial portraits remained very much the same, as mediating the presence of the person himself.[65] The role of the emperor parallels that of a saint in Christian tradition, which ironically may have been a clearer separation from divinity than the difference between a *divus* and a *deus* in the previous era. And from this point on, the emperor's image could be equated with the image of the saint. As Glen Bowersock explains:

> Any religious institution [the imperial cult] that lasted over four hundred years and could accommodate both pagans and Christians was not without vitality. It endured so long because it succeeded in making multitudes of citizens in far-flung regions feel close to the power that controlled them. It did not, for most of its duration, respond to those desperate human anxieties over salvation in the next world and disease in this one; but at least it kept a Roman citizen from feeling helpless and alone in a faceless crowd.[66]

Not long after the elevation of Constantine and Christianity's transition from a persecuted cult to an imperially sanctioned one, Christian theologians referenced the mediatory function of the imperial image to explain the equality of natures within the Trinity. Athanasius, speaking of the identity of natures between the Father and the Son in his *Third Discourse against the Arians*, explained the passage from the Gospel of John, "The one who has seen the Son has seen the Father" (John 14:9) by analogy to the image of the emperor:

> And we may perceive this at once from the illustration of the emperor's image. For in the image of the emperor is the shape and form of the emperor, and in the emperor is the shape which is in the image. For the likeness of the emperor in the image is exact; so that a person who looks at the image, sees in it the emperor; and the one who sees the emperor, recognizes that it is he who is in the image. . . . Accordingly the one who worships the image, in it worships the emperor also; for the image is his form and appearance.[67]

Likewise, in his treatise on the Holy Spirit, Basil of Caesarea uses the analogy of the emperor's image to illustrate his proof that the First and Second Persons do not constitute two different gods:

> For the Son is in the Father and the Father is in the Son; since such as is the latter, such is the former, and such as is the former, such is the latter; and herein is the Unity. So that according to the distinction of Persons, both are one and one, and according to the community of natures, one. How, then, if one and one, are there not two gods? Because we speak of a king, and of the king's image, and not of two kings. The majesty is not cloven in two, nor the glory divided. The sovereignty and authority over us is one, and so the doxology ascribed by us is not plural but one; because the honor paid to the image passes on to the prototype.

His last observation would one day be critically important to the theological justification for venerating saints' icons, of course. Basil concludes his comparison by pointing out its basic flaw. Whereas the imperial portrait is an image only by virtue of its being an imitation, the Son shares the actual nature of the Father and thus is in full communion with the Godhead.[68]

According to the record, four hundred years later (787 C.E.) at the conclusion of the Seventh Ecumenical Council when the devotional function of icons was finally pronounced as an important precept of orthodoxy, a one-time iconoclast, Bishop Theodosius of Ammorium, confessed his faith and asked to be reinstated as an orthodox believer. Insisting he now had no theological objection to the veneration of the portraits of saints, he explained his change of heart as the result of his noting a common practice: "For if the people go forth with lights and incense to meet the '*laurata*' and images of the Emperors when they are sent to cities or rural districts, they honor surely not the tablet covered over with wax, but the Emperor himself."[69] Theodosius may have been influenced by the persuasive arguments of Theodore the Studite, who died in exile during the reign of the last iconoclast emperors and who cited both Basil and Athanasius to this very effect.[70] With the passage of time and assurance that the emperor was himself Christian, any remaining scruples about offering honor to his images had disappeared, and he could be seen as mortal representative of the heavenly King. The rituals associated with the old Roman emperor-cult had survived the transition to Christianity and were incorporated into Byzantine court ceremonial.[71]

The Images of the Gods

Even though the attacks launched against idolatry by Christian theologians from Paul to Athanasius would suggest that the adherents to conventional Greco-Roman religions were confirmed idol worshipers, surviving documents actually show that the intellectually inclined of the ancient world were ambivalent about the myths, rituals, and idols of the traditional cult. Although the polytheism of Roman Late Antiquity embraced many gods and had incorporated or absorbed many of the varied local or foreign deities, the educated classes tended toward a kind of enlightened deism, interpreting the myths as poetic allegories and eschewing overly materialistic beliefs that localized or limited divinity to a particular statue or image.[72] Nevertheless, in order that they might remain favorable, the gods still received devotion and prayerful petitions from the devotees. For this purpose, their images, carved and painted, were produced in impressive quantities, ranging from the highest art forms to the crudest and most mundane. Temples as well as markets were filled with figures of the gods; shrines and altars in public spaces, street corners, shops, and private homes were well supplied. Representations of the gods were simply everywhere, as Christian teachers reluctantly noted, and since they were almost impossible to avoid, Christians were urged to avert their eyes, or blow or spit on them.[73] Some of these images were by famous sculptors, but more often were knock-off copies of famous statues. Countless others were simply made from molds. Wall paintings, portable images, and mosaics also decorated the homes of those who could afford them.[74]

Dio Chrysostom, a first-century orator and philosopher, listed artistic representations of the gods as one of four or five basic sources for human conception of the divine (along with the innate understanding and knowledge gained from poets, lawgivers, and philosophers). To him, skilled craftspeople who made statues or likenesses, whether in stone, wood, metal, wax, or paint (and he listed many of the greatest artists known to him), gave their patrons "ample and varied conception of the divine" by producing all sorts of figures of different gods, in a variety of poses. Dio pointed out, however, that artisans were reticent about one thing—they shied away from innovations, preferring to adhere to the images described by the poets and to maintain some consistency with one another in their representations. Nevertheless, he added, a few had dared to contribute their own ideas and thus became the poets' rivals as well as fellow craftsmen—primarily out of positive impulse to honor the divine beings and to win their favor.[75]

The artist's particular contribution to the work of making an image of a god might make it truer than a simple copy or imitation of a standard figure, at least in the view of some exponents. According to his third-century biographer Philostratus, Apollonius of Tyana objected to the Egyptians' representation of their gods as animals or birds. Such things seemed to him irrational and indecent, and he thought that by doing this the Egyptians showed that they ridiculed rather than believed in the gods. His Egyptian companion, offended by his view, sarcastically asks Apollonius how artists like Phidias or Praxiteles could know how the gods appeared—had they gone up to heaven to make the images they reproduced in their sculpture or was there some other means by which they produced their figures of the gods?—for what besides imitation could be a basis for such representation? Apollonius answers that the artist's imagination is a subtle thing, "pregnant with wisdom and genius," and that work incorporating this imagination is far superior to and more awe-inspiring than any mere imitation or copy, "for imitation can only create as its handiwork what it has seen, but imagination equally what it has not seen; for it will conceive of its ideal with reference to the reality, and imitation is often baffled by terror, but imagination by nothing; for it marches undismayed to the goal which it has itself laid down."[76]

Although the ubiquity of such images suggests that they were often merely commonplace objects of domestic decoration more than focal points of deep religious piety, what all these widely varying images of the gods had in common was their superficial recognizability. The viewer should be able to identify the god in the image, at least from certain characteristic attributes (details of garb, props, hair or beard style, and so forth). Images were the necessary props for the cult of a god, without being the actual focus of it—representing the gods but not actually identical with them (since so many replicas existed). The almost countless little altars, shrines, or dedicatory inscriptions that are still extant demonstrate the widespread and deeply entrenched habits of Roman polytheism. Such things were undoubtedly part of one's cultural identity and expressions of a kind of local, civic, or national pride that was exemplified to some extent in the gods one worshiped. Significant exceptions to this conventional perception of the deities existed, of course—the statue of Artemis in Ephesus, for instance, or the mysterious black stone Baal of Elagabalus, which seem to have had a more powerful hold on the imagination of their devotees.[77]

However, traditional polytheists might also be wary of too much superstition in regard to such things. Plutarch, for one, expressed contempt for persons who made divine images in the likenesses of human beings and dressed them up and worshiped them.[78] Nearly three hundred years later (at the end of the fourth century), Emperor Julian was determined that people should distinguish between the images and the gods themselves, just as they should distinguish between the image of the emperor and the emperor himself. Still, he declares, the images had a powerful function, and the attraction that they held was based on the degree of affection that the viewer had for the model:

> For our fathers established images and altars, and the maintenance of undying fire, and generally speaking everything of the sort, as symbols of the presence of the gods, not that we may regard such things as gods, but that we may worship the gods through them. . . . For just as those who make offerings to the statues of the emperors, who are in need of nothing, nevertheless induce goodwill towards themselves thereby, so too those who make offerings to the images of the gods (though the gods need nothing) do nevertheless thereby persuade them to help and to care for them. . . . Therefore, when we look at the images of the gods, let us not indeed think they are stones or wood, but neither let us think they are the gods themselves; and indeed, we do not say that the statues of the emperors are mere wood and stone and bronze, but still less do we say they are the emperors themselves. He then who loves the emperor delights to see the emperor's statue, and he who loves his son delights to see his son's statue, and he who loves his father delights to see his father's statue. It follows that the one who loves the gods delights to gaze on

the images of the gods and their likenesses, and should feel reverence and shudder with awe of the gods who look back from the unseen world.[79]

Cult images were equally important for the ancient and traditional Roman gods (for example, Jupiter, Juno, Mars, and Minerva) as for imported or regional deities like Mithras, Cybele, and Dea Caelestis, who tended to have a more self-selected group of devotees or provincial transplants. They played a key role in the religious revivals (and political propaganda) of particular emperors, such as Augustus, who associated his family with Venus and himself as a special favorite of Apollo. These cult images of gods had generally recognizable appearances, even when their identities were conflated (as in Apollo/Sol/Helios). Jupiter, for instance, was presented as the supreme ruling god (a mature potent male), with full dark beard and abundant hair. He was usually pictured as enthroned and holding a scepter or other props of the ruler of heaven, with an eagle at his feet. Depending on their rank or authority, other male gods might have a similar appearance. Neptune and Asclepius also appear with full beards and heads of hair as do Mars and Hades. Gods associated with Jupiter (Zeus), such as Liber or Serapis, were given very similar facial features but with their own distinctive attributes (in Serapis's case, the small grain measuring basket or *modius* on his head; fig. 35). Mars, on the other hand, was sometimes shown in full military dress including an ornate breastplate (*cuirass*), while at other times appeared nude except for his military cloak, quiver strap, and helmet; the nude depictions are rare, although some exceptions exist (for example, the Jupiter Column at Mainz). Artistic representa-

Fig. 35. Busts of Roman Gods, now in the British Museum, London (Photo: Author).

tions of this group of gods intended to project dominion, authority, and an uncontested right to rule and to judge.

Another group was made up of the younger male gods (such as Apollo/Sol, Hermes, the semidivine Hercules, and sometimes Mars), gods associated with the mystery cults (Dionysus, Mithras, and Orpheus), or heroes (such as Meleager, Hercules, and Adonis). Members of this group were often shown as youths with flowing locks and beardless (or nearly beardless) faces, although they could also be shown as mature figures with beards and older body types (especially Dionysus and Hercules). While Jupiter and the older gods of the Pantheon were usually shown bare-chested but draped, these younger gods often appeared nude, with almost pubescent bodies. This is especially true, for example, of Dionysus and Apollo (fig. 36). Mithras and Orpheus wore typical clothing identifying them as "eastern" in origin (see fig. 69, p. 149) while Hercules—although nude—was usually bearded and was more ruggedly masculine. These gods, on the boundary between youth and maturity and even, in some cases on the boundary between female and male, projected sensuality and could be polymorphic. They were the mediators between the upper and lower worlds, managing the transition from life to death or bringing messages from heaven or Hades. Sol/Helios was also a kind of mediator, riding his chariot over the heavens to turn night into day.

Fig. 36. Dionysus with panther, Archaeological Museum of the Phlegraean Fields, 1st cen. C.E., Roman reconstruction of Greek original, Castello di Baia (Photo: Author).

Given the familiarity of the traditional images, foreign gods and heroes who were introduced to the Roman pantheon often entered by means of conflation with known deities. Jupiter was conflated with the senior gods of other nations (such as Sabazios or Serapis), just as the younger gods were often linked with one another. Apollo was variously associated with Helios and Sol, for example. Their representations then borrowed the facial types, postures, or sometimes attributes from one another. According to Lucian, Heracles was transformed into Heracles Ogmios by the Celts, who kept his general garb and equipment (lion's skin and club, bow and quiver) but transformed his physical appearance, from that of a young hero to a balding old man, and gave him a very dark complexion.[80]

Although often confused with one another, the female gods were most easily recognized by details of their attire, headdresses, props, or other attributes. Diana was nearly always equipped with a bow and quiver, and she, like Apollo, was associated with one of the celestial deities (Luna). Athena wore a quite recognizable helmet. Isis generally was shown with particular Egyptian accoutrements, including her special rattle (*sistrum*). She was sometimes shown with the child Horus on her lap and a bared breast to feed him, an image often asserted to be the prototype of the Virgin Mary with child (fig. 37).[81] Venus (also known by her Greek name, Aphrodite) was almost always at least partially nude, draped so as to accentuate her physical beauty, while Juno was usually presented as

Fig. 37. Harpocrates on the lap of Isis, wall painting from house in Karanis, now in Cairo (Photo: George R. Swain, by permission of the Kelsey Museum Archives, the University of Michigan).

modest and matronly. Reclining Tellus (Earth) holds her cornucopia, which makes her difficult to distinguish from Ceres, Italia, or even Pax, as she appears on the Ara Pacis in Rome (fig. 38). There were other female personifications too: Pietas, Salus, Fortuna, and Concordia each had a particular prop or attribute to identify her. Winged Victory held out her crown. In a similar way, Roma became the personification of the state and received temples and cult, usually in conjunction with the emperor. Such personifications were adapted by the Christian church to represent virtues of its own (faith, hope, or charity), or even the church (Ecclesia) "herself," just as the later Madonna iconography borrows from the various representations of both virgin and mother goddesses (Persephone and Isis, for example). The practice of adding necessary identifying attributes of traditional gods and goddesses was clearly carried over into the images of the saints from the fifth century onward.[82]

The function of the actual images of the gods can be difficult to specify and, indeed, was subject to a variety of interpretations. Like the portrait of the emperor, images of the gods served a kind of representative role. They did not entrap the spirit of the deity in a particular place or statue but rather mediated a presence that was understood to be in many different places simultaneously. At the same time, the image of the god was a central aspect of the religion, since this was the way that devotees recognized the presence of the god and were called to reverence. To venerate a divine image was actually to exhibit a pious respect (if not actual devotion) to its model. And yet the power and efficacy of these objects continued as an open question well into the era when polytheism was waning, after the death of Julian the Apostate. For instance, in *City of God*, Augustine cites a debate between Hermes Trismegistus (the "thrice holy") and Asclepius about the nature and operation of divine images that suggests the question was still a live one at the beginning of the fifth century.

In this document, Hermes contrasts the gods created by the Supreme Deity with images made by human hands but acknowledges (according to Augustine) that human artisans had a technique for attaching immortal spirits (or demons) to material bodies. In this way "the visible and tangible idols are in some way the bodies of gods; certain spirits have been induced to take up their abode in them and have the power either to do harm, or satisfy many of the wants of those who offer them divine honors and obedient worship." Yet, even so, this is only an imitation of divinity, and Hermes predicts a time when all images will finally be destroyed as "delusional and pernicious." Augustine interprets Hermes' words as referring to the arrival of Christianity, which then casts the debate as an example of pre-Christian prophecy.[83]

Taking advantage of divine images' power, the emperors, their wives, children, mothers, and even favorites sometimes were depicted in the guise of one of the gods, a tradition that may have begun with the representations of Alexander as Zeus. Augustus appeared enthroned with the goddess Roma, his portrait bearing some of Jupiter's attributes but holding an augur's staff rather than a thunderbolt. His wife, Livia, appeared in the guise of several goddesses, including Ceres and Magna Mater. Her representation as Ceres Augusta in the theater at Leptis Magna is a famous example.[84] Nero (like several subsequent emperors) identified himself with Helios or Apollo and had himself represented with a radiate halo.[85] Hadrian's lover Antinous was variously portrayed as Bacchus, Apollo, and Silvanus, the god of the forest.[86] At the end of the

Fig. 38. Tellus (Mother Earth) from the Ara Pacis Augustae, Rome 13–9 B.C.E. (Photo: Author).

second century, Commodus appeared with the lion's skin and club of Hercules in a famous bust found on the Esquiline and now in the Museo del Palazzo dei Conservatori, perhaps modeled after an earlier such representation of Domitian (fig. 39).[87] His mother, who appears in many portraits, has been identified as the face upon the figure of Venus in a modestly draped group sculpture of Venus and Mars (her husband, Marcus Aurelius, appearing as Mars).[88] Julia Domna, the mother of Caracalla and Geta, was portrayed, just as Livia had been earlier, in the guise of the protective mother and fertility goddess Ceres (or Demeter) or given the attributes of Juno and Isis.[89] In most cases, such representations did not intend to identify the mortal ruler as a particular immortal god (*deus*), but to associate the one with the other, and to give the imperial personage quasi-divine status (*divinitas*). The intention was to legitimize their earthly authority by associating it with immortal divinity. At the same time, adopting the iconographic aspects or attributes of the gods imparted a sense that these particular character traits belonged likewise to the ruling individual. In some cases, the emperor even adopted the halo of the gods for himself.[90]

Fig. 39. Commodus as Hercules, 191–192 C.E., Museo del Palazzo dei Conservatori, Rome (Photo: Author).

Like most of the earlier emperors, the first Tetrarchs—Diocletian, Maximian, Constantius Chlorus, and Galerius—were associated in their portraiture with the gods, in their particular case with Jupiter and Hercules according to their senior rank as Augustus or junior rank as Caesar, an identification that was reflected on the iconography of their coinage (fig. 40). Claiming to be in some sense human representatives of these deities, they adopted the divine names into their own and in so doing reaffirmed Roman religion, repudiating the quasi-monotheistic cult of the Unconquered Sun instituted by Diocletian's predecessor, Aurelian. The distinction between Jupiter and Hercules was significant with regard to the division of authority and role among the four rulers. Jupiter is the ruler and judge who sits upon his throne in majesty, while Hercules is the active agent, known for his wondrous deeds. Such distinctions came to play a role in the iconography of Christ, whose facial features suggest that he plays both roles—on the one hand as the enthroned ruler, and on the other as the active and incarnate agent of the Divine Trinity.[91]

However, when Constantine I ascended to power and began to con-solidate his rule, the divine patron was Sol. This may have been a way for him to signal a break with the Tetrarchy. The critical moment for this adoption (or conversion) was reported to be a vision that Constantine had while visiting a sanctuary of Apollo in Gaul.[92] Since the worship of the Sun already held an official position and significant following, when Constantine had his vision of the cross (or *chi rho*) and "converted" to the Christian faith, he may have conveniently confused the Christian God and Sol, or perhaps allowed a certain ambiguity between their respective symbolism. In this respect, Constantine tried a different approach from that of the earlier Roman emperor, Elagabalus (218–222 C.E.), who also tried to establish the worship of the Syrian god of the sun under the Roman name "Sol Invictus" but who identified himself with the god, rather than taking that god as his personal patron. In any case, images of Sol, shown as a youthful nude god wearing a cape and radiate crown (or halo), remained on the coin reverses of Constantine until the mid 320s (fig. 41). Later, during the last of the revivals of polytheism, Julian the Apostate made similar attempts to promulgate the worship of Sol, whom he associated not only with Mithras (into whose cult he had been initiated) but also with the language of Neoplatonism and even echoes of Christian teaching (his former, but renounced faith). King Helios, as he calls him, is the Son and Image of the Idea of the Good and coexistent with the Good from eternity.[93]

The religious and social culture in which Christianity emerged and developed understood viewing images of heroes, deceased family mem-bers, emperors, and gods as an essential part of one's engagement with these persons or beings and with their personal patronage and authority. The center of one's gaze, specifically, was the face—the access point for this subject-object relationship. Whatever its degree of "likeness," the face mediated the representative or real presence of the model as no other part of the body (or being) might allow. The portrait thus had a distinct function, more than a didactic, memorial, or even inspirational one. It also offered a mode of encounter or experience of theophany not avail-able in the same manner through a narrative image. God was apparent in events and deeds but now even more so in the holy face itself.

For these reasons, external appearance was more than mere illusion, more than a record of a transitory and superficial exterior. It was a way to establish a connection between realms, whether of the dead and the living, the royal and the lay, or the mortal and the immortal. It became a

Fig. 40. Gold coins (*aurei*) showing Diocletian and Maximian (obverses) with Jupiter and Hercules on their respective reverses, minted in Trier, 294 C.E. (Photo: Courtesy of the American Numismatic Society).

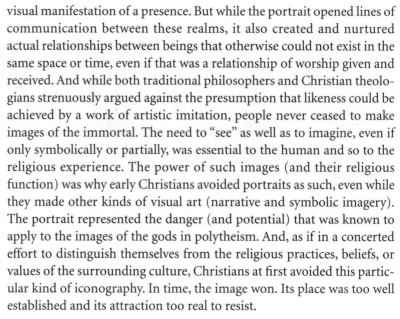

visual manifestation of a presence. But while the portrait opened lines of communication between these realms, it also created and nurtured actual relationships between beings that otherwise could not exist in the same space or time, even if that was a relationship of worship given and received. And while both traditional philosophers and Christian theologians strenuously argued against the presumption that likeness could be achieved by a work of artistic imitation, people never ceased to make images of the immortal. The need to "see" as well as to imagine, even if only symbolically or partially, was essential to the human and so to the religious experience. The power of such images (and their religious function) was why early Christians avoided portraits as such, even while they made other kinds of visual art (narrative and symbolic imagery). The portrait represented the danger (and potential) that was known to apply to the images of the gods in polytheism. And, as if in a concerted effort to distinguish themselves from the religious practices, beliefs, or values of the surrounding culture, Christians at first avoided this particular kind of iconography. In time, the image won. Its place was too well established and its attraction too real to resist.

Fig. 41. Three Constantinian coins with slightly different reverse types, minted in Ticinum, 316 C.E. (Photo: Courtesy of the American Numismatic Society).

THREE

The Invisible God and the Visible Image

AROUND THE TURN of the third century, just before the earliest known date that Roman Christians began to adorn the walls of their burial places (with figurative art), a professional advocate and North African Christian convert, Marcus Minucius Felix, summarized a (probably fictional) debate between a Christian named Octavius and a polytheist named Caecilius. The dispute was over the credibility, morality, and value of Christian faith, and, although at the end Caecilius is converted, he offers some expected pagan criticism of Christian teachings and practices, including their lack of divine images. That Christians did things in secret surely indicated their shame and perversity. That they believed their god to be invisible, omniscient, and omnipresent demonstrated their gullibility:

> Why else should they go to such pains to hide and conceal whatever it is they worship . . . why do they have no altars, no temples, no publicly known images? . . . Besides, look at the fantastic, unnatural creature that these Christians have devised! They make that god of theirs—whom they are unable to show to others or see for themselves—they make him pry with scrupulous care into the morals and actions of all men, even down to their words and hidden thoughts; he has to rush to and fro, he has to be present everywhere![1]

Octavius answered Caecilius's objections by asserting God's essential transcendence of human vision and knowledge:

> Now you think that if we have neither temples nor altars we are concealing the object of our worship? But what image would I fashion for God, seeing that humans rightly consider themselves the image of God? What temple would I erect to him, seeing that this entire universe, the work of his hands, cannot contain him? Would I enclose the might of such majesty within the

confines of a single chapel, while I, a man, may lodge more spaciously? It is a better course, you must agree, that he should be dedicated in our minds, or rather consecrated in our hearts.[2]

Octavius's response clearly echoes Paul's speech to the Athenians, as recounted in Acts 17. The text suggests that Paul's address was given at the behest of devout Jews as well as Stoic and Epicurean philosophers, with whom he had been arguing. Although he was distressed to see that their city was full of idols, Paul opened, somewhat surprisingly, by complimenting his audience on their extreme religiosity. In particular, he noted, they had an altar dedicated to an "unknown god." Making this altar his object lesson and undoubtedly hoping to find some common ground with his intellectually sophisticated listeners, Paul announced that Christians worship this "unknown God," a god who "does not live in shrines" and is not made of gold, silver, or stone, "an image formed by the art and imagination of mortals" (Acts 17:22-29).

Octavius, like Paul, draws upon the teachings of Greek and Roman poets and philosophers to support his contention that the Christian God is far above needing a human shelter or service, far beyond human vision or knowledge. This God, he says, "cannot be seen; he is too bright for sight. He cannot be grasped; he is too pure for touch. He cannot be measured; he is too great for our senses—a boundless infinity, sharing with himself alone the knowledge of his vastness." Octavius continues, denying that anyone can know the magnitude of God or seek a name for God. Titles or personal names distinguish individuals in a group, but God is unique. "Should I call Him father, you would consider that He is earthly; should I call Him king, you would suspect that He is made of flesh; should I call Him lord, you would certainly understand that He is mortal. Remove the aggregate of names and you will see clearly His splendor."[3] All these truths are well known to the common people as well as poets and such philosophers as Pythagoras, Antisthenes, Epicurus, Aristotle, Zeno, and Plato. All these philosophers hold opinions "pretty well identical with ours."[4]

After pronouncing those who fail to understand the definitive unknowability of the unique, unrepresentable, and unnamable God, Octavius goes on to ridicule anyone deluded and superstitious enough to offer prayer or sacrifice to images of the pagan gods. No matter how artistically elegant, these things could be nothing more than dead objects made by ordinary human craft. Even animals, birds, and insects realized their worthlessness as they trampled over, perched on, and built nests or webs in such idols, leaving them for "you to wipe, clean, and scour, thus protecting, and yet dreading gods you have made yourselves."[5] Anyone, he says, who would take part in rituals involving these images or their supposed gods is both laughable and pitiable, deluded and of unsound mind.

Justin Martyr: Refutation of Idols and Divine Theophanies

Mocking the inanimate statues of pagan gods was a well-used ploy long before Minucius Felix wrote his dialogue. Justin Martyr, who lived a century before Minucius Felix, similarly regarded honoring images of the gods as foolish, but he also believed them to be actively dangerous. According to Justin, these senseless, fabricated items actually had the names and forms of wicked demons who deceive gullible humans into worshiping them and offering religious service to corruptible (and corrupted) human-made objects. Instead, the true deity that Christians worship, he proclaims, has an ineffable appearance and glory, which cannot be imitated or represented. This nameless God, the source and provider of all things, has no need of constant caretaking and requires human virtue rather than material offerings.[6]

Like many of the Christian apologists and writers who followed him (including Minucius Felix), Justin acknowledges that Christians agree in certain respects with the teachings of pagan poets and philosophers. He identifies issues that he and his audience may hold in common, and he appeals both to their intellectual sophistication as well as to their common sense: "For why need we tell you, who already know, into what forms the craftsmen, carving and cutting, casting and hammering, fashion the materials? And often out of vessels of dishonor, by merely changing the form, and making an image of the requisite shape, they make what they call a god?"[7] All intelligent persons, he asserts, shun the idols of the gods as mere "works of mortal hands" and, as such, inferior to the artisans who made them.[8] And although philosophers and poets have already said this, Justin argues that Christians teach such truths more fully and offer proof of their assertions. In this way, Justin elaborated the teachings of this new religion in opposition to pagan idolatry and by (positive) comparison with philosophy.

Thus, despite his characterization of the popular culture as making and worshiping idols, Justin maintained that Christian profession of the invisibility and incomprehensibility of God was compatible with certain tenets of the pagan philosophers—an argument that may have been intended to make the new faith seem more intellectually (and culturally) acceptable to an educated pagan audience. At the same time, the Christian assertion that God is utterly transcendent of human vision and without describable features seems contradicted by certain Scripture passages, and this required some explaining. Justin was acutely aware of and probably somewhat embarrassed by the frequent biblical portrayals of God as appearing with human characteristics and habits. For example, Adam and Eve "heard the sound of the LORD God walking in the garden at the time of the evening breeze" (Gen 3:8). God smells the pleasing odor of Noah's burnt offering (Gen 8:21). The Lord appears and speaks to Abram in several places (Gen 15:1, a vision; 17:1; and 18:1), appears to

Isaac (Gen 26:24), and (apparently) wrestles with Jacob at Peniel (Gen 32:24-30). God called to Moses out of a burning bush, and "Moses hid his face for he was afraid to look at God" (Exod 3:2-6). Although the elders of Israel are allowed to see God (Exod 24:9-11), when Moses asks to see God's glory he is denied, since no one may see God's face and live. Instead, God puts Moses in a rock cleft, covers him with his "hand" while God passes by, and allows Moses to have a look at God's "back" (Exod 33:18-23). God has heaven as a throne and earth as a footstool (Isa 66:1), gathers the lambs in "his arms," carries them in "his bosom," and measures the waters in the "hollow of his hand" (Isa 40:11-12).

The prophets Ezekiel and Daniel both describe visions of a divine being with the "likeness of a human form" (Ezek 1:26) or the Ancient One with white raiment and hair like pure wool (Dan 7:9). Justin, who repudiated the polytheists' material and anthropomorphic images of the pagan gods and proclaimed instead that God was beyond human conception or form, was challenged by these texts. He claimed continuity with certain teachings of ancient philosophers, which were (rather safely) critical of certain pagan religious practices. However, so long as his community retained the holy books of the Jews as their own, he needed to resolve these awkward manifestations of God in their Bible. At the same time, he elaborated the differences between Christian teachings from beliefs he attributed to Jews, in order to demonstrate the unique and salvific character of Christian faith.

For example, in his first *Apology* Justin asserts that "all the Jews" understand that it was the "nameless God" or "Father of the Universe" who appeared or spoke to the patriarchs or prophets in Holy Scripture. This belief, he claims, clearly demonstrates that Jews are both ignorant of God as well as of the fact that God's Divine Word (*logos*) is also God. Furthermore, Justin continues, the Logos appeared to and spoke with Moses and the others, sometimes as fire, but also sometimes in the guise of an angel or apostle. And when the voice out of the bush said to Moses, "I AM WHO I AM" . . . "the God of Abraham, the God of Isaac, and the God of Jacob" (Exod 3:14-15), it signified that all of these departed patriarchs now belong to Christ (the Word who has come in the present age as a human being).[9] Justin thereby explains all the Old Testament theophanies as christological events.

In his debate with the Jew Trypho, Justin further elaborates his argument that the attributes ascribed to God in the Scriptures actually describe the Divine Logos, and the Being that the patriarchs and prophets heard or saw actually was the Divine Word rather than the Supreme God. To this end, Justin cites the story of Abraham and his three visitors at Mamre (Genesis 18). Believing Moses to be the author of Genesis, he notes that the prophet declares that the one who appeared to Abraham under the oak in Mamre is God, "sent with the two angels in his company to judge Sodom by another who remains ever in the supercelestial places, invisible to all men, holding personal intercourse with none, whom we believe to be Maker and Father of all things."[10] Here Justin recounts the story in Genesis that begins "the Lord appeared to Abraham as he sat at the door of his tent in the heat of the day" (Gen 18:1) and continues through the destruction of Sodom and Gomorrah (Gen 19:1-28), and asks Trypho and his colleagues if they fully understood the passages. They assert that they do understand, but according to their understanding, God first appears to Abraham, and then subsequently three angels appear—two of whom go on to destroy Sodom while the third brings the joyful news to Sarah that she will become pregnant with a son. Justin, promising to persuade his listeners that these passages could only refer to another God who is subject to the Maker of all things (who is also called an Angel), begins to attend to the various titles and modes of address in the texts as they appear in the Greek text of the Old Testament (*Septuagint*).[11]

Leading Trypho through a cross-examination he points out that the one who spoke to Sarah is called "the Lord" (Gen 18:10 LXX) and that this one appears again at the birth of Isaac. Trypho, conceding that that this title "Lord" might indicate that God and two angels appeared to Abraham (rather than God, followed by three angels), still does not see the necessity for a second divine being.[12] Like other Jews, Trypho apparently can accept the biblical statement at face value. If the text says that God appeared, then God appeared. Justin, however, having gotten Trypho to acknowledge that the title "Lord" refers to the Divine Being, draws Trypho's attention to the section of the story that names *two* distinct beings as "Lord." After the two angels safely whisked Lot and his family out of Sodom, "the LORD rained on Sodom and Gomorrah sulfur and fire from the LORD out of heaven" (Gen 19:24). To strengthen his argument, Justin then points out other places in the Scriptures where more than one being is called "God" or "Lord" (*Kurios*). For example, he points to Ps 45:6-7, where God appears to be anointed by another God ("your God"), and Psalm 110 where the psalmist writes: "The Lord says to my lord, "Sit at my right hand until I make your enemies your footstool" (Ps 110:1).[13]

Toward the end of his debate, Justin summarizes his position—that all passages of Scripture in which God is said to act, to move, to speak, or even to be seen, refer to the Word rather than the Unbegotten God. In other words, every scriptural allusion to God as being seen or heard (for example, Moses and the bush or Jacob wrestling with the man at Peniel) should be understood as a manifestation of God the Son or Logos.[14] In addition to asserting the superior Christian understanding of the Scriptures (including a claim that Christian believers were the heirs that God promised Abraham), this clear distinction between the First and the Second God is absolutely necessary in Justin's mind, in order to protect the utter transcendence and incomprehensibility of the First: "For the ineffable Father and Lord of all neither has come to any place, nor walks, nor sleeps, nor rises up, but remains in his own place, wherever that is, quick to behold and quick to hear, having neither eyes nor ears, but being of indescribable might. . . . Therefore, neither Abraham, nor Isaac, nor Jacob, nor any other person, saw the Father and ineffable Lord of all (and also of Christ), but saw him who was according to his will his Son, being God."[15] According to Justin, as a divine agent of the Unbegotten God, the Word can approach and interact with the material and mortal realm. Such agency protects the Supreme God's transcendence, while allowing interaction with the creation through God's Word. After all, while mixing with creation was tough and dirty work, someone had to do it.

Irenaeus: The Unity of God against the Gnostics

Around the same time, but for different reasons, Irenaeus similarly tried to reconcile the contradiction between God's essential invisibility and ineffability with biblical accounts of divine theophanies. In his *Refutation of Heresies*, Irenaeus, like Justin, stresses the utter transcendence of the First Person, but since he also wants to protect the unity of the Godhead, he could not simply resort to distinguishing between the Logos and God by the Logos's direct interaction with the created world. The differences between Justin's and Irenaeus's arguments reflect their different aims. Whereas Justin explains the theophanies of the Old Testament as appearances of the Word in order to establish the duality of the divine actors (against a Jew), Irenaeus is motivated by a different theological purpose and circumstance; he needs to defend the unity of God, the eternal consistency of the divine plan for salvation, and the essential goodness of creation against Gnostics. In addition, although Irenaeus draws upon Scripture, when he refutes the teachings of the Gnostics, he cannot use it as authoritative proof text in the way that Justin did in his dialogue with a Jew.

Irenaeus realized that a teacher like Valentinus could simply allege that the biblical accounts of divine theophanies proved the existence of a different God—in this case neither the Divine Word nor the Invisible God, but an inferior Creator who was sullied by association with the material realm. Justin's solution (that the Second Person was the subject of these theophanies) seemed also to pose this danger. For this reason, Irenaeus resists making a clear distinction between the two Divine Beings prior to the incarnation. He emphasizes the profound significance of the incarnation as the unique way in which God appears to humankind more than as demonstrating the existence of a Second Person in the Godhead. As a result, Irenaeus repeatedly insists that the future is presaged in these biblical stories of God's manifestation to humanity. And this was his proof of God's initial and well-ordered plan for human salvation, which includes both the First Adam's fall and the

Second Adam's redemptive coming in the person of Jesus. In addition to his belief in God's unity, consistency, and providence, however, Irenaeus may have been conscious of the potential mythological parallels. Assigning the divine theophanies to the pre-incarnate Word comes perilously close to the stories of divine manifestations in pagan or Gnostic myths in which a divine being (deity, angel, or demon) temporarily took on mere human appearance, but such theophanies did not and could not involve taking on actual human flesh. Moreover, the fact that God came in different forms, appearing differently to different individuals was a sign of God's inclusive generosity, so that all persons might be included in God's providence irrespective of their individual intelligence or ability to perceive or understand an esoteric truth.[16]

Therefore, Irenaeus proclaims, what the patriarchs saw was a *vision* of the Divine Word who, as God, is invisible and boundless, but who, as Word, has the capacity to become visible and would do so at some point in the future, out of God's infinite goodness and love for creation, to those who have faith.[17] The Word, who makes God known to humans through the gift of prophecy and visions, grants certain individuals a glimpse of a new thing that would come to pass in the "last times." In other words, the prophets and patriarchs *foresaw* the *eventual* manifestation of God—in Christ. Those "ignorant ones," who insist that the prophets saw a different God than the "invisible Father of all," understand neither the nature or God nor the function of prophecy. According to Irenaeus, the coming of Christ was the singular way in which God appears to mortals, and the mode by which God is fully present within creation.[18] And this unique earthly appearance (always part of God's original intention for the ultimate perfection of the world) is what the prophets saw and foretold. Furthermore, when mortals ultimately see God's full glory, it will not be out of their natural capacity, but due to God's own self-revelation, to whom God chooses and in the way that God chooses—as Christ says in Matt 5:8, "Blessed are the pure in heart, for they *will* see God."

At the end time, according to Irenaeus, the Logos will lead those blessed ones who love God into the Presence and they will partake of its brilliancy. By this sight, they receive immortality ("incorruption for eternal life") and know both God and themselves in truth. As the writer of 1 John puts it: "Beloved, we are God's children now; what we will be has not yet been revealed. What we do know is this: when he is revealed, we will be like him, for we will see him as he is" (1 John 3:2). In the interim, the incomprehensible, infinite, and invisible God will be made perceptible and knowable, "prophetically through the Spirit, and adoptively through the Son."[19] In this way, the invisible God is partially and provisionally visible in the present, and humans are enlivened by recognition of God's providence initially in creation and subsequently through the manifestation in Christ. Asserting that God can be perceived both in the beauty of the natural world as well as in actual human flesh was clearly anti-Gnostic. In the interim, certain persons are granted a foresight of the future incarnation, when the "incomprehensible will be known by means of the comprehensible, and the invisible by the visible." All these glimpses of the Divine come to humans through the agency of the Word, so that mortals might know God and continue to exist. "For the glory of God is a human made alive, and the life of the human consists in behold-ing God."[20]

Irenaeus illustrates these points by citing the examples of Isaiah and Moses. God's refusal to grant Moses a face-to-face interview was offset by a prophetic consolation prize—a look at God's back—that Irenaeus interprets as the divine assurance of special consideration in the future. God's putting Moses in the cleft of the rock symbolized the incarna-tion—the time when God would be wrapped in matter. Eventually, God grants Moses' request when he (Moses) and Elijah are allowed to confer with the transfigured Christ "face to face" (Matt 17:1-8 and parallels).[21] In the meantime, the prophets could have an intimation or tantalizing "backside" glimpse of that glory and splendor, which would temporar-ily satisfy and prepare them to receive that which will be revealed later on. This is why, when Ezekiel recounted his visions of God (with the four beasts and the wheels), he took care to clarify that "this was the appearance of the likeness of the glory of the LORD" (Ezek 1:28).[22] If, he says, what Moses, Elijah, and Ezekiel saw (he might have added Isaiah and Daniel) were celestial "similitudes" of divine splendor and "prophe-cies of things to come," then it is manifest that God is indeed invisible. Even John's vision of the Apocalypse is a preview of the future, but as such it almost kills him (Rev 1:17), since "no one shall see me and live" (Exod 33:20). Irenaeus continues with an assertion that it is not by means of visions or words alone, however, that God is shown forth or the incarnation prefigured, but through actual works, known to the prophets and later fulfilled in the church.[23]

In his *Demonstration of Apostolic Preaching*, Irenaeus asserts that it is the Divine Word who appears to Abraham at Mamre, Jacob at Peniel, Moses at Horeb, and the Israelites in the wilderness (as a pillar of cloud or fire). But, he clarifies, all these appearances were revelations of the Begotten One who would one day come into the midst of human com-pany. Hence, Abraham, Jacob, and Moses can be called prophets, because they "see things to come, which were to take place in human form."[24] However, as if aware that the ability to appear might imply the inferiority (mutability) of the Word to God, Irenaeus stresses that *both* are God, and "in the substance and power of his being there is shown forth one God; but according to the economy of our redemption both Son and Father."[25] Thus, sometimes appearing is no sign of inconsis-tency, but it is rather the evidence of God's benevolent and gracious intention for creation.

Consequently, unlike Justin, Irenaeus avoids distinguishing the divine persons in terms that imply subordination, but (like Justin) uses these stories from Scripture to refute the Jews who "imagine that they could know the Father by himself, without the Word, that is, without the Son."[26] At the same time, Irenaeus also combats Gnostics who vainly declare that the purpose of the text "No one knows the Father except the Son" (Matt 11:27; Luke 10:22) was to introduce another, unknown God. Against this, Irenaeus declares that the Logos is the one who was manifest and who, in this way, "chooses to reveal God so that God might become known."[27] Working simultaneously against different opponents, Irenaeus denies that God was humanly visible prior to the incarnation of Jesus, which is his way of protecting the unity of God as well as affirming the divine economy that claimed that God appeared uniquely in Christ for the sake of the world's salvation. This divine initiative toward humans did not imply God's mutability, however, since Christ's coming as human was *always* a part of God's plan. Adam and Eve's fall was not a miscalculation of the deity or an inherent cosmic flaw; rather, it was a necessary part of a long and intentional process of maturation, culminated in the appearance of God as the Incarnate One (an appearance foreseen in the prophets) and to be completed in the end time with the salvific vision of God's full glory.

The way Irenaeus understands the Word to show forth God is through the agency of creation and—in the incarnation—the works of ministry and redemption, as much as through the visions and words seen and heard by the Hebrew prophets and patriarchs. Washing the disciples' feet and feeding them at the Last Supper were ways that God "exercised providence" toward those who earnestly desired to behold God, but in this way, "according to their capacity." Finally, just as the theophanies of the Old Testament allow the patriarchs and prophets to see and know Christ, Iranaeus claims that contemporary Christians who share these same visions are themselves represented in those ancient texts. The church appears in the Old Testament, and God's redemption is extended to all humanity from creation, not just to those who were born after the time of Tiberius Caesar.[28]

Tertullian: The Dignity of the Incarnation and the Distinction of the Persons of the Trinity

Tertullian, like his fellow North African Minucius Felix, ridiculed those who worshiped inanimate statues or images of the gods that were fashioned out of everyday materials. In his *Apology*, he points out that they are merely pieces of matter—"headless" objects that "have no sense of the injuries and disgraces of their consecrating, as they are equally unconscious of the honors paid to them." Tertullian then defends Christians against those who would persecute them for refusing to participate in such foolishness: "We surely cannot be made out to injure those [gods] whom we are certain are nonentities."[29] In his treatise *Against Idols,* he is even more blatantly contemptuous, declaring that those who make these things not only receive no help from them, but are like them—they can neither see nor hear, feel nor smell, and "their hearts are ashes and earth" (cf. Ps 115:8).[30] Against these vain idols, Tertullian insists that the object of Christian worship is the One God, whom the eye cannot see although he is spiritually visible. This God is indescribable, though discernible in grace, beyond all thought or conception, but yet manifest in that very transcendence. Human inability to conceive of God actually allows mortals to understand who God is. Furthermore, humans are by nature aware of God. They cannot possibly be ignorant of God since God's existence is demonstrably shown everywhere in nature and through the working out of history and every time a soul gives thanks or cries out for justice.[31] God is, therefore, something humans do not see, but yet perceive from evidence all around them, even in their own instinctual behavior.

In his refutation of heretics, however, Tertullian condemns those who misunderstand the eternal nature and human incarnation of the Word. Against Marcion, who denies the reality of the true fleshly incarnation of Christ and claims that he was actually some kind of spiritual, "angelic" being, Tertullian insists that there was nothing unworthy or degrading about the Divine Being assuming human flesh. However, in order to protect the transcendent majesty and invisibility of God, Tertullian further contends that it was the "Son of the Creator" who actually appeared to and conversed with the prophets and patriarchs and was later incarnate in human flesh. Only the Begotten One may know the Parent, he says, citing Matt 11:27, since no (mortal) one may see God and live (Exod 33:20). On one hand, Tertullian agrees that the attributes that Marcion uses to describe God, such as invisibility, inapproachability, and immutability, are appropriate. On the other hand, Tertullian insists that those degrading human qualities that Marcion would deny to God, such as being seen, heard, or encountered in bodily form, were necessary for human salvation and thus worthy of and becoming to God. But, he clarifies, we believe that the Word was that member of the Godhead who actually conversed with the prophets and patriarchs from the beginning, making himself a "little lower than the angels" (cf. Ps 8:5) and, by this lowering of himself, actually learned about and practiced (rehearsed) being in the human state that he "was destined in the end to become." And this was the One who descended to earth to interrogate or argue with humanity, with the authority and in the name of God (who was never visible); the One who alone "knows the Father" (Matt 11:27).[32]

For this reason, when Tertullian turns to the scriptural accounts of divine theophanies, he argues for the actual human and fleshly reality of the divine appearance. For example, in his view, the three guests of

Abraham in Genesis 18 truly appeared as three men. And while he judges that these were not ordinary men, but two angels and Christ, he also holds that they materialized in real human flesh. However, their flesh was not that given at the birth from a human mother, since the birth of a heavenly being from a mortal woman was reserved only for Christ at the moment of his nativity. Rather, the flesh of the three ("from whatever source derived") did not have to undergo birth, because it was not going to die. In contrast, the flesh of Christ on this occasion was also obtained without benefit of human birth, since it was at this juncture also not subject to death. But, it was meantime "learning to hold intercourse amongst mortals." After all, Tertullian concludes, if God can one day make humans into angels, God certainly can make angels into humans (just as even God can become human).[33]

Tertullian elsewhere cites the story of Abraham's visitors and Jacob's wrestling match to show that the taking on of human flesh indicates no loss of dignity to the Second Person. For even if one imagines that all those angels were mere angels (and not one of them Christ), one would have to believe that their assumption of human form did them no harm, even though they must be assumed to be inferior to the Son. Accordingly, the assumption of human flesh was an action that confirmed Christ's superiority, his invulnerability to the dangers of bodily change, and his transcendence of all the known physical laws. At the same time, the Second Person is the one of the Trinity who is able to undergo external change and to take on another (human) nature.[34]

Toward the end of his fifth book against Marcion, Tertullian refers to Paul's letter to the Colossians to support his contention that Christ was the visible appearance of God to the prophets and patriarchs of Scripture. Just as Paul calls Christ the "Image of the Invisible God," Tertullian proclaims, "we similarly say that the Father of Christ is invisible, for we know that it was the Son who was seen in ancient times . . . as the image of the Father himself."[35] Such a role for the Son, he simultaneously cautions, must not be understood to demonstrate a difference between a visible and an invisible God, since the Son, as the Eternal Word and First Begotten of the Father, cannot be distinguished from the Father in terms of action, will, time, or substance. The two divine Persons are coeternal, the same in essential being, and united in intention and deed. Their distinction, for Tertullian, rests on the dispensation by which one can appear to humans *in real human flesh* while the other does not.

When Tertullian refutes the teaching of the modalist Praxeas, however, he does not have to affirm the reality and dignity of the incarnation in human flesh, or to demonstrate the unity of the invisible God of Scripture with the One who appears to the patriarchs. Rather, against the modalists' radical idea that the single God appears in three different "modes" or roles, Tertullian upholds the plurality of God while showing the distinctions of the three persons of the Trinity. Here Tertullian shares Irenaeus's concern to show the action of God along with the Logos and Holy Spirit in both creation and redemption. According to Tertullian, Praxeas had attempted to protect the unity of God by denying the essential distinction between God, Christ, and Spirit. In particular, Praxeas taught that the Supreme Father was born into the world (and thus temporarily visible) as the Savior. Such a teaching necessarily implied that when appearing as Christ, the One God suffered and died. This led Tertullian to accuse Praxeas of "crucifying God [the Father]."[36]

To refute Praxeas, Tertullian demonstrates the definitive necessity of divine plurality by showing the practical distinction between the invisible God and the visible Word and by turning to various scriptural testimonies of God's appearance. Tertullian proclaims that while humans may not see God in God's full majesty, they may see the Second Person, by virtue of "the dispensation of his derived existence."[37] The Supreme God is *predicated* by invisibility, while the eternal Logos is not. Therefore, while the First Person is absolutely invisible, God the eternal Word may be invisible or visible. Since invisibility is not one of the Word's unconditional qualities, it may become visible, even before the incarnation, in visions and dreams. The First Person, by contrast, can never be seen.

Tertullian candidly acknowledges that the Scripture seems self-contradictory, however. He notes that in certain places the text asserts that no one may see God and live (cf. Exod 33:20), while in other places it gives examples of those who *did* look upon the face of God and survived—for example, Jacob at Peniel (Gen 32:30) and Moses in Deuteronomy whom the "Lord knew face to face" (Deut 34:10). Noting these apparent discrepancies can lead to the conclusions that either the Scripture is false or misleading or it distinguishes between different divine "faces." Praxeas and his followers would have claimed that such texts merely revealed the different divine modes, perhaps a bit like royalty who sometimes refer to themselves in the third person and sometimes in the first.

Tertullian lets the contradiction prove his point about the distinction of the persons (one whose face might be seen, one whose face may not), but he also sees an opportunity to play on the word "face" and contends that such contradictions should be understood as an enigma or riddle, borrowing the lines of Paul: "now we see through a mirror in an enigma, but then face to face" (1 Cor 13:12, author's translation).[38] For instance, he says, why does Moses ask to see God's face in Exod 33:13 and 18, when he has just seen it, according to verse 11? Or why does God refuse in verse 20, when God had already shown Moses his face? Can seeing one divine face be mortally dangerous while seeing the other be beneficial? Tertullian's way out of this conundrum is to claim that the appearance of the Son shows forth the "face of the Father" to whom he belongs and by whom he is begotten. Tertullian thus reiterates Paul's assertion: "he is the image of the invisible God" (Col 1:15).[39]

Finally, Tertullian concludes, the Gospels and Epistles reveal both a visible and an invisible God, "under a manifest and personal distinction in the condition of both."[40] However, in the incarnation, the invisible and visible become reconciled, and Christ shows us his "face" (the "Father"). Tertullian may have been thinking of Paul's description of the face of Jesus showing forth the "light of the knowledge of the glory of God" (2 Cor 4:6). Such an argument thereby resolves such seeming contradictory statements as John 5:37: "you have never heard [the Father's] voice or seen his form," and John 12:45: "whoever sees me sees him who sent me."[41] Because of its "derived existence," the Pre-incarnate Word is visible by will, and because of its human existence, the Incarnate Word is visible by (its human) nature.

Clement of Alexandria:
Philosophical Aniconism and the Futility of Idols

Clement, in very much the same tone as Tertullian, ridiculed the worship of idols and, by exposing its futility, hoped to convert those who followed such practice. In his *Exhortation to the Greeks*, he offers to set some images up for inspection and promises his audience that "you will, as you go over them, find how truly silly is the custom in which you have been reared, of worshiping the senseless works of human hands."[42] He describes a great catalogue of examples to demonstrate his point, including an image of Artemis made from a tree trunk, one of Jupiter made from bones, and of Dionysus made from rocks. Exasperated, he finally claims to pity the miserable wretches who take such things seriously and, praying to images, get the same result as they would if they talked to the walls of their houses. Not particularly dangerous, but utterly foolish, he asserts:

> The senseless earth is dishonored by the makers of images, who change it by their art from its proper nature and induce people to worship it; and the makers of gods worship not gods and demons, but in my view earth and art, which go to make up images. For truly, the image is only dead matter shaped by the artisan's hand. But *we* have no sensible image of sensible matter, but an image that is perceived by the mind alone—God, who alone is truly God.[43]

Like Justin and Minucius Felix, Clement also understood that Christians were not unique in their teaching that God is invisible. In fact, for him even more than those others, this is an important weapon to combat idolatry. In this same proselytizing treatise, he cites Socrates, Plato, Xenophon, Cleanthes, Moses, the Pythagoreans, and the cynic philosopher Antisthenes (a student of Socrates and the founder of Cynicism) as exemplars of non-Christian philosophers who had insisted on the transcendent perfection and invisibility of the divine being. Moreover, he adds, such knowledge is native to humans whether educated or not, for if they think about it all, even against their will, they will realize that God is one, unbegotten, indestructible, and that "somewhere on high in the outermost spaces of the heavens, in a private watch-tower, God truly exists forever." And he follows this up with a quotation from Euripides: "What nature, say, must we ascribe to God? Who sees all and yet never is seen?"[44]

According to Clement, Plato had taught that mortals are incapable of a sustained view of the divine, since its beauty transcends the reflections of it in both nature and the imitative arts, and since neither immortality nor absolute perfection can be achieved by humans. God can be contemplated through the human faculty of reason but cannot be seen by the ordinary eye. Clement also claimed that Plato believed that certain humans might achieve the capacity to see the truth, and these people had anticipated both Jesus' declaration that "blessed are the pure in heart, for they will see God" (Matt 5:8) and Paul's assurance that while now "we see through a mirror in an enigma, then we will see face to face" (1 Cor 13:12, author's translation). In the meantime, such beatific vision is partial or fleeting, and prior to the "final perfection" can only be received in the mind or soul.[45] This final perfected vision is the goal of those who seek intellectual and spiritual enlightenment. And, consciously drawing upon philosophical tradition, Clement concludes that the Supreme One is not merely invisible but transcends ordinary sight and expression, existing far beyond earthly space and time.

In his exploration of the nature of God in the *Stromateis,* Clement refers to the teachings of a number of philosophers, especially the Pythagoreans and Stoics, although he anchors his readings of them to the basic tenets of the "truth-loving" Plato, to whom he returns with great predictability. And yet, he says, Plato and the others were not only indebted to the teachings contained in the five books of Moses, but they anticipated all that would be proclaimed in Christian Scripture. For example, Moses' prohibition of temples or altars in more than one place indicated that he knew that God could not be contained or circumscribed within space. Zeno echoed this when he claimed that humans ought to refrain from making either temples to or images of the gods, as did Plato when he asserted that nothing made by mortal builders and mechanics could be regarded as holy. Clement completes his case by citing Paul's speech in Athens, when he declared that the God that made the world and all things in it does not dwell in temples made by human hands (Acts 17:24). A little later in his discussion, Clement claims that Plato's argument, that it is impossible to declare the Maker of the Universe to everyone (since such a thing is beyond the ordinary kind of instruction), was derived from his (Plato's) hearing that Moses only took part of the people of Israel with him up to the holy mountain. Also, according to Clement, Plato had heard about Moses entering the thick darkness where God was, and he (Plato) interpreted this to mean that "God is invisible and beyond expression in words." Plato had even described the Divine Trinity when he wrote in the Timaeus of two other divine beings surrounding the God of Gods.[46]

Ancient Roman Precedents for Christian Aniconism

For Minucius Felix's character Octavius, that Christians had no images of their God was a point they shared in common with Greek and Roman poets and philosophers. Athenagoras, another late second-century apologist, tried a different approach to establishing a respectable, and even more ancient, precedent for Christian lack of divine images. Although he also presents the usual pre-Christian philosophical arguments regarding the unity, invisibility, and immutability of God and (like the other apologists) claims that Christians do nothing other than teach these same things in a manner more true and complete than these others, he argues that images of the gods in the popular cult are a relatively new invention.[47]

Athenagoras contends that failure to distinguish created things from the Uncreated God places the perishable on the same plane with the imperishable and values the artifact above the skill of the artisan. Anyone may see, however, that idols constructed of ordinary matter are sensible, rather than intelligible things. They are also of recent origin. According to his information, prior to Homer and Hesiod, the Greeks lacked any representations of the gods and only began to make them at the time drawing was invented. Recounting the legend of Saurias, who first sketched the shadow of a horse in the sun, or the story of the girl who traced the outline of her lover on a wall as he slept, Athenagoras asserts that no existing image of a god is older than four hundred years, and most are clearly the work of human artisans and thus even younger than those who made them. Before the invention of sculpture and painting, humans had no images of the gods. He poses his objection in a question: "If these are [real] gods, why did they not exist from the beginning?" "Why did they need the assistance of artists to bring them into being?"[48]

But even the gods, whose images these idols portray, did not exist from the beginning, he points out. The poets invented their names, characters, and exploits. Because they came into being, they are no more immortal or eternal than their images.[49] Athenagoras draws upon the ancient theory of Euhemerus in the fourth century B.C.E. that claimed the classical gods were really nothing more than ancient kings or heroes, often with scandalous reputations, who had become mythologized over time. Those who worshiped the images of these gods, he charges, were drawn to them by demons eager to eat the blood of the sacrifices and invade the minds of the worshipers, filling them with empty visions as if coming from the idols themselves. Such perversity only causes the victims to be even more addicted to idols.[50]

Athenagoras's claim that the known images of the gods were no older than four hundred years (when, according to him, the Greeks began to make visual art) dates the oldest artifacts to around 225 B.C.E. This is a relatively late date, compared to a more traditional formula in circulation at the time, which assigns the first divine images to a century and a half after the founding of Rome, or sometime in the late sixth century B.C.E. Clement also cites this historical datum in his first book of the *Stromateis*, where he claims that Numa, the first king of Rome, was a Pythagorean, and "aided by the precepts of Moses, prohibited [the Romans] from making any image of God in human form, and of the shape of a living creature." And so, he says, for the first hundred and seventy years, "though building temples, they made no base or graven image. For Numa secretly showed them that the Best of Beings could not be apprehended except by the mind alone." This teaching, Clement asserts, had flourished in antiquity among the nations, including the Greeks, Egyptians, Chaldeans, Assyrians, Druids, and even the Magi of the Persians, "who foretold the Savior's birth and came into the land of Judaea guided by a star."[51]

Plutarch may have been Clement's source for this legend about Numa, since his *Life of Numa* told much the same story: "Numa forbade the Romans to revere an image of God which had the form of man or beast. Nor was there among them at this early time any painted or graven likeness of Deity, but while for the first hundred and seventy years they were continually building temples, and establishing sacred shrines, they made no statues in bodily form for them, convinced that it was impious to liken higher things to lower, and that it was impossible to apprehend Deity except by the intellect."[52] Plutarch, like Clement, credited Pythagoras as the influence on Numa but, unlike Clement, said nothing about Numa's being "aided by the precepts of Moses."

Tertullian also knows and cites this presumption of ancient Roman aniconism during the time of King Numa. In the middle of an especially vitriolic attack on the various Roman gods and religions of his day, he refutes the argument that Roman religion contributed significantly to Roman prosperity and greatness. Even during the time of Numa, he says, religion was vain superstition, although at least "not yet a matter of temples and images." This older Rome was "frugal," and its "rites were simple," with no fancy capitals or altars. The Greeks and Etruscans had not yet flooded the city with the "products of their art."[53] Whereas Clement puts forward Moses as the source of ancient contempt for idols, consequently aligning philosophy with ancient Hebrew teachings, Tertullian proposes that Christians have inherited and maintain ancient Roman religious values and thus are more faithful than their idol-worshiping neighbors to their own tradition.

This traditional attribution of aniconic worship to the original Romans continues through the fourth and into the fifth century c.e. In Augustine's *City of God,* the legend is attributed to first-century b.c.e philosopher and antiquarian Varro. According to Augustine, Varro maintained that the ancient Romans worshiped the gods for a hundred and seventy years without making any images of them, and that "if that habit had been continued, the worship of the gods would have been conducted with greater purity." Augustine also says that Varro credited Jewish aniconic tradition as evidence for this assertion, adding that Varro believed that divine images ultimately led to disrespect for religion and that "those who first set up images of the gods for the people were responsible for the abolition of reverent fear in their communities and for the increase of error" because "it was easy to despise the gods because of the insensibility of their images."[54]

Further on in his encyclopedic tome, however, Augustine cites Varro again as his source but judges him more negatively, since Varro also maintained that when the images of the gods finally were invented, they were fashioned in such a way that "those who had been initiated into the mysteries" could fix their eyes upon them and "thus apprehend with their minds the true gods, namely the Soul of the World and its manifestations." Furthermore, according to Varro, the human form was chosen for many of these statues because "the human body most nearly resembles the Immortal Spirit." And, while Augustine acknowledges that the development of cult images in human form recognized something of the constitutive nature of God (since the human spirit most nearly resembles the Immortal Spirit and is contained in the vessel of a human body), he also disapproves. He accuses Varro of losing the insight that had enabled him to see that Romans in the remote past had "offered a purer worship, without images."[55]

While contemporary historians hold different views on the question of Roman aniconism, many argue that the earliest Roman cult, from the time of Numa to the ascendancy of the Etruscan kings (about a hundred and seventy years) was indeed an imageless one.[56] Whatever the historical truth of the matter, the fact that Christian theologians were able to claim an ancient Roman tradition of imageless worship gave them some leverage with their critics, who regarded their rejection of images as an indication that they were atheists without traditional values. According to Christian writers, although the Romans eventually lost their original purity of worship, some among them continued to have an aversion to divine images and subscribed to a Platonic repudiation of artistic imitation, Aristotelian materialism, and Stoic monotheism. In the first century b.c.e, for example, Cicero had ridiculed the idea that gods have forms that could be fashioned by art and especially chided Epicureans for deeming such images (and their gods) worthy of worship:

We have an idea of god implanted in our minds, you say. Yes, and an idea of Jupiter with a beard, and Minerva in a helmet: but do you therefore believe that those deities are really like that? The unlearned multitude is surely wiser here— they assign to god not only a man's limbs. For they give him bow, arrows, spear, shield, trident, thunderbolt; and if they cannot see what actions the gods perform; yet they cannot conceive of god as entirely inactive . . . but your gods [Epicureans'] not only do no service that you can point to, but they don't do anything at all. "God," [Epicurus] says, "is free from trouble." Obviously Epicurus thinks, as spoilt children do, that idleness is the best thing there is.[57]

The Philosophical Argument in the First Four Centuries C.E.

We have seen how the early Christian writers cited the views of ancient poets and philosophers as being in general harmony with Christian teaching on the invisibility of God and the vanity of the idols. The previous passage from Cicero's treatise *De Natura Deorum* partially summarizes his teaching about the gods in one of the three main philosophical schools—the Epicureans, the Stoics, and the Academics. In religious matters, Cicero generally sides with the Stoics, who traditionally objected to divine images, following the teachings of their founder, Zeno, who was famous for his opposition to temples and statues. In fact, the conflicting positions represented by Stoicism and Epicureanism in first-century Athens on the matter of divine images may lie behind Paul's speech to the Athenians in Acts 17.

The mention of the Epicureans and Stoic philosophers in Acts actually suggests an interesting background to Paul's speech. Christianity might have been seen by this audience as addressing current debates within two key philosophical schools and aligning itself with those who challenged the traditional religious practices of Roman and Greek culture with its images and temples for the gods.[58] Paul's commendation of the altar to the unknown god (Acts 17:23) as a possible way for acceptance of the Christian God, who does not live in shrines or appear by means of artistic representation (cf. Acts 17:24), has clear parallels with contemporary Stoic thought. At the same time, as Paul himself points out, the Athenians (and the foreigners who lived in Athens) love to hear and tell about something new (Acts 17:21).

Around that same time (the first and second centuries C.E.), a philosophical movement now known as Middle Platonism was indeed forming a "new" syncretistic blend of religion and philosophy, especially Platonic, Aristotelian, and Stoic elements. This movement's influence on Justin Martyr is apparent, but it is even clearer in the thought of Clement of Alexandria, who refers to the writings of philosophers as well as the ancient poets in his exposition of Christian teachings about God. Middle Platonism's best-known ancient representative, Plutarch, echoes Zeno's and Plato's critique of temples and images (also cited by

Clement) as well as Paul's address to the Athenians when he criticized the Stoics for their inconsistency regarding the images of the gods. Although they scoff at the building of shrines, they continue to act in a traditional manner in other respects:

> Moreover, it is a doctrine of Zeno's not to build temples of the gods, because a temple not worth much is also not sacred, and no work of builders or mechanics is worth much. The Stoics, while applauding this as correct, attend the mysteries in temples, go up to the Acropolis, do reverence to statues, and place wreaths upon the shrines, though these are works of builders and mechanics.[59]

In the next century, Plotinus also combined the ideas of Plato, Aristotle, and the Stoics into a system that had enormous influence on Christian writers of the late fourth and early fifth centuries—particularly Augustine, whose encounter with this system was partly mediated by the works of Plotinus's student Porphyry. Plotinus's view of the divine image bridged that of Plato and Aristotle, incorporating both the value of the particular sensory experience and the assertion of an ideal Form. This allowed him to elaborate the value of art as a mode of participation in the reality to which it pointed—a Form that existed in a higher reality that lay somewhere outside the individual human mind.

Plotinus agrees with Aristotle that artists begin by examining the natural world. In Plotinus's view, the order and structure they experience in nature, however, leads artists to discover the transcendent world of ideals and finally the experience of pure intellectual beauty, which they attain only through contemplation. Comparing two blocks of stone, one worked and the other unworked, Plotinus sees in the worked block a Form, introduced by the idea in the mind of the artist. This Form exists outside the stone, and outside the work of art itself. The original idea transcends the material creation, even though its existence is, in fact, revealed in the artist's product. Consequently, works of art are not mere imitation of natural objects (which are imitations themselves—imitations of a higher reality), but draw upon the Form itself and, in fact, perfect what is sometimes lacking in nature. For Plotinus, this is as true for a painting of a bowl of fruit as a portrait, or even an image of a god: "Thus Phidias wrought the Zeus upon no model among things of sense but by apprehending what form Zeus must take if he chose to become manifest to sight."[60]

In other words, according to Plotinus, great artists like Phidias produced works that were superior to nature by incorporating their vision of the ideal and by their ability to portray that vision. The influence of this thesis on Augustine is apparent in the *Confessions*, where Augustine wrote that artisans who create objects out of their mind have "the power to impose the form which by an inner eye [the mind] can see within itself." This form derives from the translation of inward vision to external (material) objects, using that vision to judge whether the work was "well done." Of course, for Augustine, the ultimate source of the artisan's vision is above the human mind; it is put there by God.[61]

That this argument of Plotinus's is germane to the question of divine images is evident in the example he chooses—the image of Zeus. For Plotinus, however inferior images may be to their prototypes or models, they can still serve a higher religious purpose. While statues or paintings of the gods could not pretend to contain or communicate divine truth in themselves, by their very existence they demonstrated that such truth could be comprehended. In other words, although the gods were not portrayed in their actual being, they were present in a representational sense. Their images provided a kind of proof of their existence, just as objects in the natural world provided proof of the higher reality of which they were a reflection.

Despite this view, Plotinus never stopped being deeply suspicious both of the material world and of visual images (including his own portrait). His followers, however, gradually found a place for images in their religious practices as a way to help worshipers experience the presence of the divine. The conditional rehabilitation of images drew upon the rituals associated with the mystery cults and with the esoteric blend of magic and religious rituals known as theurgy, whose purpose was to mediate nonmaterial theophanies of the deity (what today we might call "spiritual encounters").[62] Such theophanies were also possible through the mediation of a human being (an ancient "medium"). Porphyry's student Iamblichus constructed a whole system of philosophy and ritual that depended upon images and sacrifices. This system so won the enthusiasm of Julian, the emperor who converted from Christianity to polytheism, that it led to a revival of a kind of philosophically based pagan cult.[63] Augustine's paraphrase of a dialogue between the gods Asclepius and Hermes Trismestus in his *City of God* illustrates the contemporary popularity of this movement. In one passage Hermes describes statues of the eternal gods as "endowed with souls, fully equipped with sensibility and spirit; statues which perform such great and wonderful works; statues which foreknow the future and foretell it by means of the lot . . . which send diseases upon men and also cure them, bestowing sadness or joy, according to deserts."[64]

For those who subscribed to this practice, images served a mediating function, calling the viewer to recognize that the object had a source, a prototype that must exist in order to be communicated through the inferior material form. The image is, actually, the proof of the prototype—an idea derived from Platonic theory and central to the later theology of icons. Of course, a nonphilosopher may not have understood the theory or realized that the goal was to move the eye of the mind beyond the image to the prototype. Even so, the average person might have agreed that the plentiful statues and paintings of the various gods were ample proof that the gods existed and that they merited venera-tion. Such images also mediated a divine presence and functioned effec-tively within religious cult.

First-Century and Early Rabbinic Teachings on the Invisible God

We have seen how second-century Christian writers like Justin and Clement credited Greek philosophy with recognizing God's invisibility and singularity. As a legitimizing parallel for their own claims, the wis-dom of the Greeks on this point served as an invaluable resource for the early apologists. The Hebrew Scriptures represented another such ancient and authoritative tradition. Christians saw these Scriptures as the original source not only of Christian teaching about God's inde-scribability but also of Greek wisdom on the subject, since they often presented Moses as the source of Greek philosophy as well as of Chris-tian theology—although pointing out that whereas Christians had got-ten the truth of the matter, the Greeks (and later Romans) persisted in a flawed and insufficient understanding. Such a view is particularly char-acteristic of Clement's writings, but it can also be seen in the works of other Christian apologists.[65]

However, Justin Martyr, in his first *Apology*, states that "all Jews" believed that God actually appeared to Abraham and the others who had theophanic visions in the Bible, and Trypho is presented as agreeing with this basic assertion.[66] Justin, who agrees that the Divine Word might appear in human form, further criticizes Jews for their literal-mindedness, claiming that they misunderstand figurative speech and suppose that "the Father of all, the unbegotten God, has hands and feet, and fingers and a soul, like a composite being; and for this reason teach that it was the Father Himself who appeared to Abraham and Jacob."[67] Still, whatever second-century Jews actually believed about the appear-ances of God in Scripture (even the anthropomorphic ones), they apparently refrained from representations of God in visual art. Josephus explains in his treatise *Against Apion* that while God may be seen in cre-ation, God's form and magnitude are completely beyond human ability to describe and that no materials, however precious, could be used to fashion an image of God. Moreover, no individual possesses the ability to conceive of or make such an image. God is so far beyond human vision that even to contemplate the act of representation of the divine One is impious. The like of him we have never seen, we do not imagine, and it is impious to conjecture.[68] Tacitus confirms this from the Roman perspective, saying that Jews conceive of only one god, and that with the "mind alone," regarding those who make divine representations as impious since the supreme and eternal divine being is neither destructi-ble nor able to be depicted.[69]

Philo clearly agrees with this position, but he expands somewhat on the simple prohibition of divine images. In his exposition of the Second Commandment, he explains that although all those who worship objects in creation rather than the Creator are in grievous error and have done great injury to the human race, God does not equally condemn those who worship the divine in natural phenomena (for example, the stars or the sun) as those who venerate "graven images." According to Moses, he says (using an argument that would appear in later Christian apologetic writing), those who worship heavenly bodies offend less than those who worship idols, because the latter do not perceive that human-made objects are inferior to and younger than both their makers and their models. Nevertheless, each group of idolaters has cast away a main support of the soul—the proper conception of God.[70]

Philo also anticipates Clement and Origen in interpreting the biblical theophanies as mystical and not as corporeal appearances. For example, according to Philo, Moses' request to see God's face was made even though Moses realized that such a request could never be granted, but still he persists until he enters "into the thick darkness where God was—that is, into a conception regarding the Existent Being that belongs to the unapproachable region where there are no material forms. . . . And out of this quest there accrues to Moses a vast boon, namely to apprehend that the God of real Being is apprehensible to no one, and to see precisely that He is incapable of being seen."[71] Such a mystical exegesis resolves the contradiction between the superficial implications—and even the apparent contradictions of the text of Exodus—and Philo's assertions that nothing can be said descriptively of God's appearance and that no one may have an actual physical view of the Divine.

Philo also claimed that certain biblical statements of God must be understood in a figurative and not a literal sense. For example, he says, when the text says that "The Lord went down to see that city and that tower" [of Babel, Gen 11:5], it did not mean that God actually came down and walked around as if God had a human body, but rather that God fills all places at once and both contains and pervades everything in the universe. The Divine Being, he says, is both invisible and incomprehensible, and at the same time everywhere and in everything.[72] For Philo, however, asserting that the invisible God also had an "image" was necessary, since the first chapter of Genesis claims that humanity was created in that image (and "after the likeness," Gen 1:26). Philo, however, as the Christian Alexandrians do later on, associates the image with the preexistent Word of God—the agent of creation and the model for humanity whose likeness may be achieved through the practice of intellectual and moral virtue. The likeness that humans bore to this original image was not according to any external appearance, then, but according to the degree that humans shared in Divine Reason. Philo insists that no one could "represent this likeness as one to a bodily form; for neither is God in human form, nor is the human body God-like."[73]

On the other hand, the rabbis of Justin's time and later may well have emphasized the human-like appearance of God, especially as they considered the epiphanies portrayed in the books of Exodus and Daniel. According to Elliot Wolfson, some of the rabbinic authorities from the tannaitic period "assumed an anthropomorphic manifestation of God in concrete, visible forms was a basic part of biblical faith."[74] For example, Wolfson cites the midrashic collection *Mekhilta de-Rabbi Ishmael* on the book of Exodus and expounds on the polymorphic appearance of God as noted in these texts: "'The Lord is a man of war' [Exod 15:3]. Why is this said? For at the sea he appeared as a warrior doing battle, as it says, 'The Lord is a man of war.' At Sinai he appeared as an old man full of mercy, as it says, 'And they saw the God of Israel etc.'"[75]

Wolfson sees an anti-Christian polemic at work in these Jewish traditions. Just as Irenaeus was concerned that Gnostic teachers might interpret these theophanies as the appearance of a lesser God, the rabbis were aware that Christians were proposing that they demonstrated the existence of a second divine person. The polymorphous representations of God (sometimes as a warrior, sometimes as an old king on a throne, sometimes as a bridegroom, for instance) were not as worrisome as the claim that Christians like Justin or Tertullian made that these were epiphanies of God's Son or Logos. By way of combating such Christian readings, the rabbis might wish to assert that the manifold and diverse manifestations of God in the Bible were an essential means of presenting a truth about God—that God appeared in reality and not just as a figure in the prophet's imagination and, at the same time, God transcends ordinary (or banal) morphic consistency.[76] The invisible God's occasional manifestation to select individuals at particular moments gives the people assurance of God's presence, but, at the same time, it demonstrates that God cannot be limited in any sense or by any single form or outward appearance.

Theophilus, Novatian, and Origen: Salvific Vision ("Seeing God and Living")

Theophilus, a late second-century bishop of Antioch, attacked pagan idolatry and expounded his views on the visibility of God in his apology *To Autolycus* (his only certain surviving writing). In this work, Theophilus begins by setting out the occasion of the dialogue. Autolycus has boasted of his gods of wood and stone, carved or cast, and scornfully asked Theolophilus to "show me *your* god." In response, Theophilus impugns Autolycus's character, saying that God is seen only by those who are pure in heart (Matt 5:8), who have cleansed themselves from all sins, impurities, and evil occupations (adultery, robbery, slander, envy,

pandering, and so forth). Only these are able to behold God, with puri-
fied "eyes of the soul." Iniquities cloud the internal eyes of sinners, like a
cataract, and prevent them from perceiving the light, or seeing God.[77]

But, when asked how God will appear to one once he or she achieves
this sight, Theophilus answers with a long discourse on the folly of
image worship and the utter inadequacy of any description of the
Divine. This description had much in common with the writings of the
Stoics and of Philo, and it incorporates both negative terminology and
well-known titles for the Divine Being. For example, he begins: "The
appearance of God is ineffable and indescribable, and cannot be seen by
eyes of flesh. For in glory he is incomprehensible, in greatness unfath-
omable, in height inconceivable, in power incomparable, in wisdom
unrivalled, in goodness inimitable, in kindness unutterable." Following
this, he turns to the descriptive names one could give to God, including
Light, Word, Mind, Spirit, Wisdom, Strength, Power, Providence, Kingdom, Lord, Judge, Father, and Fire. Each of these titles, according to
Theophilus, refers to a particular aspect of God's being. "Light," for
instance refers to God's work, and Fire, a noticeably Stoic borrowing, to
God's anger.[78]

However, Theophilus continues (following the precepts of Paul and
echoing the arguments of Irenaeus), even though God is invisible to the
external eye, God can be perceived in the world—through God's work.
One can *see* God's providence and mighty deeds in the evidence of
nature and in the fact of one's very existence. And furthermore, if an
individual recognizes this and lives righteously, *then* he or she will see
God—after dying and being raised in the flesh. For only the immortal
may behold the immortal. Thus, again sounding much like Irenaeus,
Theophilus describes an end-time vision, when the mortal will contemplate the divine in its full glory. Theophilus, however, does not claim this
beatific vision to be the *cause* of immortality (as Irenaeus does), but
rather it will be the *result* of immortality, which is itself the reward for
righteousness (the purification of the soul from all iniquities).

Like all the other Christian apologists, Theophilus attacks the images
of the pagan gods, saying that it is absurd to think that human artisans
might shape worthless materials into images of the gods that could
merit sacrifices or receive prayers. Further, he points out, the stories told
about these gods clearly show that they are no more than human beings,
elevated erroneously to the status of gods. However, in the midst of his
account of creation, he digresses. Clearly aware that God is presented in
Genesis as having human characteristics, he recognizes that he must
clarify how the invisible and uncircumscribable God could be described
as walking around Eden and calling out to Adam. Theophilus explains
that it was God's Word who "assumed the person of the Father and Lord
of all," who went to the garden in the guise of God and talked with Adam
and Eve. In addition, the voice that Adam heard was none other than the

voice of the Word who is God and is generated from God. This Word goes wherever and for any purpose that God wills and is able to be both seen and heard in that designated place. Theophilus is careful to specify that the Word is not like other "sons of the gods" begotten through sexual intercourse, but it was the "firstborn" of creation and the eternal Reason of God, by which all things came into existence. On the basis of his argument regarding the appearance of the Logos to Adam and Eve, one can assume that Theophilus, like Justin, believes that the Word is the visible form of God, and the Divine Being who can interact with human beings, and the One who appears to the prophets, sometimes in human guise even prior to the incarnation.[79]

In the mid-third century, Novatian offered his view of God's ineffability in his treatise *On the Trinity*. He, too, recognizes that Scripture often presents God with human form or characteristics, but he explains that when the ancient text describes the tablets of the law as "written with the finger of God" (Exod 31:18), or a prayer that asks God to "incline your ear . . . open your eyes" (2 Kgs 19:16), it merely shows how the people thought of God at that time, but does not reflect how God really was. God was never limited, but human perception was. But, after the coming of Christ, things changed; the faithful no longer imagine that they may confine God in a temple or on a mountain. Quoting the Gospel of John, Novatian asserts, "God is spirit; and those who worship God must worship in spirit and in truth" (John 4:24). Hence, when God is described as having eyes or ears, it merely implies that God sees and hears all things. A reference to God's finger is really a reference to God's will, and a mention of God's feet is a metaphor for God's ubiquitous presence, and so forth. By concession to the needs of humanity, God may even be called "spirit," "light" or "love," but these are mere figures or analogies, not sufficient expressions of what God really *is*.[80]

However, when Novatian addresses a specific problem, like the appearance of the three persons to Abraham or the One who wrestled with Jacob, he seems to adapt Tertullian's position and maintains that Word was the Divine Person who had the essential capability of being seen, and not the Ineffable God. Since Scripture surely cannot lie, he argues, truly God was seen, but "it was not the Father who was seen, since he never was seen, but the Son, who has both been accustomed to descend, and to be seen because He has descended."[81] Moreover, he adds, that this appearance was a concession to human frailty, that seeing the Divine Word was a step in the process of gradually being able *one day* to see God. This is because "things that are great are dangerous if they are sudden." Novatian then compares the need for gradual adaptation to the vision of Divine glory to the blindness experienced by those coming out of pitch darkness into the bright light of day. The appearance of the Word to the prophets, in his view, was a one-step-at-a-time means of preparing humanity for a future beatific vision, as well as the means by which they might apprehend God in the meantime. Jacob could call the place that he wrestled with the angel, "The Vision of God" (Peniel), but this identification could only refer to his having seen God the Word or Christ (the Word made flesh).[82] And while Tertullian speaks of these manifestations of the Word as the means by which God becomes accustomed to human appearance (and future incarnation), Novatian understands them as a way for humans to become gradually accustomed to seeing God. Through these occasions, Novatian asserts, "the weakness and imperfection of the human destiny is nourished, led up, and educated by him; so that, being accustomed to look upon the Son, it may one day be able to see God the Father himself also as he is, that it may not be stricken by his sudden and intolerable brightness, and be hindered from being able to see God the Father, whom it has always desired."[83]

Origen, no different from all these others, absolutely believed that invisibility was essential to God, along with incorporeity, immutability, and incomprehensibility. This assertion of God's utter transcendence of human sight or knowledge led Origen to be particularly cautious about speaking of God even as "spirit," since that terminology might imply a kind of physical or substantial existence.[84] In this respect, Origen sounds a bit like Novatian (who was his younger contemporary). In contrast to Justin, Tertullian, or Novatian, however, Origen maintained that the invisibility of God extended also to the Divine Word, who (in Origen's view) shared this essential characteristic with the Unbegotten God. Given his position on the matter (not to mention his abhorrence of pagan idols), Origen's example of two statues to answer the question of whether God has a body or could be visible in any sense seems somewhat infelicitous.[85] The analogy (see below) comes within Origen's clarification of the way humans are created after the Divine Image, however, and he uses it to demonstrate how an image functions as a perceptible representation of an imperceptible model.

Origen also sees the incarnation as the way God shows forth an otherwise invisible, but also unbearable, divine glory. In language clearly reminiscent of the myth of the cave from Plato's *Republic*,[86] Origen explains that mortal eyes cannot bear the light of God directly but require an intermediary brightness that assists them little by little, until they can become accustomed to "bear the light in its clearness." Because of limited human abilities, Origen says, a mediating image is necessary—one that alone knows God (Matt 11:27) and that can express or reveal the form of God to those who are capable of it. And this, Origen says, is why the author of Hebrews can call Christ the "brightness of God's glory," as well as "the express image of God's substance or subsistence" (Heb 1:3).[87] In order to make this principle more understandable, Origen uses an analogy that he acknowledges at both outset and conclusion is problematic, since it borrows from "the realm of material things":

Let us suppose, for example, that there existed a statue of so great a size as to fill the whole world, but which on account of its immensity was imperceptible to anyone, and that another statue was made similar to it in every detail, in shape of limbs and outline of features, in form and material, but not in its immense size, so that those who were unable to perceive and behold the immense one could yet be confident that they had seen it when they saw the small one, because this preserved every line of limbs and features and the very form and material with an absolutely indistinguishable similarity.[88]

Origen defends his use of such an analogy, claiming its only purpose is to show how the Son of God, being "brought within the narrow compass of a human body," could become "an express image of God's substance or subsistence" (Heb 1:3), which could not be perceived in its full glory or its "immense and invisible brightness." In terms very much like Novatian's, Origen asserts that God is light and the only-begotten Word is the "brightness of that light," whose purpose is to assist eyes that were in the dark to become gradually adjusted to and able to endure the source of that brightness.[89]

But, he clarifies, the divine image that humans see in Christ is not in his physical appearance (his human nature) but rather through his deeds, which reveal the works of God in their transcendent majesty and power.[90] Here Origen may have been thinking of Paul's text regarding those perishing folk for whom the gospel is veiled: "In their case the god of this world has blinded the minds of the unbelievers, to keep them from seeing the light of the gospel of the glory of Christ, who is the image of God. . . . For it is the God who said, 'Let light shine out of darkness,' who has shone in our hearts to give the light of the knowledge of the glory of God in the face of Jesus Christ" (2 Cor 4:4, 6). But Origen here echoes Irenaeus as well, who argued that one knows God not only by visions and words but also in actual works.

Later in the treatise, Origen refutes those who claim that the God of the Hebrew prophets and patriarchs is distinct from and inferior to the Supreme God revealed by Christ. Like Tertullian, Origen candidly admits apparent contradictions in Scripture that arguably refer to two different Gods, one visible and the other invisible. But while Tertullian was more engaged with contradictions within the account of Moses' request for a vision of God's face, Origen expanded his discussion to examine the supposed dissimilarity between the God of the books of Moses and the Prophets and the God revealed in the New Testament. For example, Origen juxtaposes the Fourth Gospel's claim that "no one has ever seen God" (John 1:18) with the stories of God's appearances to Moses and the others. Origen admits this apparent contradiction might support the assertion that the God whom Moses proclaims (the Creator) is visible, while the God whom Jesus teaches is invisible. But, he points out, an utterly *invisible* God would have been invisible even to the Savior himself, a snag that would make it impossible for Jesus truthfully to say that no one has seen God except the one from God, as in "he has seen the Father" (John 6:46), or that "whoever has seen me [also] has seen the Father" (John 14:9).[91]

As a result, Origen concludes, the language of seeing is not meant in a literal sense, but rather as a metaphor or an allegory. "We must suppose Moses to have seen God, not by looking at him with eyes of flesh, but by understanding him with the vision of the heart and the perception of the mind, *and in this part only*."[92] And here Origen restates his position that God can have no body that could be perceived or known but is incorporeal and utterly outside human sensate knowledge. Jesus' statement in Matthew's Gospel ("no one knows the Father except the Son," Matt 11:27) in some sense clarifies the meaning of his statement in John, since the language of "seeing" is equivalent to and best replaced by the language of "knowing." As he says, it is "one thing to see and be seen, another to perceive and be perceived, or to know and to be known."[93] Origen's understanding of the power and nature of words as symbols, however, opens the way for a theology of image that will come to apply to things actually seen by the eye.

Origen might have made the same argument with respect to the whole text of John 1:18: "No one has ever *seen* God. It is God the only Son, who is close to the Father's heart, who has made him *known*" (emphasis mine; Greek = *exēgēsato*, trans. "exegeted" or "interpreted"). This argument also allows the words preceding the claim of John 14:9 to explain its actual sense: "If you *know* me, you will *know* (Greek = *gnōsesthe*) my Father also. From now on you do *know* him and have *seen* him. . . . Have I been with you all this time, Philip, and you still do not *know* me?" (John 14:7-8, emphasis mine).[94] Moreover, Origen argues that this nonsighted "knowing" also characterizes the way humans encounter the whole Trinity, since the ability to be seen properly belongs only to corporeal bodies, which excludes the Divine Triad, which by its very nature "transcends the limits of vision." Incorporeal and intellectual nature is only capable of knowing and being known. It is *never* seen, even by itself.[95]

Using the language of sight as a metaphor for intellectual perception, Origen interprets the stories of God's appearance to the Hebrew patriarchs allegorically. For example, in his fourth homily on Genesis, he gives the story of Abraham's divine visitation at Mamre a moral and mystical meaning. He focuses on the differences between the ways Abraham and Lot receive and treat their guests, the significance of the place name (Mambre, the name Origen uses, means "vision" in "our language" according to him), the symbolic rather than superficial meanings that one can draw from the fact that Sarah was standing behind Abraham, or that God speaks of "descending to see the iniquities of Sodom," and so forth. Origen is apparently uninterested in the actual identity of the three mysterious guests. They obviously cannot be God, since all three Persons of the Trinity are invisible.[96] Similarly, in his commentary on the Song of Songs, Origen suggests that the time of the visit to Abraham (midday) denotes the soul's pursuit of the clear, bright light of knowledge (cf. Song 1:7).[97] Later, he identifies the call of the lover to the dove in the clefts of the rock, "let me see your face" (Song 2:14), with Moses also in the shelter of the rock, where he could see God's back, since he was not allowed to see God's face. The bride of the Song is accorded something Moses was not until the transfiguration: she may contemplate the glory of God with "unveiled face" (cf. Exod 34:33-35; 2 Cor 3:7-18; 2 Cor 4:3-4).[98]

Such interpretations emerge out of Origen's essential understanding of how humans were created according to the image of God and how they will be redeemed through the renewal of that original image. Origen's view, which was similar to that of his Alexandrian predecessor Clement, was that the human likeness to God was an invisible and spiritual likeness, not an external or corporeal one. The divine likeness resides in the inner person, which was made immortal, incorruptible, and invisible. To think otherwise would be to suppose impiously that God could look like us or have a human form. But, he clarifies, humanity was created according to the image of God, the Savior, who is the "the exact imprint of God's very being" (Heb 1:3), the "image of the invisible God" and "the firstborn of all creation" (Col 1:15). And, this is why Jesus can say, "he who has seen me has seen ["known"] the Father" (John 14:9). Since anyone who looks at an image of someone sees the original model, so also does anyone who sees Christ perceive God.

Such perception is the beginning of human spiritual progress, which is the renewal of that inner, invisible image given to men and women at their creation. Origen believes that the thing one beholds is what one becomes. If one contemplates the image of God, one will gradually recover that likeness. If one turns instead toward the Devil, one will become like the Devil. Sin erases one's original image and begins to implant another. Understanding the dynamic power of vision is critical since human salvation depends upon it.[99] In his debate with the pagan Celsus, Origen validates the theory of participation, so long as the contemplation of sensible things leads to the contemplation of the intelligible world. However, he points out, too often those who have been enabled to form the material or sensible representations are drawn back to them and slip back into the foolish error of offering veneration to created things, exchanging the sublime for the base and making the truth of God into a lie.[100]

In a different homily on Genesis, Origen again takes up this theme, citing the parable of the woman and the coin (Luke 15:8-10) and interpreting it as an allegory of the soul's lost image. In order to find that lost coin (the image), the woman had to light a lamp and sweep and clean her house (the soul), removing the filth and rubbish that had been built up over a long period of sloppy housekeeping. So long as the inner person is covered with dirt or dust, the image is obscured—an echo of Paul's promise in 1 Cor 15:49: "Just as we have borne the image of the man of dust, we will also bear the image of the man of heaven."[101] Here, Origen's disparagement of the materiality of human flesh in favor of recovering a spiritual and incorporeal original verges on agreeing with the Gnostic repudiation of created matter. Visibility is a signal of the fallen state (the soul was bound to the earthly body as a punishment), and the progressive reversal of that condition makes humans more and more perfectly, invisibly spiritual. Yet Origen refuses to specify that in the end "bodily nature" will perish, since he asserts "we believe that to exist without material substance and apart from any association with a bodily element is a thing that belongs only to the nature of God, that is of the Father, the Son, and the Holy Spirit." The perfected or spiritual nature will still be bodily in some sense but no longer visible to the degree or in the same way that its lower form was.[102]

Later in this same homily, Origen once again employs an analogy from visual art to explain this progressive spiritual renewal of the original image. In this case, however, rather than describing the Logos as a smaller version of an incomprehensibly enormous statue, Origen speaks of the Logos as the original of a painting as well as the artist who paints it, and he compares the human soul to the copy or reproduction. Because the painter is God, the image is indelible—it can be obscured but cannot be destroyed. Humans can paint over that image with an earthly one made up of colors derived from lust, covetousness, rage, pride, and other sins, but once humans turn again toward their original, God can remove those muddy and reddish colors like an art restorer, uncovering and freshening the luminous originals.[103]

Origen's analogy does not mean to downplay the human participation in this work of restoration, since the sinner both draws the image of the "earthly" person over the original and must be engaged in cleansing the soul, guided by a vision of the True Image. In this respect, Origen sounds rather like Theophilus, who accorded the vision only to those whose righteousness allowed them to attain immortality. Origen's idea of spiritual renewal is grounded in moral conversion, aided by intellectual discipline and conforming to Scripture. However, Origen's process is more gradual. Those being converted or restored must always keep their (inner) eye on the model. And the transformation from the muddy darkness of sin and confusion to the clear radiance of divine likeness comes in stages, at least up to the point when the soul is finally able to withstand the full brightness of divine glory. However, in contrast to Theophilus, Origen, like Irenaeus, would say that seeing is itself transformative and salvific, rather than the sign of salvation already achieved. Irenaeus believes that vision of the Divine in its full brilliant glory ultimately grants humans immortality and eternal incorruptibility, while Origen speaks in terms of a time when the "form of the world will pass away" (1 Cor 7:31), and "bodily substance will be so pure and refined the we must think of it being like the ether."[104]

In conclusion, although most of these ancient writers, whether Christian, pagan, or Jewish, affirm that God is invisible and utterly beyond human knowledge or encounter, they show an enormous range and variation in how they understand and defend this basic assertion. All three groups criticized anyone who might actually assume that the divine could be circumscribed by a statue or contained within a temple, and in various ways each one might accuse the others of atheism or idolatry, depending on what was at stake.

At the same time, the biblical assertion that human beings were created in the image of God and therefore bear some kind of likeness to God raises the problem of what the term "likeness" might mean and to what extent it has anything to do with external appearance. And although the statement that God is invisible seems simple enough by itself, the whole matter is complicated when Scripture relates certain epiphanies of God to select individuals. Furthermore, as the Divine Word is incorporated into the essential structure of the Godhead in Christian teaching and then identified by some Christian teachers as the one who "appeared" in these texts, new complications arise, especially with regard to arguments about the plurality or unity of God and the relationship of the Word to the Father. Furthermore, the Christian declaration that the Word became incarnate in visible human flesh calls for a theory about the relationship among theophany, beatific vision, divine perception (knowledge), and human salvation. Moses was told that he could not look at the face of God and live, but Christian teaching suggests just the opposite—that seeing God "face to face" is the sum and substance of being truly alive.

FOUR

Seeing the Divine in the Fourth and Early Fifth Centuries

ORIGEN'S ANALOGY of a painting's restoration to human salvation (discussed in the previous chapter) has a close parallel in the writings of the fourth-century Alexandrian theologian Athanasius. In his treatise *On the Incarnation,* Athanasius likewise speaks of the Incarnate Logos as a painter or art restorer and of the human soul, made in the image of God, as a blemished or soiled painting, obscured and damaged through the careless accretion of sin. The Logos, as the True Image of God, then comes to renew the painting "effaced by stains from without" so that the portrait may be renewed and restored. Borrowing metaphors from the actual practice of portrait painting on wooden panels, Athanasius maintains that the board and the outlines exist and may be reused, but the colors need to be filled in again and the likeness redrawn.[1] In another place, Athanasius, again echoing Origen, depicts the mortal soul, stained by the filth of lust, as needing to be washed until the foreign matter has been removed and the likeness to the image is returned to its original created state: "then surely this latter [the soul] being thoroughly brightened, the soul beholds as in a mirror the Image of the Father, even the Word, and by this means reaches the idea of the Father, whose Image the Savior is."[2]

Despite their use of similar analogies, Athanasius takes a very different position from Origen's on the importance of God's corporeal appearance and the degree of human effort involved in the process of the restoration of the image. Whereas for Origen, the Divine Image is essentially invisible and incorporeal even when it is brought "within the compass of a human body," for Athanasius the Incarnate One was necessarily visible because visibility was essential to his saving mission.[3] Athanasius relies on the actual, material corporeality of the incarnation as a medium of salvation. The renewal of the divine image in humankind happens through sensible means. Seeing God's image in Christ was important to both Athanasius and Origen, but they would have said that they were looking at different things. Origen believed recovery was a matter of the renewing of the inner spirit and illumination of the mind, while Athanasius believed the human fleshly reality itself was redeemable, as demonstrated in the incarnation and resurrection of the body of Christ.

At the same time, Athanasius holds a more pessimistic view of humanity's ability to progress on its own than Origen does. According to Athanasius, fallen humans lack adequate awareness of the dim and obscured image within themselves even to recognize their own state of decrepitude. Mortals cannot come to knowledge of God by their own power since they are hopelessly mired in confusion, blinded by sin, and deceived by demons. They are thereby rendered insufficient to withstand the vanity of idols. He asks, "If someone cannot see, how can he or she be reeducated?"[4] The signs of God in creation are not enough, for if it were, humanity would not be in such a state. Even the Divine Word showing forth the truth of God as in former times was not enough—for humans had missed seeing this before and moreover now kept their eyes downcast. The only means left was for God to condescend to humanity's need for a corporeal appearance, to come down to the world of nature and of sense, to take on a mortal body so that—meeting them halfway—humans might finally perceive the truth in three dimensions and recognize the True (incorporeal) God by means of what the Incarnate One effects through his body. Thus, seeing the resurrection of the Savior, those who were drawn to worship idols or to mistake them for gods were made aware of their error, by comparison.[5] And since Christ's corporeal appearance and his visible acts and deeds were a critical part of human salvation, the Savior once born could not immediately offer himself for sacrifice on the cross and resurrection from the dead:

> For by this means he would have made himself invisible. But he made himself visible enough by what he did, abiding in it and doing such works, and showing such signs as make him known no longer as human, but as God the Word. For by his becoming human, the savior was to accomplish both works of love, first in putting away death from us and renewing us again; secondly, being unseen and invisible, in manifesting and making himself known by his works to be the Word of God, and the Ruler of the Universe.[6]

For Athanasius, the sensory knowledge that comes through the external eye was crucial for humans to become attracted to Christ, "and center their senses on himself," so that they could see his works (healing the blind and the lame, changing water to wine, and so forth) and come to recognize that this was not human only but also the Divine Word and Wisdom of the True God. For the sake of human salvation, the invisible had to become visible. God had to come down to the human level, to "show up" in a body so that humanity might see the Truth and through the Incarnate Christ recognize God (the Father).[7]

Athanasius consequently proposes that seeing serves an important function in the working of salvation, which in his view now requires the recognition of God who appears in human form in addition to those previously available signs in creation, Holy Scripture, and history. Since so far these other means had not succeeded, God chose to "meet humanity halfway" and took on its physical reality. In Christ's earthly performance of works and wonders, as well as in his birth, death, and resurrection, Athanasius sees God's nature, love, and redemptive plan revealed. More than Origen, Athanasius believes that seeing was a critical *means* of knowing, not a metaphor for it. In the incarnation, the human race was directly and physically confronted with its potential. Now with a visible model of its true self, it could both see its origin and recognize its destiny. In a more literal sense, the Origenist proposal that what one looks at is what one becomes is extended to the principle "look and live." Simultaneously, the emphasis on Christ as the physical and incarnate model of salvation opens the possibility of seeing an actual painted portrait as an instructive and beneficial image, rather than as a deceitful idol. The prototype may be recognized through its representation and incorporated into the human idea of itself.

The Invisible God in the Fourth Century

Shortly before Athanasius wrote his treatise on the incarnation, Arnobius, a Numidian convert and teacher of rhetoric, launched a late—but vehement—attack on traditional polytheism. His extremely zealous denunciation of his former religion may have been partly explained by the timing of his writing during the Great Persecution (303–311 C.E.) and by his hope to convince others to convert as he did. But it also revealed much about the state of Roman religion at the time. His treatise *Against the Nations* answers pagan charges that the Christian religion was bringing Rome to ruin and, in one long section, reprises the familiar apologetic ridicule of image worship, particularly among his North African neighbors: "And so, unmindful and forgetful of what the substance and origin of the images are, you, rational beings and endowed with the gift of wisdom and the discretion, sink down before pieces of baked earthenware, adore places of copper, beg from the teeth of elephants good health . . . and while it is plain and clear that you are speaking to senseless things, you think that you are heard, and bring yourselves into disgrace of your own accord, by vainly and credulously deceiving yourselves."[8] In his work Arnobius also follows the pattern set by the apologists and assails the polytheistic practice of localizing their

gods in a temple or image and of presuming that they have need of sacrifices and gifts. And, like his earlier counterparts, he defends the Christian practice of refusing both temples and images to God. But within a
few generations, Arnobius's critique must have seemed dated, due to the
gradual demise of traditional Roman religion and the spread of Christianity in the Empire. Within a generation or two, the attention of
Christian teachers shifted away from condemning external idolatry and
focused instead on attacking internal error. Idolatry was no longer a
serious threat to the faith—heresy was.

After the Edict of Milan, the function of the image began to take on
new significance in the dogmatic discussions of Christian theologians.
Like Athanasius, later fourth-century theologians discussed the matter
of divine images at a whole new level, possibly because they felt less
threatened by pagan idolatry but also inspired by their debates about the
nature and relationship of the Divine Beings of the Trinity and by their
efforts to find appropriate terminology for God, Logos, and Holy Spirit.
The earlier pattern of speaking of the Logos as the visible member of the
Trinity (as seen in Justin or Tertullian) continues, but within the polemical struggle to assert the unity and shared nature of the Godhead. For
example, Basil of Caesarea's treatise, *On the Holy Spirit* (written around
375 c.e.), emphasizes the unity of the Three Persons against those who
would divide or enumerate the Persons into a plurality of divine beings
or reduce the Holy Spirit to the status of a mere creature, thus falling
into the error of polytheism. To illustrate his point, Basil employs an
example well known to his contemporaries, the portrait of the
emperor—an illustration that would have been unthinkable a century
earlier—and argues that the Divine Image and Prototype share the same
nature, which is not divided by the fact that one is seen and the other
unseen:

> How, then, if one and one, are there not two gods? Because we speak of a king,
> and of the king's image, and not of two kings. The majesty is not cloven into
> two, nor the glory divided. The sovereignty and authority over us is one, and
> so the doxology ascribed by us is not plural but one; because the honor paid
> to the image passes on to the prototype. Now what in the one case the image
> is by reason of imitation [the emperor's portrait], that in the other case the
> Son is by nature; and as in works of art, the likeness is dependent on the form,
> so in the case of the divine and uncompounded nature, the union consists in
> the communion of the Godhead.[9]

Basil here specifies the important assertion that will later belong to the
defense of icons: that any honor paid to the image passes on to the
prototype. He continues by maintaining that the relationship of the
Word and God is that of image and prototype, and he says that when
one gazes at the beauty of the image, one is drawn up to the spectacle of

the archetype. Much influenced by the teachings of Greek philosophers, Basil sees vision as a dynamic activity of the senses and a spiritual aid, since it leads the viewer beyond the external appearance and on to the perception of invisible truth, thus forming a critical link between the philosophical theory of participation and the later defense of the place of icons in liturgy and devotional prayer.[10]

Basil, however, does not have painted images in mind in his treatise, and he prefaces this discussion with a traditional insistence that God is ultimately invisible and ineffable, a Spirit that must be worshiped in spirit and in truth. In his earlier writings against the neo-Arian Eunomius (ca. 363–364 C.E.), who claimed that knowledge of God was possible, Basil insists on God's incomprehensibility and defends a metaphorical or allegorical reading of the theophanies in Scripture against a reading of Scripture that would take the anthropomorphic descriptions of God literally (which Eunomius probably did not actually do).[11]

Correspondingly, in his refutation of Eunomius, Basil's brother, Gregory of Nyssa, addresses the problem of names applied to the deity and their source as well as their validity. Gregory argues that the mind might supply terms, but that ultimately God's essence is incomprehensible, and that the only true descriptions of God are in terms of negative constructs (for example, "pretemporal," "incorporeal," "imperishable," or "ungenerate"). Elaborating on the unknowability of God and human incapacity to give name or description to this ultimate reality, he asserts: "For this inability to give expression to such unutterable things, while it reflects upon the poverty of our own nature, affords an evidence of God's glory, teaching us as it does, in the words of the Apostle, that the only name naturally appropriate to God is to believe God 'above every name' [Phil 2:9]. That God transcends every effort of thought, and is far beyond any circumscribing by a name, constitutes a proof to us of this ineffable majesty."[12]

Gregory's friend Gregory of Nazianzus was of the same mind, insisting that God was beyond expression and impossible even to conceive because of the "darkness of this world and the thick covering of the flesh" that serve as an obstacle to the complete understanding of the truth, not merely to the ignorant and careless but also to those who "are highly exalted and who love God." Gregory denies that even "higher natures" and "purer intelligences" (he presumably means angels) are able to perceive fully, but, "because they are illumined with all his light, [they] may possibly see, if not the whole, at any rate more perfectly and distinctly than we do . . . in proportion to their rank."[13] Thus, the appearances to Abraham or the visions of Isaiah, Ezekiel, or even Paul (when he was caught up into the third heaven; 2 Cor 12:2-4) are partial and provisional glimpses of an indescribable mystery. In another place, Gregory speaks of the Son as the perfect image of the Father, the "pure seal and his most unerring impress" by way of explaining Jesus' statement that "whoever has seen me has seen the Father" (John 14:9). But, he insists, the kind of seeing meant in this text is mental, not sensible, perception.[14]

In what may have been his last work, probably written in the 390s, Gregory of Nyssa proposed Moses as an exemplar of how a mystical theologian approaches the infinite by consistently removing concepts, analogies, or metaphors that would describe (or circumscribe) God. The soul seeking perfection must be on a journey that has an unattainable goal, and yet the journey itself is the progress that the soul makes toward perfection. The analogy for this absolute transcendence and infinity of God, and for Moses' story, becomes the figure of the soul striving to see what it cannot see, yet driven by that very desire, making gradual progress toward spiritual enlightenment that comes from desiring what is beyond attainment. Thus Moses "shone with glory. And although lifted up through such lofty experiences, he is unsatisfied and desires more. He still thirsts for that with which he constantly filled himself to capacity, and he asks to attain as if he had never partaken, beseeching God to appear to him, not according to his capacity to partake, but according to God's true being." And, citing the text of Exod 33:20 ("You cannot see my face . . . and live"), Gregory explains that this does not mean that the sight of God's face causes death, but rather that the expectation that God can be known is a misunderstanding deadly to the soul: "This Being [God] is inaccessible to knowledge. If then the life-giving nature transcends knowledge, that which is perceived certainly is not life." Gregory concludes by asserting that the Divine by its very nature is infinite, enclosed by no boundary, and transcends all characteristics.[15]

Around the same time (ca. 386–387 c.e.), and in somewhat the same context although in his particular style, John Chrysostom preached five sermons at Antioch on the subject of the incomprehensible nature of God, also against the neo-Arian position that it is possible to know God as well as God knows God. In these homilies, John blasts Eunomius for arrogantly insisting that God's nature could be apprehended through human reason, and he defends the absolute ineffability of God and the mystery of God's being.[16] John elaborates his arguments with careful attention to the scriptural appearances of God to the patriarchs and prophets, but especially to the visions of Isaiah, Daniel, and Ezekiel. He points out that these texts emphasize the unapproachable glory of God, unbearable to human eyes. Isaiah, for example, cries out in fear at the vision, Ezekiel fell on his face, and Daniel was terrified. But, even these, according to John, were not actual visions of God's divine essence but only God's self-revelation in a form that the visionary could receive within the limits of mortal life. Citing 1 Timothy, John affirms that God "dwells in unapproachable light, whom no one has ever seen or can see"

(1 Tim 6:16). This unapproachable light not only indicates God's infinite glory but also protects God's absolute ineffability.[17]

From this kind of theological discussion, the invisibility of God finds its place in the mystical tradition. The invisible, immortal, and incomprehensible God is above all form and even imagining. Those who would wish to meditate on the nature of God must empty their minds of all images or even propositions through a process of negation known as apophatic theology. In the late fourth century, for instance, Evagrius of Pontus (345–399 c.e.) developed these teachings into a form of spirituality, and, along with other aspects of an Origenist theology, he emphasized the nonsubstantiality and utter unknowability of the Divine nature. In his *Chapters on Prayer* he gives directions: "When you are praying do not fancy the Divinity like some image formed within yourself. Avoid also allowing your spirit to be impressed with the seal of some particular shape, but rather, free from all matter, draw near the immaterial Being and you will attain to understanding."[18] By keeping the mind free of any image (even metaphorical) for God, Evagrius believed that the human spirit also was kept free of misleading concepts or finite figures, which would trap the human soul in a materialistic dead end.

This gradual freeing of the mind from the image in order to understand mystically the invisibility or incomprehensibility of God continued to occupy a central place in Christian theology and spiritual practice through the fifth century. Scriptural exegesis of the visions and appearances of God also shored up an "orthodox" position on the knowability of God in such writers as Theodoret of Cyrus in the mid-fifth century.[19] The idea would reach a kind of high point at the beginning of the sixth century in the writings of Dionysius the Areopagite (Pseudo-Dionysius), who has been described as a spiritual heir of both Gregory of Nyssa and Evagrius (as well as Philo).[20]

In his treatise *Mystical Theology* the author also presents Moses as a prototype of the one who attains a vision of God by first seeing God in earthly manifestations but finally ascending into the "cloud of unknowing" on Sinai.[21] The one who wishes to know God is advised to emulate Moses' process, by gradually negating all possible descriptions, affirmations, names, or attributes assigned to the Divine One (cataphatic theology), since all these are ultimately only human and limited constructions that fall far short of the truth. At the beginning, however, the author assigns an initial value to images or visible symbols, which serve as the first step on the ladder of ascent toward higher awareness (by negating all these images or attributes), until one finally transcends perceptible qualities and arrives at a mystical vision of and union with God. In another treatise (*Divine Names*), he summarizes the way that a seeker proceeds from the negation of the perceptible and then the conceptual, finally to arrive at the invisible:

> On no account therefore is it true to say that we know God, not indeed in His nature (for that is unknowable, and is beyond any reason and understanding), but by the order of all things that He has established, and which bears certain images and likenesses of His divine paradigms, we ascend step by step, so far as we can follow the way, to the Transcendent, by negating and transcending everything and seeking the cause of all.[22]

For Dionysius, this process is an anagogical one, in which the symbols or images that humans apply to God that are useful at the start of the ascent must be finally abandoned. At last, the mystic comes to meet God at the point that all words or images, even ideas, are gone, and the seeker, like Moses, enters the silence of unknowing.

The Anthropomorphite Controversy

However, minds do not eradicate images easily, especially when the thinking process itself calls forth images constantly. Resistance to conceiving of God in an anthropomorphic form belongs to the spiritually adept and aware, but not easily to the general population. Furthermore, Scripture itself seems to encourage such visualization. In the late fourth and early fifth centuries, certain anti-Origenist (and so also anti-Evagrian) groups among Egyptian monks and Syrian followers of a certain Audius posited a corporeal and anthropomorphic understanding of God's appearance, following the text of Gen 1:26-27 ("Let us make humankind in our image, according to our likeness . . ."). According to the Christian historian Socrates (380–450), the question caused much strife and contention; one group (the "more simple ascetics") favored the opinion that God is corporeal and has a human form, while another contended that God is incorporeal and free from all form whatsoever. Socrates reported that Bishop Theophilus of Alexandria (384–412) inveighed against those who held the anthropomorphite position, expressly teaching that the Divine is incorporeal, a position that, when it reached the ears of the "simple Egyptian monks," emptied out the monasteries as they rushed to Alexandria to protest, accusing the bishop of impiety and threatening to put him to death.[23]

This dispute got entangled in the larger Origenist controversy partly because these monks demanded a condemnation of Origen's "spiritualizing" theology, and Theophilus could not afford to alienate them. In the meantime, he may actually have saved his own skin and pacified the angry crowd by telling the monks that "In seeing you I behold the face of God."[24] For a while, enemies of Origenist theology may have sought "anthropomorphite" support for their condemnation of Origen's generally negative position on the human body. The monks, however, were simply being defensive about their own traditions, in which they imagined God as having a body like theirs (and thus their own potential to attain the divine form through ascesis). They realized that when they prayed they held a mental image of God. According to them, inhibiting such imagination would have made it impossible for them to pray.

John Cassian recounts an event in his tenth Conference that captures the essence of this movement and the monks' attachment to their image of God. He tells the tale of a monk named Serapion, who had lived a life of dedicated austerity and discipline. Despite his age, merit, and holy life, however, he was a little ignorant of theology, and to him the teaching that God's appearance was incomprehensible made no sense. It seemed an invention of intellectuals and a direct contradiction of the Scriptures. However, when a certain deacon named Photinus explained that the "image and likeness" of God was to be understood in a spiritual sense (for God could have no corporeality), the old man finally gave in and accepted the teaching. His assent to orthodox teaching gave great joy to all in his community, who had feared losing his soul to heresy, and they gathered to pray and give thanks for the rescue of this simple-minded brother. "And then, amid these prayers, the old man became confused, for he sensed that the human image of God which he used to draw before him as he prayed was now gone from his heart. Suddenly he gave way to the bitterest, most abundant tears and sobs. He threw himself on the ground and with the mightiest howl he cried out: "Ah the misfortune! They've taken my God away from me. I have no one to hold on to, and I don't know whom to adore or to address."[25] A visual idea of God, even one only imagined, was, if not impossible, at least terribly difficult and even debilitating to expunge from the mind.

Augustine and the Problem of the Invisible God

Augustine's approval of ancient Roman aniconism (in the time of King Numa) is consistent with his general position on making visual images of God. He clearly believed that such things were indicative of simple-minded materialism and needed to be eradicated.[26] However, despite efforts to free Christians from the errors of idolatry, Augustine lamented in one of his sermons that idols and images had nevertheless found a place in the church and even generated justifiable criticism of this "Christian superstition" by some of their educated pagan neighbors. Reminded that these same pagans defend their own practice of image veneration by claiming that they "don't adore images, but what is signified by the image," Augustine challenges their logic. He asks why they go to the trouble of making certain images, when the model is so often directly available to them, as in the case of the sun or the moon: "But since they can see the sun, which is signified by the image of the sun, why do their turn their backs to what is signified, and their faces to the sign it is signified by?" He acknowledges that if pagans only made their images of things that were otherwise invisible, they might actually be acting in a logical manner. As it is, however, the action of offering worship or prayer to an image of something otherwise visible or available is parallel to asking a favor from a portrait, rather than from the actual person portrayed:

> How can you expect him to hear you, when you abandon him, and turn to some false and totally misleading image of him? It's as if you went to the house of some landowner to beg for something, and he was standing in his courtyard while you turned your back to him and faced his portrait; and if you not only poured out your heart to a picture and not to a man, but did so in the presence of the man portrayed in the picture, wouldn't he assume you were making fun of him, or put you down as crazy, and in any case have you thrown out of his house?[27]

But, as if suddenly realizing that his arguments might be used to justify the visible images of invisible things for the sake of prayerful petition, Augustine adds that seeing things and seeing God are two different operations. He tells his listeners that God "made you one thing to see these things with, another with which he himself might be seen—for seeing these things he gave you the eyes in your head, for seeing himself he gave you a mind—you cannot therefore be allowed to say in that inane way, 'I can't see him.'" In the same way, Augustine continues, one cannot see a person's soul but can know that it exists from the evidence of its work to move and control the body.[28] His argument here is paralleled in a homily on the Gospel of John in which he distinguishes between seeing the visible miracles of Christ with the external eye and perceiving the transcendent and invisible reality to which those miracles point with the mind. By analogy, he contrasts the way one superficially sees the whole of a picture in one glance with the fact that one must read a text through to understand its meaning.[29]

Augustine's concern for protecting the invisibility of God is also evident in his responses to several letters written between 408 and 414. The first, written to a widow named Italica, offers some comfort in her loss but at the same time refutes a popular idea that, in the resurrection, God will be seen by bodily eyes. He assures her that such an idea is absurd, since God is a spirit and cannot be seen as a body. At the same time, he also reassures her—that a vision of God is promised as a reward of faith. That vision will not, however, be a bodily one, but a spiritual one.[30] He similarly admonishes a layman named Consentius, who has trouble thinking of God as disembodied, like some abstract virtue (for example,

Fig. 23. Porphyry group portrait of the Tetrarchs, ca. 300 C.E., originally from Constantinople, now in St. Mark's Square, Venice (Photo: Author).

Fig. 29. Sarcophagus from Church of Santa Maria Antiqua, late 3rd cen. C.E., Foro Romano (Photo: Author).

Fig. 32. Christian funerary mosaic from Tarbarka, 4th cen. C.E., Bardo Museum, Tunis (Photo: Author).

Fig. 39. Commodus as Hercules, 191–192 C.E., Museo del Palazzo dei Conservatori, Rome (Photo: Author).

Fig. 48. Lamb of God, mid-6th cen. C.E. mosaic in the presbytery vault, San Vitale, Ravenna (Photo: Author).

Fig. 54. Detail, Trinity creating Adam and Eve. Dogmatic Sarcophagus, Museo Pio Cristiano, Vatican (photo: Author).

Fig. 64. Christ giving the new law to Paul (and Peter), Apse mosaic, mid-4th cen. C.E. from the Mausoleum of Constantina, Rome (© The International Catacomb Society. Photo: Estelle Brettman).

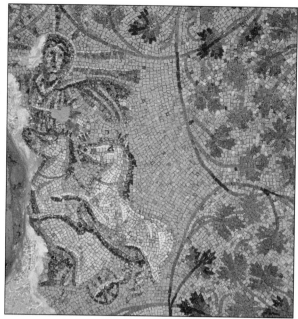

Fig. 66. Christ as Helios, Mausoleum M (or the Julii), 4th cen. C.E. mosaic, Vatican Necropolis (© The International Catacomb Society. Photo: Estelle Brettman).

Fig. 70. Christ as Orpheus from the Catacomb of Domitilla, Rome (©The International Catacomb Society. Photo: Estelle Brettman).

Fig. 75. Jesus as teacher, 4th cen. C.E. mosaic from the Chapel of San Aquilino, Basilica of San Lorenzo Maggiore, Milan (Photo: Michael Flecky, S.J.).

Fig. 78. Jesus enthroned, ca. 400 C.E. Church of Santa Pudenziana, Rome (Photo: Author).

Fig. 80. Jesus before Pilate, mosaic, early 6th cen. C.E., San Apollinare Nuovo, Ravenna (Photo: Author).

Fig. 84. Apse mosaic, mid-6th cen. C.E., San Vitale, Ravenna (Photo: Author).

Fig. 86. Transfiguration mosaic, mid-6th cen. C.E., apse of San Apollinare in Classe, Ravenna (Photo: Author).

righteousness or piety). Augustine admits that it is difficult for humans to conceive of a being without a body, because of their familiarity with visible, bodily things. Still, he says, the invisible, incorporeal, and immutable Trinity is unbounded and omnipresent. This is only known through true reason and not through carnal experience.[31] Augustine then outlines three kinds of things that can be seen: first, actual corporeal things that one may see in reality; second, those bodily things that one imagines or dreams; and finally, those things that have no bodies but are mentally conceived, such as wisdom. The Trinity, however, is none of these, since it cannot even be grasped fully by the mind—something as he says, one somehow grasps as through a glass and an enigma (1 Cor 13:12). Thus, Augustine urges his reader to drive out and deny even those mental images that would give God the likeness of a body.[32]

A few years later, Augustine takes up the same theme in his response to a letter from a woman named Paulina. Apparently, Paulina had asked Augustine to write (something lengthy and detailed) "about the invisible God and whether he can be seen by bodily eyes." Complying with her request, Augustine wrote a book-length treatise that he later called On Seeing God, in which he asserts that humans can see God, not as we can see the sun or earthly objects, but rather with the "gaze of the mind" as we see ourselves inwardly. Citing Matt 5:8 ("Blessed are the pure in heart, for they will see God"), Augustine distinguishes between bodily seeing and mentally comprehending (as well as between present and future sight), since we believe much of what we cannot see (from details about our family history to Christ's virginal conception), and he then tries to reconcile Scripture texts that claim that certain persons have seen God over against those that say that such sight is impossible.

In the treatise, Augustine specifically comments on particular passages from the Hebrew Scriptures in which God appears, including Jacob's assertion that "I saw God face to face and my soul was saved" (Gen 32:30), the statement that Moses spoke with God "face to face" (Exod 33:11), and Isaiah's testimony that "I saw the Lord of hosts sitting upon a throne" (Isa 6:1). Note that these passages are difficult to coordinate with the seemingly opposed claim that "no one has ever seen God" (John 1:18). Drawing his reader's attention to the teaching of his mentor, Ambrose, Augustine argues that sensible things and God are not seen in a similar manner, since God can will to be seen or not to be seen, whereas all other objects or beings cannot choose to become invisible. Nor can someone choose to "see" God, for God's appearance is only at God's own initiative. "By nature, therefore, God is invisible, not only the Father but also the Trinity itself, one God, and because he is not only invisible but also immutable, he appears as he wills in what form he wills so that his invisible and immutable nature may remain whole within him."[33]

Then, referring to the rest of the text of John 1:18 ("It is God the only Son, who is close to the Father's heart, who has made him known"), Augustine allows that some argue that the Son was the Person who appeared to Abraham, Jacob, Moses, and Isaiah, and this would refute certain adoptionist heretics (the Photinians), who assign a beginning to the Son at the human birth from the Virgin. However, he continues, the meaning of the line "no one has seen God" was not meant to distinguish the Persons of the Trinity but to establish that no one can see God in the fullness of God's divinity, and, moreover, that which is "made known by the Son" is a vision more of the mind than the eyes. "A form is seen, but a power is made known. . . . God is not sought by bodily eyes, nor enveloped by sight, nor perceived by his walk." And even Christ is no longer seen in the flesh, but only in terms of the Spirit.[34]

But, in a modified fashion, Augustine argues, the righteous ones of old did see God, to the extent that God willed to be seen. Citing Ambrose again, Augustine asserts that to assign this appearance to the Son would be to accept the teachings of the Arians, who believe that the nature of the Father is invisible but that of the Son is visible. Hence, one must assert that all three Persons of the Trinity are equally invisible, and, to the extent that they appear, they do so in the form chosen by their will and not according to their nature—the Holy Spirit appearing as a dove, for example.[35] Finally, the distinction between seeing with the eye and comprehending with the mind is resolved in the end time, when the righteous will receive the grace to see God as God is (1 John 3:2). The unrighteous, however, will not be able to do so, even in the resurrection. Only those who are "clean of heart" (Matt 5:8) shall receive this gift. All others, including the Devil, are excluded from such sight, "without a doubt."[36]

Finally, speaking of humans' desire to see God, Augustine argues that, rightly understood, this desire is not to see a particular aspect of God, but rather to perceive the Divine nature itself. Moses' petition to see God "openly" (Exod 33:11) was such a case. But, Augustine continues, such vision can only be obtained after the cleansing of the heart and when the mind is drawn away from all carnal senses, which is why the Scriptures testify that "no one can see the face of God and live." Once the mind is turned away from any sensory knowledge, the person has a sort of out-of-body experience similar to death, which may happen in a state of advanced ecstasy, a condition attained by certain saints prior to death when they were granted the perfection of revelation, like that described in 1 John 3:2 ("when he is revealed, we will be like him, for we will see him as he is"). When humans rise to eternal life, Augustine contends, their vision shall be like that of the angels, "for we shall then be equal to them" and will be able to see things that were in this life invisible and inaccessible. And in language that would really have upset the anthropomorphist Egyptian monks, Augustine asserts: "And so, one who can invisibly see God invisibly can cling to God in an incorporeal way."[37]

In other places, Augustine offers more simple admonitions that, despite the many anthropomorphic depictions of God in the Bible, God does not have a physical body like humans: he has no lap or arms, no bosom or hands. In his third tractate on John's Gospel, he explains this and even goes on to say the eyes that see God are not the eyes of flesh but the eyes of the pure heart. And this is even true of the Son prior to the incarnation. Only those who cannot "grasp the invisible" are held by the visible and thus slip into idolatry.[38] Even so, Augustine allows that the scriptural "appearances" of God to the patriarchs suggest that bodily eyes see some intimation of the divine, although not a full or complete vision of God.

His examination of these Old Testament appearances, however, distinguishes Augustine from earlier Christian writers on the subject. Based on his argument about the invisibility of the Divine, he refused to allow that Abraham's visitors were an actual manifestation of the Holy Trinity, or an appearance of the Divine Word with two angels. On the other hand, he countered the still-prevalent view that proposed the Divine Word as the Person able to be visible in creation even before the incarnation—a view that became commonplace in the late fourth-century polemics against neo-Arians, among others.

For example, in the early to mid-fourth century, Eusebius of Caesarea had argued that only the Second Person could change shape and take on the form of a human and appear to Abraham, and that it would be impious to suggest that the unchangeable, Almighty God could have been meant by the story.[39] Eusebius's interpretation of the appearances of God in the Hebrew Scriptures, unlike Irenaeus's or Tertullian's, does not emerge out of a polemic with Gnostics or even from an early effort to establish the distinction of three Persons of the Trinity against a Sabellian theology, as much as out of a careful exposition of the question of how the Divine was manifest to humanity before the incarnation. In his exegesis of Isaiah 6, Eusebius asks what (or whom) the prophet actually saw when he described his vision of the Lord sitting on a throne.

Citing the texts from the Gospel of John as evidence that no one (including Isaiah) has ever seen the Unbegotten God, Eusebius insists that the prophet could only have seen the only begotten God, who condescended to human view, and he goes on to insist that it was the Word (and not God) who appeared to Abraham, Isaac, Jacob, Moses, and Ezekiel, further noting that each of these appearances was distinct, which may have been, for him, an indication of their still incomplete or even enigmatic nature.[40] In an earlier treatise, Eusebius portrays all these as appearances of the Word, but he notes that only the "Perfect" saw him in a human form, because it was reserved only to them to be able to see beforehand its future incarnate shape. The other appearances (burning bush or pillar of cloud) inspired fear and wonder, but they also protected the people from a sight they could not bear.[41]

In Augustine's opinion, however, claiming that the Word appeared to these prophets and patriarchs undermined the equality, shared natures, and common activity of all three members of the Godhead. Augustine discussed the hospitality of Abraham in some detail in his treatise *On the Trinity*. Pointing out the problem of plural manifestation (three men) but singular address ("Lord"), he too interpreted the story as a figure of the Trinity and corrected those (for example, Justin, Ireneaus, and Tertullian) who maintain that while two were angels, one of them was the Son, "visible in his own proper substance even before he was born" since "only the Father is referred to by the words 'to the invisible and only God'" (1 Tim 1:17). Such a view was impossible in Augustine's opinion because the Son could not have been found in human form prior to his incarnation: "Surely he had not already 'emptied himself, taking the form of a servant, made in the likeness of men and found in the condition of a man'" (Phil 2:7). Moreover, he noted, none of the three appeared to be superior in stature, age, or authority to the others. And, while Abraham addressed the one who remained as "Lord," Lot bowed low before the other two and greeted them as Lords as well. Thus Augustine concluded that all three were angels but that they also served as a figure of the Trinity. The one that remained with Abraham represented the Father while the two that went on to Sodom the Son and the Holy Spirit, for the latter are said to be sent by the One who is never sent (the Father).[42]

Augustine's refusal to see the manifestations of God found in the Old Testament as actual appearances of the Word was motivated by his resistance to any kind of distinction in the Trinity and to a differentiation between visible and invisible Persons that was untenable to him. Moreover, he rejected literal readings of the texts as if God really appeared as some kind of material form. The full or true nature of the Divine simply cannot be seen. Such a position is demonstrated in his subsequent analysis of the other stories of God's theophanies, to Moses in particular (for example, Exod 3:2 and 33:21-23), as perhaps manifestations of any one of the three, since "right-minded faith understands these words of the supreme and supremely divine and changeless substance in which the one and only God is both Father and Son and Holy Spirit. All these visions, however, were produced through the changeable creation subject to the changeless God, and they did not manifest God as he is in himself, but in a symbolic manner as times and circumstances required."[43] In other words, God, whether as Father, Son, or Spirit, can be seen but only in a form chosen by the Divine will and never in its fullness, in appearances granted out of consideration for human weakness. And thus, while earlier thinkers allowed visibility only to the Son, in the fifth century Augustine, at least, eliminated it as a particular characteristic of only one member of the Trinity, yet he opened up the possibility that humans might see symbolic manifestations of the whole Godhead. And, although he doesn't have this in mind, we may speculate whether these manifestations could include visual art.

At the end of his great work *City of God,* he speaks about the kind of vision with which the saints will see God in the world to come, when the flesh will have become spiritual and bodily sight will be transformed into spiritual sight. Citing Paul's claim that our present insight is only partial (as through a mirror or in a riddle—1 Cor 13:12), he can also cite Paul's promise that someday it will be "face to face" as the holy angels already see God. Of course, this vision will be of a different order from the kind of "fleshly" or corporeal sight we now possess. God will be seen in the future time by eyes that are transformed and possess the ability to discern immaterial or spiritual truth and then "perhaps God will be known to us and visible to us in the sense that God will be spiritually perceived by each one of us *in* each one of us, perceived in one another, perceived by each in themselves. God will be seen in the new heaven and the new earth, in the whole creation as it then will be; God will be seen in every body, by means of bodies, wherever the eyes of the spiritual body are directed with their penetrating gaze."[44] Here, in a sense, Augustine adapts the Pauline notion that all creation reveals God and in all creation (including the human race) one may see God. At the same time, Augustine insists that Paul's promised future vision of God will be a kind of disembodied perception—a sight received in the mind, not through the eyes.

Portrayals of God and the Trinity in Visual Art of the Third and Fourth Centuries

Although the question of God's visibility to the human eye was a subject of much discussion by theologians, almost no surviving and parallel arguments address the related impossibility of representing God (the Father), the pre-incarnate Word, or the Trinity in visual art. Presumably, theologians who discussed the invisibility of God assumed their arguments to preclude artistic portrayal in any form but particularly as showing God with human features. In other words, the possibility may simply have been unthinkable and so not raised. On the other hand, if they were aware of some visual art that portrayed the Supreme God, they did not directly attack it.

Despite this lack of comment, however, artists' workshops, beginning in the fourth century, in fact produced a number of images that were meant either as actual figures or as symbolic representations of God, the visible Word, or the Trinity. The most obvious iconography, the popular presentations of Jesus healing and working wonders, such as we find sometimes rather crowded together on early Christian sarcophagus

Fig. 42. The Holy Trinity, 1420s
(tempera on panel), Andrei
Rublev (c. 1370–1430)
(Photo: Tretyakov Gallery,
Moscow, Russia, Bridgeman
Art Library).

reliefs, might have been a type of visual response to the writings of theologians such as Athanasius, who writes that although God is invisible,
God's power as much as God's image is manifest in the person and works
of Christ, including cleansing lepers, healing the blind, and changing
water to wine.[45] These and other miracles mentioned by Athanasius are
frequently represented on early fourth-century sarcophagi as well as in
catacomb frescoes and fifth-century mosaics (see fig. 60, p. 143).

On the other hand, certain representations, considered alongside the
extensive discussions of human inability to "see" God, suggest a level of
discontinuity between popular practice and theological argument, or
perhaps a perceived difference between artistic representation and verbal discourse. While it is possible that such images were so rare that they
were unknown to these theologians, their existence should have been
disconcerting to those who believed that such a thing should not or
could not happen.

Abraham's three visitors at Mamre was a well-known subject in
Byzantine icons, and visual representations of that scene are still
widespread today, although usually interpreted only as a symbol of the
Trinity and not as an actual visual presentation of it. The early fifteenth-
century panel painting by Andrei Rublev is the most famous of these
representations (fig. 42), but there were earlier models, including a

number of twelfth-century Bible illuminations. According to tradition, a painting of this scene also hung in the southern aisle of the church Hagia Sophia in Constantinople, over a table made from a tree cut from the very grove at Mamre.[46]

Possibly the earliest known representation of the story occurs in the fourth-century among the frescoes of Rome's Via Latina catacomb. This catacomb contains several other innovative narrative images, including Jacob's dream of the ladder and Jacob blessing Ephraim and Manasseh. Above the image of Jacob's dream is a fresco showing a seated Abraham (calf at his side) greeting three men dressed in tunics, mantles, and sandals (fig. 43). We cannot be certain that this image is, in fact, any reference to the Trinity, but its proximity to the scene of Jacob's dream suggests that it might have been meant to represent a divine theophany. On the other hand, given its placement with other "new" narrative scenes from the Old Testament, it may be merely a single image within a Genesis cycle. However, the similarity of the three visitors also suggests that the interpretation of the narrative as found in the documentary materials might have been incorporated into the iconography.

In addition to this possible symbolization of the Trinity in the iconography of Abraham's hospitality, we also have evidence of other early, but now lost, parallels. Eusebius of Caesarea mentions a drawing (*graphē*) set up at the traditional site of the visitation, a place honored by locals as a sacred place, where the tree (Eusebius calls it a terebinth, rather than an oak) can still be seen. And those who were entertained by Abraham are represented in the picture sitting one on each side of a central figure, "Our Lord and Savior," who surpasses them in honor and "thus in person from that time sowed the seeds of holiness among mortals, putting on a human form and shape, and revealed to the godly ancestor Abraham who he was and showed him the mind of his Father."[47] This description actually comes in his argument that Almighty

Fig. 43. Abraham and his three visitors, Via Latina Catacomb, Rome (© The International Catacomb Society. Photo: Estelle Brettman).

God could not have appeared, but only "our Lord and Savior," who could put on human shape and form in order to reveal himself to Abraham and show forth "the mind of his Father."[48]

The scene also appears in the mosaic cycle of biblical scenes of the Basilica of Santa Maria Maggiore in Rome (ca. 435) (fig. 44). Here, the scene is divided into two registers (Abraham appears three times in the composition). At the top of the panel, we see Abraham bowing before his three visitors and making a gesture of greeting. The three are dressed alike and have identical faces, but the central figure is distinguished from the other two by being surrounded by a *mandorla* (a full body halo similar to the almond-shaped frame of light around the image of Christ in the transfiguration). In addition, the central figure makes a gesture of speech and faces directly forward, while the other two are slightly turned in a quarter profile. Below and on the left we see Sarah preparing food (three pyramid-shaped cakes) for the visitors while Abraham instructs her ("make ready quickly three measures of choice flour, knead it, and make cakes," Gen 18:6).

Fig. 44. The Hospitality of Abraham, early 5th cen. C.E. mosaic, Basilica of Santa Maria Maggiore, Rome (Photo: Scala/Art Resource).

On the lower right, the three visitors sit under the tree at a table set with Sarah's cakes, while Abraham serves them, offering a platter with the roasted calf. In front of the table, we see an urn (perhaps filled with milk, since its color appears to be white; Gen 18:8). In this composition, the three also have nearly identical faces and dress, but the central figure is not this time specially set off by a mandorla and merely gestures toward Abraham's proffered platter. Nevertheless, given the particular presentation of the central visitor in the upper rendering, we might conclude that the visual tradition has relied on Justin's scheme, that the three are meant to represent the Son and two angels—although unlike Rublev's famous image, the three have no wings—or that the image presents a subordinationist Trinity (the Son and Spirit as inferior to the Father), although such a construal seems highly unlikely given the date and general anti-Arianism of the Roman church under Sixtus III (who supervised the decoration of the church and dedicated it).

This scene of Abraham's hospitality is only one among a whole program of mosaics in Santa Maria Maggiore, which means that interpreting the meaning of this image ought to include consideration of the wider context and cycle of iconographic program. More than twenty years ago, Suzanne Spain argued that the mosaics of both the nave and the triumphal arch (the apse mosaics were destroyed at the end of the thirteenth century and had contained a monumental figure of Mary with Jesus on her lap) all point to the broad theme of prophecy and fulfillment, in which Sarah serves as a prototype of Mary.[49] The stories of the Old Testament, included in the overall decoration, foretell the future incarnation of Christ. Therefore, the scene of Abraham and his visitors is more about the promise of progeny to Abraham than a divine theophany. At the same time, however, several of the other mosaics that appear in the nave portray a heavenly figure that might be intended to represent the visible Divine Word. For example, a figure appears in the clouds in the illustration of Abraham meeting Melchizedek, in a scene from the story of Jacob taking sheep from Laban's flocks, and in a portrayal of the manna coming to the Israelites in the wilderness.

Abraham also appears in several other places in the mosaics of Santa Maria Maggiore, including a scene on the main arch that shows Joseph and Mary's betrothal, their hands being joined by an angel. Here Abraham is shown in a posture almost identical to his greeting of the three angels (except here his hands are covered), as he bows before a vision of a woman holding a child with a halo and cross over his head, just to the left of the betrothed couple. Spain interpreted this as the final fulfillment of the promise to Abraham by one of his three guests: "your wife Sarah will have a son." The woman holding the Christ child in the mosaic is none other than Sarah, holding her great-grandchild, while Abraham finally recognizes the meaning of the event that took place at

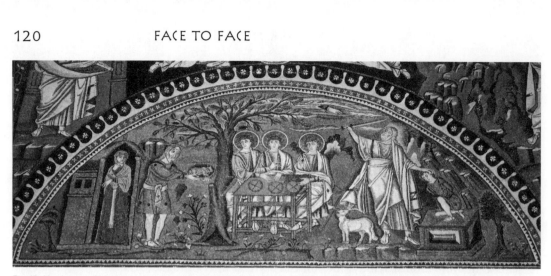

Fig. 45. Abraham and his three visitors, mid-6th cen. C.E. mosaic, San Vitale, Ravenna (Photo: Author).

Mamre. Thus, Spain argues, Sarah has become Mary's antitype (the "mother of many nations"—Gen 17:16) just as Isaac is Jesus'.[50]

Roughly a little more than a century later, a portrayal of Abraham and his visitors was set into a lunette above the presbyterium in the Basilica of San Vitale in Ravenna (fig. 45). Although in many ways very different from the composition in Santa Maria Maggiore, it also has two parts. On the right is the scene of Abraham's offering of Isaac, with the lamb at Abraham's feet and the hand of God staying his upraised knife. In the center of the mosaic, we see the three visitors seated at a table under the oak tree. The table holds three loaves, marked with crosses (perhaps resembling the eucharistic bread served during the actual liturgy). Abraham holds out a platter with the calf, and Sarah, on the left, watches from a small booth with a bemused expression. The faces of the three at the table are again identical, as are their dress and this time also their haloes.

In this presentation all three visitors gesture to the bread on the table, as if calling our attention to it. And, while the other hand of the guest on our left is hidden, the persons in the center and right make particular gestures of blessing with their right hands—their index and third fingers are extended while the fourth and fifth fingers curl down to touch the palm or thumb. The equality of the three and their function as symbols of the three distinct persons with one shared nature may be intentionally expressed by the composition. Here, however, the iconography also points to the importance of the eucharistic offering made directly below, at the altar in the center of the presbyterium. Across from the lunette of Abraham, Sarah, and Isaac is one that shows both Mechizedek, the priest-king, offering his gift of bread and wine (Gen 14:18) and Abel offering his lamb (Gen 4:4) before an altar prepared as if for a Christian liturgy.

But even earlier than these scenes of Abraham and his visitors, Christians employed visual representations for God the Father that were both less symbolic and more anthropomorphic, although still being curiously abstract—a disembodied hand, reaching down from the sky. Possibly drawn from Jewish prototypes (the divine hand also appears in the synagogue at Dura Europos), it frequently appears in scenes of Abraham's offering of Isaac and the giving of the tablets of the law to Moses (fig. 46) and continues into the fifth and sixth centuries.[51] Gregory of Nyssa describes a painting of the sacrifice of Isaac in some detail, including Isaac's bound hands and piteous expression and, as he says, "already the edge of the sword touches the body, when a voice sounds unto him [Abraham] from God, prohibiting the deed."[52] Gregory's description does not tell us how God's voice would be portrayed, but we might assume it was indicated by a hand reaching down from the sky.[53]

Oddly, the divine hand rarely appears before the sixth century in scenes of Jesus' baptism, where the descending dove is shown according to the narrative, although it appears somewhat later, beginning in the sixth century. This is particularly interesting since, in the two prior cases (the offering of Isaac and the giving of the law), the voice of God is no more significant to the narrative than it is in the story of Jesus' baptism, and because in Western medieval and renaissance art, the iconography of Jesus' baptism became a prime locus for iconography of the Trinity (sometimes with a hand of God, but often with an anthropomorphic figure of God at the top of the composition).[54] In the fourth-century mosaic in the dome of the Baptistery of San Giovanni in Fonte in Naples, however, the hand also appears out of a dark starry sky, holding a wreath of victory over a large chi-rho (fig. 47). The divine hand also appears in the seventh-century mosaic in the Basilica of San Apollinare in Classe (fig. 87, p. 167), as well in scenes of resurrection or ascension, on ivories, and on pilgrimage flasks (*ampullae*) from the Holy Land. Probably borrowing from earlier imperial imagery, the hand also appears on the coins or medals showing the apotheosis of Constantine.

Paulinus of Nola described a different strategy for avoiding anthropomorphic images of God in the late fourth or early fifth century. In

Fig. 46. Moses receiving the law and Abraham offering Isaac from a 4th cen. C.E. sarcophagus in the Museo Pio Cristiano, Vatican City (Photo: Author).

addition to his usefully distracting and didactic gallery of biblical scenes and portraits of the saints, Paulinus also commissioned an apse mosaic that portrayed the Trinity for his basilica at Nola in the early fifth century. Conscious of the error of representing the infinite and unknowable divine nature as having human features but still wanting to find a way to enlighten and inspire his congregation, Paulinus substituted symbols for figurative representations of God. In a letter to his friend Severus, Paulinus poetically praised the result:

> The Trinity shines out in all its mystery. Christ is represented by a lamb, the Father's voice thunders forth from the sky, and the Holy Spirit flows down in the form of a dove. A wreath's gleaming circle surrounds the cross, and around this circle the apostles form a ring, represented by a chorus of doves. The holy unity of the Trinity merges in Christ, but the Trinity has its threefold symbolism. The Father's voice and the Spirit show forth God, the cross and the lamb proclaim the holy victim. The purple and the palm point to kingship and to triumph. Christ himself, the Rock, stands on the rock of the church, and from this rock four plashing fountains flow, the evangelists, the living streams of Christ.[55]

Fig. 47. Dome mosaic showing the hand of God holding a wreath from the 4th cen. C.E. baptistery of San Giovanni in Fonte, Naples (Photo: Author).

The Trinity, portrayed as a lamb, dove, and something that would have symbolized a voice (or perhaps the hand of God), was based on the biblical descriptions of Jesus' baptism (including John's reference to Christ as Lamb of God, John 1:36). Paulinus's reference to the image of a voice is similar to Gregory of Nyssa's description of the scene of Abraham offering Isaac and, based on the frequent portrayals of Abraham and Isaac with the hand of God, it seems reasonable to assume that the divine voice was represented with a hand in both Paulinus's apse and Gregory's painting.

However, according to Paulinus, somewhere else within the composition a cross represented Christ, twelve doves the apostles, and the four rivers of paradise the evangelists. The Bishop of Nola, proud of his portraits of saints and prophets elsewhere in the church, also chose to substitute symbols for portraits of the apostles or evangelists in the apse of his basilica. The use of doves to represent the apostles can be seen elsewhere, for instance in the early sixth-century mosaic from the baptistery of Albenga, which also uses a triple chi-

Fig. 48. Lamb of God, mid-6th cen. C.E. mosaic in the presbytery vault, San Vitale, Ravenna (Photo: Author).

rho monogram to symbolize the Trinity. And, just as the lamb often represents Christ (as in Paulinus's basilica and in the dome of San Vitale—fig. 48), sheep or lambs frequently stand in for the apostles as well, as in the apse of the Basilica of San Apollinare in Classe (fig. 86, p. 166), or in the sixth-century apse of the Basilica of Saints Cosmas and Damian in Rome.

Arguably, a different kind of nonfigurative presentation of the Trinity is the image of the empty throne with a crown or cross set upon its thick cushion, with a descending dove often hovering above. One of the earliest examples of this comes from the mosaic program of Santa Maria Maggiore, but stunning examples may be seen in Ravenna, in the Basilica of San Vitale, and both the Arian and Orthodox baptisteries (fig. 49). The absence of a figure referring to the Holy Spirit in this case, however, is inexplicable if this is a symbol of the Trinity, although the throne may be understood as a symbol for God. The image may be a more specific reference to the kingdom of heaven, and the ascended and enthroned Christ as the Lord of that kingdom, with its parallel in

Fig. 49. Cross surmounted on throne, early 6th cen. C.E. mosaic in the dome of the Arian baptistery, Ravenna (Photo: Author).

more figurative images of the enthroned Christ, like that seen on the Junius Bassus sarcophagus (fig. 14, p. 34).

Despite these efforts to arrive at typological, symbolic, or nonfigurative visual images of God, the Divine Word, or the Trinity, certain attempts also were made in the fourth century to portray the triune God in the form of three human-appearing males. Some examples of these images showed the Trinity receiving the offerings of Cain and Abel. For instance, on a sarcophagus now in the Vatican Museo Pio Cristiano, a bearded male wearing a tunic and *pallium* and seated on a rock receives an offering from the two brothers; one has a basket of fruit, the other holds a lamb (fig. 50). The bearded figure makes a gesture of blessing over Cain's offering of fruit and grain—the same gesture made by the figures in the hospitality of Abraham mosaic described above (two fingers extended, the other three curled back to the palm). Behind his head are cut (in low relief) two other faces that might be interpreted either as onlookers (two angels?) or the other two Persons of the Trinity. If this was intended as a representation of the Holy Trinity, then the Father's older (bearded) visage, as well as the distinctions among all three profiles, may be significant, perhaps implying a subordinationist or Arian Trinity. Or, if this is an image of God blessing the offering of Cain, then

Fig. 50. Cain and Abel presenting their gifts to God, 4th cen. C.E. sarcophagus relief, Museo Pio Cristiano, Vatican City (Photo: Author).

Fig. 51. 4th cen. C.E. sarcophagus in the Musée de l'Arles Antique (Photo: Author).

the story in Genesis has been undermined in the image for some unknown reason. Later, as in the mosaics programs of San Apollinare in Classe or San Vitale, only the offering of Abel is depicted (while in a fourth-century fresco of Cain and Abel in the Via Latina Catacomb, God is not depicted).[56]

Strengthening the identity of the above image as a portrayal of the Trinity (as opposed to God and two angels) are the representations of the Trinity on two other sarcophagi from approximately the same date (early to mid-fourth century). These images appear to depict the Trinity creating Adam and Eve. One of these is now in the Musée de l'Arles Antique (and may be the older of the two), and the other is in the Museo Pio Cristiano in the Vatican. Both of them, double-registered sarcophagi, have the image of a seated male in the upper left corner, joined by two other standing male figures, perhaps meant to represent the Holy Spirit, the Son (figs. 51–52). In both cases, the "Father" has a full beard, but, in one instance (the Arles example), the "Son" is beardless while the "Spirit" has a clipped beard and shorter hair than the

Fig. 52. "Dogmatic Sarcophagus," 4th cen. C.E., Museo Pio Cristiano, Vatican City (Photo: Author).

Fig. 53. Detail, Arles sarcophagus, the Trinity Creating Adam
and Eve (Photo: Author).

Fig. 54. Detail, the Trinity
Creating Adam and Eve,
Vatican Dogmatic Sarcopha-
gus (Photo: Author).

Father (fig. 53). On the Vatican sarcophagus, the Son and Spirit bear more resemblance to the Father (fig. 54). Before this group are two diminutive nude figures, Adam and Eve at their creation. The Son puts his right hand on the head of Eve in each of the scenes (in one case Adam is still lying on the ground), and the Father makes the now-familiar gesture of blessing.[57] On the Arles sarcophagus, the apostle Paul also appears in the scene, as if presenting the "old Adam" to the "new Adam."

The images of the Trinity are presented in some cases as identical and in others as having different facial types—either older and bearded or younger and beardless. The fact that the central figure is seated while the others stand suggests that these latter two are the ones engaged with the world as agents or messengers of the Father (his "right and left hands").[58] Given the date of the images (mid-fourth century), the explanation for their age or facial distinctions may depend on whether the prevalent theology emphasized the identity and coeternity of the Persons of the Trinity or tended to subordinate the Son and Spirit to the Father. A Nicaean version of this iconography arguably would show the three faces as identical, while a pre-Nicene version would present the Son and Spirit as younger than the Father. The Son or Logos figure may also be shown as identical with or older than the figure of Christ elsewhere in the composition, artistically capturing another theological idea. On one hand, the flesh taken in the incarnation must be

Fig. 55. Adam and Eve with Christ/Logos on 4th cen. C.E. Christian sarcophagus in the Museo Pio Cristiano, Vatican City (Photo: Author).

acknowledged as younger than the Eternal Word, but, on the other hand, the "face" of Christ is the "image" and revelation of God. The face of Adam (and also possibly even Eve) may also bear a likeness to the Logos or Son, as well as to Christ, the new Adam (compare figs. 54 and 55).

Just below these Trinity representations, on both of the sarcophagi, are representations of the adoration of the three magi. In parallel position to God the Father, Mary is shown, seated in an almost identical chair, while a male figure, perhaps Balaam, Joseph, or even the Holy Spirit stands behind in the position of the same figure above (fig. 56). The juxtaposition of these images suggests the story of the original creation and the recreation of Adam in the incarnation; thus, the whole composition may refer to the economy of salvation (old and new creation, old and new Adam—which may account for Paul's appearance on the Arles sarcophagus). In addition to this, however, at least one interpreter argued that this image of the magi also suggests the doctrine of the Trinity, either that they symbolically represented the Trinity (in their number and appearance) or that they, themselves, had a theophany of the Trinity (each of them seeing a different Person).[59]

Fig. 56. Detail, Adoration of the magi on the Arles Sarcophagus (Photo: Author).

This tradition has been hard to pin down, but it may be related to an Armenian Infancy Gospel that recounts a legend of the three, each having a different vision of the Christ child (as incarnate Son, heavenly commander, or suffering sacrifice—a vision that emphasizes different aspects of Christ rather than the three Persons of the Trinity).[60] We should note that in the iconography of the two sarcophagi the first of the magi points to a group of three stars or disks, rather than to a single star, but that his pointing index finger also draws our eyes up to the image of the Trinity on the upper register. The iconographic message is conveyed through the arrangement and relationship of the images of creation and incarnation, fall and redemption. Mary and Eve are above and below, just as the Logos who presents Eve to the Father can be seen as a child on the lap of the new Eve, his mother Mary. That child, the new Adam, is then greeted by a trinity of guests, not unlike the angelic visitors to Abraham, but in this case the visitors are mortals and the host is divine.

Such a dogmatically sophisticated iconographic program suggests that at least some artisans, clients, or viewers were conscious of the way visual art may convey a complicated idea in a visual rather than verbal idiom. It also tells us that making an image of God (or at least a visual metaphor for God) was not universally held to be impossible or blasphemous. At the same time, the iconography of God did not present a portrait of God so much as a representation of God doing a particular work—creating Adam and Eve or receiving the gifts of Cain and Abel.

Even so, at the end of the fourth century, the anthropomorphic pictorial representation of God the Father goes underground until the seventh or eighth century in the West and almost permanently in the East. At the same time, the portrait of Christ, along with images of the saints, begins to emerge and in a short time becomes a dominant motif of Christian iconography. The representation of the hospitality of Abraham remains, especially in the East, but it is understood to be a symbol of the Trinity and not an actual representation of it, while the image of God as bearded older man disappears for several centuries. A condemnation of any presentation of God in actual visual art is specifically argued, finally, in the early eighth century in John of Damascus's treatise *On Holy Images*:

> For if we were to make an image of the invisible God, we would really sin; for
> it is impossible to depict one who is incorporeal and formless, invisible and
> uncircumscribable. And again: if we were to make images of human beings
> and regard them and venerate them as gods, we would be truly sacrilegious.
> But we do none of these things. For if we make an image of God who in his
> ineffable goodness became incarnate and was seen upon earth in the flesh,
> and lived among humans, and assumed the nature and density and form and
> color of flesh, we do not go astray. For we long to see his form; as the divine
> apostle says, 'now we see puzzling reflections in a mirror.' For the image is a

mirror and a puzzle, suitable to the density of our body. For the intellect, greatly tired, is not able to pass beyond the bodily, as the divine Gregory says.[61]

Throughout his treatise, John directly addresses the problem of idolatry and the divine injunction against graven images (Exod 20:4). In an earlier passage, he explains that God forbids the making of images to prevent idolatry and because it is impossible for any human to make an image of the infinite and invisible God. And he cites Deut 4:12, where Moses reminds the Israelites that "the Lord spoke to you from the midst of the fire; you heard the sound of his words and you did not see any likeness, but only a voice." But, John insists, this prohibition was given to the Jews because they were particularly prone to idolatry. Christians, on the other hand, are able to avoid such errors having received from God the ability to discern what may be represented and what cannot be.[62] Still John's claim of Christian spiritual superiority and discernment was never used to argue that Christians might depict the divine nature apart from the image of Christ. Therefore, according to John, avoiding visual representations of the First Person of the Trinity was the *Christian* way of repudiating the sin of idolatry. Christians do not make images of God because they are superior to pagans but are required to make images of Christ because they are superior to Jews.

John's arguments echo some of Athanasius's points, in much the same way that Athanasius seemed to draw from the ideas of Origen. John, like Athanasius, makes a distinction between the invisible God or Trinity, and the visible Incarnate One who came to humans in a visible, physical, and temporal form so that they might finally see and come to know. Other manifestations that had come before were inadequate for human salvation, since humans were so desperately weakened by their infinite generations of downcast eyes and clouded minds. The visible face and body of Christ were the ultimate remedy for a sinful and lost human race. And because it was visible, and the seeing itself was salvific, Christ's representation in visual art was both permissible and beneficial. The image, as Basil says, reveals its archetype and in turn accepts its honors. After all, even the disciple Thomas needed to see to believe. And, although Jesus admonishes him, saying that it is more blessed to believe without having seen, he yet condescends to human weakness and allows Thomas to put his finger into his wounds and his hand into his side (John 20:24-29).

FIVE

Portraits of the Incarnate One

AS THE previous chapters have argued, aside from the few anthropomorphic appearances of the First Person of the Trinity in the late fourth century, God the Father was universally asserted to be inaccessible to human gaze. On the other hand, the Second Person, "the image of the invisible God" (Col 1:15) might be perceived, at least in certain limited ways, according to various theological arguments about the divine activity (and presence) in both creation and redemption. Furthermore, God is known, prior to the incarnation, through God's deeds, as beheld by the prophets. According to Christian doctrine, the Incarnate Word came into the world as a human being (Jesus Christ) and shared all the aspects of ordinary human existence including an outward form (face and body) that could be seen and recognized in historical time and space. And so, in contrast to the rare representations of the Father or the Holy Spirit, Jesus (as the human manifestation of the Word) regularly appears in Christian visual art from the late third century onwards, first as a figure in narrative images (performing the deeds or wonders that revealed the divine nature) and then—at the end of the fourth century—in a portrait image that showed his face alone.

As Athanasius explained in his treatise on the incarnation, the invisible God had become fully visible in and through Christ, so that humans might finally see and comprehend their divine potential and recognize the true works and nature of God. In addition to Col 1:15, key New Testament texts were cited in support of the claim that Jesus Christ revealed the Invisible God (the Father), not only through his teaching but also through his appearance. For instance, while Jesus says in John 6:46, "Not that anyone has seen the Father except the one who is from God; he has seen the Father," he says later (in 12:45), "And whoever sees me sees the one who sent me." John's Gospel echoes these lines and elaborates (14:9b-10): "Whoever has seen me has seen the Father. How can you say,

'Show us the Father'? Do you not believe that I am in the Father and the
Father is in me? The words that I say to you I do not speak on my own;
but the Father who dwells in me does his works."[1] According to these
texts, "seeing" Jesus is also to comprehend the eternal and invisible Deity
in some sense, possibly in the same way that other biblical texts (as
well as early Christian literature) assert that the incomprehensible
divine essence is known or even mediated through angels, prophetic
utterances, or heavenly signs and symbols. The opening chapter of the
Gospel of John says while no one has seen God, the Son has made him
known, using the Greek verb *exēgeomai*, "to explain or interpret," rather
than a word like *apokalyptō*, "to reveal" (John 1:18). However, the text of
John 14 contrasts the verbs *ginōskō* and *horaō*, "to know" with "see," and
so to "see" Jesus is to both see and know God. Thus, these Gospel passages present Jesus as more than an angel or prophet. He is the actual
visual revelation of the One who "dwells" in him, whose face shows forth
the glory of God (2 Cor 4:6).

Such arguments have immense implications for Christian iconography. Jesus undoubtedly had a human face that could be seen and recognized in his lifetime. For this reason, the representation of Christ in
symbolic form as the Good Shepherd or even as Lamb of God could be
abandoned, in favor of the human representation.[2] The fundamental
question is whether the face or physical form of Jesus could be reproduced or copied into an even less "living" representation (a painting or
sculpted image), which captured only the external appearance and
which, by nature, could not contain his inexpressible interior reality—
his essence. In light of the philosophical arguments regarding the limi-
tations or even deception inherent in portraits of even ordinary
humans, the visual portrayal of a divine human seems all the more
problematic—even impossible. The issue of visually representing divinity was the basis of Eusebius's ostensible objections to Constantia in his
alleged response to her request for a portrait of Christ. Although there is
some doubt about the authenticity of the document, its christological
arguments clearly address the problem of divine representation:

> What sort of image of Christ are you seeking? Is it the true and unalterable
> one which bears his essential characteristics, or the one which he took up for
> our sakes when he assumed the form of a servant [Phil 2:7]. . . . Granted, he
> has two forms, even I do not think that your request has to do with his divine
> form. . . . Surely, then, you are seeking his image as a servant, that of the flesh
> which he put on for our sake. But that, too, we have been taught, was mingled
> with the glory of his divinity so that the mortal part was swallowed up by life
> [2 Cor 5:4].[3]

According to this argument, any visual portrayal of Christ must be inadequate since it either avoided or attempted to portray the divine nature.

To show only the human form was heretical; to attempt to portray the invisible divine form was blasphemous.

Certainly, attitudes toward visual representations of Jesus Christ differed according to different views of the nature and function of an image itself, that is, whether the image purports to represent the actual essence or being of its model, or whether it has some other kind of function (for example, didactic or merely commemorative). Put another way, the problem also lay with the way a viewer received the image. For instance, a viewer might expect to encounter some kind of living reality in an image or merely to see the image as a superficial record of external appearance that functioned as a memory aid or inspirational device. All of these possible perspectives had precedents in the art of the surrounding culture, including funerary portraits, images of the gods, and the official portraits of the emperor.

And so the complex problem of the relationship between representation and reality, and between external form and transcendent truth, comes to the fore. Added to this is an even more basic problem: what model would serve for a portrait of the Incarnate Divine One—one that should bear some resemblance to his actual appearance while on earth? On what basis could any such image be a recognizable or verifiable likeness? Should such a likeness be based on authenticated portraits "from life" or upon textual descriptions that provide enough detail as a basis for recreation of his physical appearance? Lacking either of these, how would one construct a "true" image? Finally, what sort of appearance would ancient viewers *expect* the Incarnate Divine One to possess or project?

Some early Christian documents contain references to Jesus' plain, even unattractive features. Justin Martyr, in his dialogue with Trypho the Jew, acknowledges that Christ was reported to be inglorious, obscure, and of ordinary mortal appearance. But, in his second coming, Justin says, he will appear in his full radiant glory.[4] According to Origen's philosopher-critic Celsus, Jesus had been reported to be unattractive, and this ran counter to what one would suppose for the Incarnate One (especially to the mind of a Greek, used to thinking that the gods ought to be supremely beautiful). To this point, Origen quotes Celsus as surmising:

> Since a divine spirit inhabited the body (of Jesus), it must certainly have been different from that of other beings, in respect of grandeur, or beauty, or strength, or voice, or impressiveness, or persuasiveness. For it is impossible that he, to whom was imparted some divine quality beyond other beings, should not differ from others; whereas this person did not differ in any respect from another, but was, as they report, little, and ill favored, and ignoble (*agennēs*).

Origen, on the defensive, admits that there were some recorded accounts of Jesus' appearance as "ill-favored" but not actually "ignoble" and certainly not "little." And, as a way of justifying the supposed lack of beauty in the Savior, Origen cites a passage from Isaiah (Isa 53:2): "He has no form or majesty, and we beheld him, and he had no form nor beauty; but his form was without honor and inferior to that of the sons of men."[5] Going further, Origen points out (in a self-contradictory way) that Celsus had overlooked a key line in the Psalms (Ps 45:2) that addresses the Mighty One as "the most handsome of men." Generations later, John Chrysostom cited this psalm in order to assert that Christ was extraordinarily handsome. From that time, reports of Jesus' unattractiveness seem to have been forgotten.[6]

Traditions and Legends regarding Jesus' Appearance

Other than the cryptic allusions to Jesus' physical appearance in Justin or in Origen (who cited the text of Isaiah as if it were historically descriptive), only a few references to eyewitness descriptions of Jesus' appearance occur in the literature. On the other hand, traditions that actual portraits were made "from life" were more widely known. Among the rare textual witnesses is a letter supposedly written by a fictitious governor of Judea, Publius Lentulus, to the "Roman People and Senate." The oldest version of this document is found in a fifteenth-century manuscript, included with the "Life of Christ" by Ludolph the Carthusian and purportedly found in 1421 by a certain Giacomo Colonna among some ancient Roman documents. In this letter, Lentulus describes Jesus as a man of medium size with a venerable appearance; his hair was brown, curly, and parted in the center "after the pattern of the Nazarenes." Jesus' brow was smooth and unwrinkled, his complexion ruddy, his expression cheerful and his abundant (but not particularly long) brown beard divided at his chin. Lentulus's description concludes: "He is the most beautiful among human beings" (*pulcherrimus vultu inter homines*).[7]

Lentulus's depiction conforms to many of the earliest portraits of Christ and, in one detail, finds a parallel in a fourth-century letter to the Emperor Theodosius from Epiphanius of Salamis. Epiphanius opens his letter by denying that any ancient Christian "father" could have painted an image of Christ either for a display in a church or in a private house, and he argues that any who do "lie" by representing the Savior with long hair. This, he claims, they arrive at "by conjecture because he [the Savior] is called a Nazarene, and Nazarenes wore long hair." Epiphanius justifies his denial that Jesus was a Nazarene (with long hair) because while Jesus drank wine, Nazarenes do not. According to him, those who make such pictures invent physical types according to their whim, even though logic contradicts them. For, how could the Savior have had long hair he asks, when his disciples all had short, cropped hair? If he were that different looking from his apostles, there would have been no need for Judas to identify him (with a kiss) to the Roman authorities, and the Pharisees could have saved their money![8] Interestingly, Epiphanius's objections are contradicted on many early Christian works of art, where a juxtaposition of long-haired Jesus and short-haired apostles is fairly common (see figs. 13, 20, and 32, for example).

Lentulus's description also more or less agrees with the details of Jesus' features in a famous account of a "from life" portrait of Jesus: the miraculous image acquired by King Abgar of Edessa, who, suffering from a dread illness, sought a miraculous cure from Jesus the healer. Several different versions of the legend exist, but according to a general outline, Abgar sent his personal scribe to Jesus with a letter imploring him to come to Edessa to aid the ailing king. Jesus could not come himself, but he wrote a reply promising that one of his apostles would arrive in his stead. Sometime after Jesus' ascension, Thaddeus arrived in Edessa and performed the cure as well as evangelizing the court.[9] In later versions of the Abgar story, however, that cure was effected by contact with a portrait of Christ that returned to Edessa with Abgar's messenger scribe, who either painted it himself or was given a miraculous image (made without hands), when Jesus wiped his face upon a towel.[10]

However the story was told, the image that Abgar's servant brought back to Edessa was revered as an authentic and miraculous image of Christ. It became one of the holiest images in the East, known as the *Mandylion*. The sanctity and power of the portrait was demonstrated by its ability to destroy competing religious idols and to save the kingdom of Edessa from enemy invasions. In the sixth century, Evagrius recounted how the cloth had been used to repel a Persian attack. Hidden in the city walls and then rediscovered in the tenth century, the relic was removed to Constantinople, where Emperor Constantine Porphyrogenitos commissioned an official history of the *Mandylion*.[11] Although multitudes of copies of the original portrait were made (possibly one found its way to Egypt where it was seen by the Piacenza pilgrim), the actual *Mandylion* itself was lost, finally disappearing from Constantinople when Christian crusaders sacked that city at the beginning of the thirteenth century.[12]

Despite its variants, the story of the miraculous image of Edessa was regarded not only as proof of the divine approval as well as the validity and power of holy images, but also as a record of how Jesus "really looked." So, while the original *Mandylion* was lost, its innumerable copies, found throughout the Eastern Christian world in particular, share certain basic features. Most particularly, the portrait of Christ only shows his face and hair on an otherwise empty field (the linen cloth). Christ's eyes look straight out, under well-defined brows and high forehead. His nose is long and narrow, with a small mouth beneath a rather drooping mustache and above a beard that comes to two points (fig. 57). The hair of his head is parted at the center and hangs to his shoulders.

The story of Abgar and his miraculous portrait has a Western parallel in the legend and subsequent tradition of the veil of Veronica (also called the *Sudarium*). This famous image was also made "without hands" when Christ's face left its imprint on a cloth held out to Jesus by the woman Veronica, while he was going through Jerusalem toward Calvary. Veronica's name means "true image," of course, and she is sometimes identified with the woman with the hemorrhage whom Jesus healed. Although neither the portrait nor the Veronica legend can be clearly dated any earlier than the twelfth century, the cloth was accepted as authentic, was promoted by Pope Innocent III in the thirteenth century, and quickly found its place among the most sacred objects of the Roman church (kept among the treasures of Saint Peter's Basilica). A representation of Veronica and her image became a permanent fixture

Fig. 57. Mandylion, 20th cen. icon in the Holy Trinity Greek Orthodox Church, Nashville, Tenn. (Photo: Author).

in Catholic piety when it became the sixth station of the cross. Like the *Mandylion*, however, this actual *Sudarium* disappeared in the sack of Rome by German troops in 1527 and was reportedly sold in a tavern by Lutheran soldiers.[13] Rediscovered in the seventeenth century, it generated a vast number of copies that were distributed all over Europe (fig. 58).

Fig. 58. Saint Veronica, Master of Saint Veronica, ca. 1400, oil on wood, National Gallery, London (Photo: Erich Lessing/ Art Resource, N.Y.).

Fig. 59. Christ Pantocrator, 6th cen. C.E. encaustic on panel, Monastery of St. Catherine, Mt. Sinai (Photo: Egypt Ancient Art Collection, Bridgeman Art Library).

Like the *Mandylion*, the Veronica portrait shows the face of Christ without any background. It often appears (as does the *Mandylion*) as a feature of a larger painting, the portrait upon the cloth held by Veronica herself, saints, or angels. The face of Jesus is bearded and dark, with curling long hair, parted in the center and reaching to his shoulders. Jesus' nose is long and straight; his mustache droops down to meet a forked beard. These two traditional images have much in common with another "miraculous image," the Shroud of Turin, as well as bearing significant resemblance to the earliest (sixth-century) Byzantine panel paintings of Christ, like the Teacher from the Monastery of Saint Catherine on Mount Sinai (fig. 59). Earlier portraits of Christ also bear some similarities, however, including the fourth- and early fifth-century portraits of Christ from the Catacomb of Commodilla (fig. 11, p. 31).

These two miraculously received images and their legends (including their amazing travels and rediscoveries) became rather entwined with one another in the Middle Ages, and their details are difficult to distinguish. And while these stories clearly have enormous implications for the Byzantine and Western cult of images, neither the details of these stories nor the questions of their veracity are as important to this discussion as the matter of what constitutes an authentic portrait of Christ. In both of these cases, a claim is made not only that the portrait of Christ was made from life but also that it was produced miraculously. However, a much simpler assertion, that a certain artist painted an image of Jesus during his lifetime, can be dated fairly early—the reference by Irenaeus to the Carpocratians' possession of a portrait of Jesus "from life," made by Pilate.[14] Since Irenaeus shows no obvious doubt about this, one wonders whether other such claims were in circulation.

Furthermore, since the details of Christ's appearance on the *Mandylion* and *Sudarium* are quite similar (long dark hair parted in the center, forked beard, and so forth), the matter of their bearing an actual "likeness" is mutually supported. Unlike ordinary portraits, however, these images "made without hands" were alleged to be imprints produced by direct contact with Christ's body, making them "reverse" or "mirror" images. Thus, an artist who wished to base a portrait on either of these "true" images would need to transpose the facial features of Christ in their paintings. This process, of course, raises the problem of how carefully a copy would be patterned after an authenticated archetype and of whether the validity of the image might be based on the degree to which it was a good or faithful reproduction. Arguably, once a claim was made that "*this* is what Christ looked like," the task was one of faithful reproduction rather than producing work from an individual imagination. However, even though the similarity of a particular portrait to its archetype was crucial for establishing the validity of the representation, some variation did not necessarily undermine the acceptance of an image as authentic.[15]

Other miraculous and "from life" images of Christ are known in the tradition, including the Volto Santo (Holy Face) of Lucca, a twelfth-century version of which is still on display in the cathedral of that Italian city.[16] Yet, despite the claims made at various points in history for portraits that had been made "from life" and the perceived importance of consistent iconography for Christ, one famous authority indicates that no such tradition was known or recognized (in the West), either for Jesus or any of the saints. In his treatise on the Trinity, Augustine points to the variations in the ways Jesus is portrayed in visual art as a kind of proof that no one possessed any one record of his actual physical appearance, and then adds that (to his mind, at least) the matter really was of very little importance. As long as one recognized that as he was a human being, Jesus must have had some kind of appearance; this is necessary for the reality of the incarnation. For him, the work of art's validity is not a matter of its verisimilitude or its faithful reproduction of a copy. Since imagination fills in what cannot be known, one naturally will imagine Jesus with some kind of human face and form, and that is as far as Augustine wished to go:

> Even the physical face of the Lord is pictured with infinite variety by countless imaginations, though whatever it was like he certainly had only one. Nor as regards the faith we have in the Lord Jesus Christ is it in the least relevant to salvation what our imaginations picture him like, which is probably quite different from the reality. . . . What does matter is that we think of him as a man; for we have embedded in us as it were a standard notion of the nature of man.[17]

Jesus' Variant and Changing Appearances in Literary Sources

Augustine's recognition that everyone who imagines how Jesus (or one of the saints) looked conjures a different image has parallels in earlier documents, some which even assert that Jesus actually had a variable or polymorphous physical appearance, particularly (but not always) in his postresurrection manifestations. Of course, the various presentations of Christ in the four canonical Gospels are testimony in themselves to a general acceptance of variation in the narrative of Jesus' life, at least, but some of the noncanonical literature adds to this variety in respect to how Jesus appeared to those who saw him. In the *Acts of Peter* for example, Peter speaks of his experience of seeing the transfigured Jesus "in such a form as I was able to take in." Further on, in his preaching to gathered believers, Peter described Jesus as "this (God) who is both great and little, beautiful and ugly, young and old, appearing in time and yet in eternity wholly invisible. . . . He is all things, and there is no other greater than he."[18] In the Syriac *Acts of Thomas*, the account of the deeds of Jesus' "twin," Jesus himself is addressed as being "of many forms."[19]

Another apocryphal (and probably originally Gnostic) book, the *Acts of John*, also contains two separate assertions of an inconsistency in Christ's appearance, but, in these cases, as testimony to Christ's divinity. The first instance concludes a section of the story of Drusiana and her husband, Andronicus, and leads into the section of John's preaching the gospel. Here, Drusiana describes a vision of the Lord in the sepulcher where her furious husband had imprisoned her: "The Lord appeared to me in the tomb in the form of John and in that of a young man." The second was an episode recounted by John himself, since John (who was listening to Drusiana) realized that her audience was confused by her description of her vision. Thus he explained: "Men and brethren, you have experienced nothing strange or incredible in your perception of the Lord, since even we whom he chose to be his apostles have suffered many temptations."[20]

In order to elaborate, John gave an example from his own experience, so that his hearers might know of the glory of Christ. John told of the time when Jesus had already chosen Peter and Andrew and then came to his brother, saying, "James, I need you." And his brother James came to John and said:

> "'John, what does he want, this child on the shore who called us?' And, I (John) replied, 'Which child?' And he answered me, 'The one who is beckoning to us.' And I said, 'This is because of the long watch we have kept at sea. You are not seeing straight, Brother James. Do you not see the man standing there who is handsome, fair and cheerful-looking?' But he said to me, 'I do not see [that man], my bother, but [let us go, and] we will see what this means.'"

And so the two beached their boat (with "his" help) and left to follow him, and he then "appeared to [John] as rather bald but with a thick flowing beard, but to James as a young man whose beard was just beginning." And while the two became most perplexed about this changing appearance, an even more amazing thing happened. John tried to see him "as he was," but Christ's eyes never closed and remained open. Sometimes he looked to John like a small, unattractive man, and at other times he seemed to be looking up to heaven. And he had another odd characteristic, as John reclined on Jesus' breast; sometimes it was hard and sometimes smooth and soft.[21]

The instability of Christ's appearance and bodily features disconcerted John, but also made sense to him, given that the being he was looking upon was no ordinary mortal. Surely Christ would and could appear differently to different persons and in different circumstances, sometimes a child, sometimes a young man who is handsome, fair, and cheerful looking (in contrast to Lentulus's description above). At other times, he might vary between being a young man with the beginning of a beard or an older man, bearded and balding. Sometimes he even appeared to look like someone else, including John himself. In the *Apocryphon of John,* the author tells of a vision of the Savior, first as a child, then as an elderly person, then as a young person, and finally as a multiform figure with three distinct forms appearing through one another. These changes were meant to reveal that the Savior is simultaneously Father, Mother, and Son.[22] Such variation in appearance was even based on the need or ability of the viewer, according to Origen, again in his debate with Celsus:

> Although Jesus was only a single individual, he was nevertheless more things than one, according to the different standpoint from which he might be regarded; nor was he seen in the same way by all who beheld him. . . . And that when seen he did not appear in like fashion to all those who saw him, but according to their several abilities to receive him, will be clear to those who notice why, at the time when he was about to be transfigured on the high mountain, he did not admit all his apostles (to this sight) but only Peter, James, and John, because they alone were capable of beholding his glory on that occasion and of observing the glorified appearance of Moses and Elijah, and of listening to their conversation, and to the voice from the heavenly cloud. . . . He did not appear the same person to the sick, and to those who needed his healing aid as to those who were able by reason of their strength to go up the mountain along with him.[23]

For Origen, Jesus' appearance changed to accommodate the different needs of the viewers or to show forth the different stages of his own earthly life.

Cyril of Jerusalem offers something rather similar in his lectures to those about to be baptized, borrowing the biblical metaphors to show that Jesus adapts himself according to the need of an individual believer—changing in his mode of being present to different people, while at the same time remaining stable and unchanging in his divine nature. As for Origen, this variable image had less to do with a display of power or divinity than with a concern for the care of souls and Christ's self-extension to persons in a way that could be most easily and helpfully received:

> The Savior comes in various forms to each person according to need. To those who lack joy, he becomes a vine, to those who wish to enter in, he is a door; for those who must offer prayers, he is a mediating high priest. To those in sin, he becomes a sheep, to be sacrificed on their behalf. He becomes "all things to all people" remaining in his own nature what he is. For so remaining, and possessing the true and unchanging dignity of Sonship, as the best of physicians and caring teachers, he adapts himself to our infirmities.[24]

And while these texts imply that adaptability of Jesus' appearance was a mark of his divinity as well as of his loving concern for those who "according to their need" saw him in different guises, the construction of a visual representation of Christ ultimately came down to the dogmatically oriented problem of how an artist might show both his humanity and his divinity (his two complete natures rather than his varying physical appearances). As we have seen, the Roman gods were shown with certain attributes that suggested their divinity, such as the use of gold, haloes, relative size (compared to mortals), or other signs of their power and transcendence. Images of Jesus would seem to demand the same kind of distinction, to signal to the viewer that this was no ordinary mortal, even if he was born into a human body. But, at the same time, Christian confessions also insisted on his full humanity. Perhaps this is why his divinity was signaled through certain traditional signs (a halo, for instance) while at the same time images showed him as having a human appearance and being proportionally "ordinary" when depicted next to other humans in artistic compositions (fig. 60, for example), instead of being "larger than life" or having a dominating stature.

Jesus' Variant and Changing Appearances in Art

Although later (Byzantine and early medieval) representations of Jesus have a remarkable degree of consistency, the earliest artistic portrayals of Christ (in the third and fourth centuries) show significant inconsistency. Sometimes Christ appears as youthful and beardless, sometimes as older, with full beard. Of course, he is also shown (or symbolized) through the familiar visual metaphors of shepherd, lamb, or even fisher. One possible explanation for these varying presentations is that it simply took time for artists and their clients to achieve the "right look" for Jesus, perhaps struggling to find the key combination of features and attributes that conveyed his dual natures, while still honoring some ancient traditions or memories concerning his physical appearance.

Fig. 60. Sarcophagus with Old Testament and New Testament scenes, 4th cen C.E., Museo Pio Cristiano, Vatican City (Photo: Author).

A survey of the extant examples (coming mainly from the environs of Rome) shows us that most of the earliest *recognizable* iconography of Jesus presents him as a beardless and beautiful youth, although in rare instances he also appears as bearded and more mature in appearance. When he appears as youthful, he most often is shown within narrative compositions referring to his role as healer and wonderworker (fig. 60). In the earliest examples of Jesus shown with a beard, he generally appears as a teacher (figs. 61–62). By the mid-fourth century, the bearded type began to appear in nonteaching contexts, a shift that may be linked with a general trend away from narrative images of healing and wonderworking and toward visual references to his passion, ascension (enthronement in heaven), and the giving of the new law (fig. 63). At the end of the fourth century, when the first true "portraits" of Jesus began to appear, the dark and bearded appearance was becoming standard and seems to be the precursor to the standard iconic presentation of Christ's image in the later Byzantine period.

Fig. 61. Sarcophagus fragment, early 4th cen. C.E., Museo Nazionale (Palazzo Massimo alle Terme), Rome (Photo: Author).

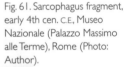

Fig. 62. Christian sarcophagus, 4th cen C.E., Musée de l'Arles Antique (Photo: Author).

Fig. 63. Jesus giving the Law on 4th cen. C.E. sarcophagus, Musée de l'Arles Antique (Photo: Author).

Fig. 64. Apse mosaic, mid-4th cen. C.E. from the Mausoleum of Constantina, Rome (© The International Catacomb Society. Photo: Estelle Brettman).

However, the final transition to a bearded iconic type happened gradually, and for some time both types (youthful and mature) coexisted, sometimes juxtaposed within a single space without raising apparent concern (or at least not enough to warrant removal of one or the other image). For example, in the mausoleum of Santa Constanza (Constantine's daughter) are two markedly different presentations of Jesus—although some scholars see them as representing God the Father and Jesus. Although both mosaics are clearly from the same date and workshop, they may be slightly later additions to the building (perhaps in the late fourth or early fifth century) and their extensive restoration makes scholars doubtful about their original composition. However, the contrasting Jesus iconography still appears to be both intentional and ancient.[25] In one, Christ is youthful, fair-haired, and light skinned, with blue eyes. He has only the hint of a blond beard (no mustache) and stands upon the rock of Calvary, handing a scroll of the law to Paul. He wears a white tunic (with blue stripes, *clavi*, from shoulder to hem) and *pallium*. In the other, Christ (or perhaps God the Father) is shown having a full beard and is seated upon the orb of the cosmos. His tunic is a rich, royal purple with two gold stripes. Both figures have haloes in shades of blue, but otherwise their presentation is strikingly different (figs. 64–65).[26]

One explanation for the continuance of these contrasting images is that such a variation made a theological point or argument in a visual mode. Perhaps a polymorphous presentation of Christ was seen as truer than a single static and consistent visual appearance. The texts, after all, suggest that during his life Jesus may have taken on different manifesta-

Fig. 65. Apse mosaic, mid-4th
cen. c.e., from the Mausoleum
of Constantina, Rome (Photo:
Author).

Fig. 65. Apse mosaic, mid-4th cen. c.e., from the Mausoleum of Constantina, Rome (Photo: Author).

tions, projecting different exterior features, perhaps in response to the need, expectation, ability, or even requirements of different viewers. From this vantage point, the Christian God recognized and accommodated viewer subjectivity as well as capacity for variety. Moreover, a changing exterior also paralleled Christ with the other gods and then trumped them, too. Christ's presentation in different guises was then less a result of confusion than an aim to show his superiority to the gods of the Roman pantheon, who also could appear in different forms or guises but for sometimes less beneficent purposes (according to Christian writers).[27] In any case, divine ability to change form was a certain sign of a god's power and craft.

Jesus as Savior and Healer: The Beautiful Youth

These issues lay right at the heart of the development of Christian art that first emphasized Jesus' work on earth, as a savior who performed certain deeds. These deeds, as they were represented in visual art, were directly related to specific textual narratives. The art of the early fourth century did not try overtly to display Jesus' divine nature, or to suggest that he showed forth the visible face of God, but rather it concentrated on narrating the actions or the stories that were told about him. For instance, the earliest representations of Jesus display no haloes or even other signs of divinity that were already in use for images of the gods or of the deified emperor, or even the golden or purple robes associated with royalty or the supreme deities of the Greco-Roman pantheon. The earliest images of Jesus showed him dressed much like the other figures in a composition, in simple tunic and pallium and sandaled feet. He is not shown "larger than life" but rather as of the same stature as his disciples and followers. The only props he holds or attributes associated with him usually are related to the narrative itself (baskets of loaves for multiplying or jars of water for transforming). His posture is far from imposing, since he usually stands or walks among a crowd of others, rather than riding a chariot or sitting upon a throne. Apart from his significantly distinctive facial appearance, Jesus looks like the other figures in the compositions.

Of course, there were some interesting exceptions, at least at first—and perhaps their very rarity proves the rule. In the famous early fourth-century mosaic said to be of Christ Helios in the dome of the mausoleum of the Julii in the excavations under Saint Peter's on the Vatican (fig. 66), we see a figure that may have been meant to represent Christ as Sol or perhaps as a rival to Sol riding in a chariot, surrounded by a golden sky, and adorned with a radiate halo. This rather glorious

Fig. 66. Christ as Helios, Mausoleum M (or the Julii), 4th cen. C.E. mosaic, Vatican Necropolis (© The International Catacomb Society. Photo: Estelle Brettman).

Fig. 67. Columnar sarcophagus in the Museo Pio Cristiano, Vatican City (Photo: Author).

image corresponds with biblical language about Christ as the light (for example, John 1:1-5 and Eph 5:14) and with some textual references to Christ that employed solar imagery, including Clement of Alexandria's description of Christ as the "Sun of Righteousness" who rides in his chariot over all creation and "who has changed sunset into sunrise and crucified death into life."[28]

But while Jesus' stance, stature, dress, and general demeanor in the earliest iconography could be interpreted as a clear emphasis on his humanity, certain key aspects of his facial type are absolutely distinctive

Fig. 68. Good Shepherd statuette, probably 3rd cen. C.E., Museo Pio Cristiano, Vatican City (Photo: Author).

and, perhaps in a different way, offer a visual construction of his immortal nature. In contrast to later depictions of Christ as a dark, bearded judge as found in Byzantine icons, the art of the catacombs and the early sarcophagus reliefs almost always shows Jesus as a beautiful youth, beardless and with long curly hair. He has a gentle expression, smooth oval face; he appears to be both graceful and rather sweet natured (fig. 67). In this respect, Jesus' iconography looks much like that of the earlier images of the Good Shepherd (fig. 68), which symbolically represented Jesus as a loving caretaker of souls. More significant, however, is the similarity of Jesus' facial features to those of the gods Apollo, Orpheus, and both Dionysus and Hercules in their youthful presentations (fig. 69). In some cases, he takes on other attributes associated with them, like the radiate halo of Sol or the lyre of Orpheus (fig. 70). Jesus' representation also parallels that of certain heroes, many of whom

Fig. 69. Orpheus on sarcophagus fragment, 3rd cen. C.E., Museo Pio Cristiano, Vatican City (Photo:Author).

became deified eventually (for example, Meleager or Bellerophon). These, too, are usually shown beardless and youthful, and sometimes with long, flowing, or curly hair, their bodily postures effete and languid. The most important difference between the representations of Jesus and those of these gods or heroes, however, is that while Jesus is sometimes shown as a nude child, as a youthful adult he is fully clothed in the relatively simple garb of an ordinary Roman male (usually a tunic or a tunic and *pallium*).[29]

In these early fourth-century depictions, Jesus works wonders (multiplies loaves and changes water to wine), teaches, heals (the paralytic, the man born blind, the woman with the issue of blood), or raises the dead (Lazarus, Jairus's daughter). As noted, prior to this time, certain visual metaphors had been far more popular, in particular the Good Shepherd, which was not a portrait of Christ, but rather a representation of his attributes and a reference to the common

Fig. 70. Christ as Orpheus from the Catacomb of Domitilla, Rome (©The International Catacomb Society. Photo: Estelle Brettman).

biblical symbolism of the Shepherd, even though the Shepherd's posture and countenance were quite similar to Jesus in the New Testament narrative scenes. As we have noted, this facial type is a remarkable contrast with the apostles or other figures in the composition, who are presented as typical Roman males with clipped beards and short hair. Jesus' appearance in contrast to these others is almost startling and the nearly inescapable conclusion is that he was either a type of, or even the replacement for the young savior gods of Greco-Roman religion. In many ways, the story of his virginal birth, miracles, wonders, sufferings, and resurrection from death make him their competition as much as their counterpart.

Early Christian writers were aware of the parallels between Jesus and these heroes and savior gods. Justin Martyr had acknowledged the similarities and even argued that they demonstrated that Jesus was in no way inferior to these gods. In fact, he asserted that the parallels showed Jesus to be truly superior, if for no other reason than that these other gods were invented by devils and those who believed in them were influenced by demons (who deliberately wanted to mislead people), and thus they even had imitated Jesus (in anticipation). But, in any case, Justin could insist that anyone who could believe all these things (heroic deeds or wonders) of gods invented by poets certainly could credit them to Christ, the one who did them "truly":

> And when we say, also that the Word, who is the first-born of God, was produced without sexual union, and that he, Jesus Christ, our teacher was crucified and died, and rose again, and ascended into heaven, we propound nothing different from what you believe regarding those whom you esteem sons of Jupiter. For you know how many sons your esteemed writers ascribe to Jupiter: Mercury, the interpreting word and teacher of all; Aesclepius, who though he was a great physician, was struck by a thunderbolt, and so ascended to heaven; and Bacchus, too, after he had been torn limb from limb; and Hercules, when he had committed himself to the flames to escape his toil; and the sons of Leda, and Dioscuri; and Perseus, son of Danae; and Bellerophon who, though sprung from mortals rose to heaven on the horse Pegasus . . . and what of the emperors who die among yourselves, whom you deem worthy of deification. . . . And if we assert that the Word of God was born of God in a peculiar manner, different from ordinary generation, let this, as said above, be no ordinary thing to you, who say that Mercury is the angelic word of God. But if anyone objects that he was crucified, in this also on a par with [the suffering of] those reputed sons of Jupiter of yours . . . and if we even affirm that he was born of a virgin, accept this in common with what you accept of Perseus. And in that we say that he made whole the lame, the paralytic, and those born blind, we seem to say what is very similar to the deeds said to have been done by Asclepius.[30]

Part of Justin's apologetic strategy was to undermine the discounting of Jesus' wonders (since people were willing to believe them of the other gods), while at the same time showing that these works by themselves were not the sum of Jesus' divinity or the only measure of his legitimacy as the Son of God. Still, the similarities were obvious to many people at least, and the iconography of Jesus may have reflected that awareness.

But, as we have discussed, in whatever way Jesus and his companions are depicted in the fourth-century catacomb paintings or sarcophagus reliefs, they appear more as actors in a scene than as pure portrait types. Their faces are not revealed as the visages of holy persons, and the iconography is not intended for veneration. These figures are insepara-ble from their specific narrative compositions, which are meant to teach or reveal some meaning found in the details of the story itself. This was also the function of the various characters or episodes from the Hebrew Scriptures that referenced a particular story that also served as a typol-ogy for or prefiguration of a Gospel event, a specific Christian sacra-mental practice, or God's promised deliverance of the faithful from danger and death.[31] The frontal, static, or formal portrait-type images, intended to invite prayer rather than provide edification, appeared somewhat later in Christian art. In these earlier images Jesus' face is more often in partial profile than facing forward, and even those other figures (Adam and Eve or Daniel, for instance), who are more often pre-sented frontally, are yet characters within a sacred drama.

Thus, the figures in this kind of art take defined roles in their story sequences, and those roles are repeated and standardized. They are never distinct from the general composition or presented as subjects to be seen alone, apart from the crowd around them. However, we do see some facial and bodily distinctions that in themselves became fairly pre-dictable. In the extant iconography of the third and fourth centuries (especially in the sarcophagus reliefs), Jesus was most often represented as a beardless and beautiful youth with curly, almost shoulder-length hair. This image most frequently appears in compositions showing him performing miracles, wonders, or healing the sick, where he looks more like the savior gods of antiquity or of the mystery cults than any other divine prototypes from the pagan art of Late Antiquity. When he per-forms certain wonders, like the changing of water to wine or the multi-plication of loaves, he often does so with a wand (fig. 67). This prop associates him with the wonderworking figures of the Old Testament (especially Moses), or even with magicians known to viewers from their surrounding culture or even some mentioned in early Christian litera-ture (for example, Simon).[32] This Christ also holds the wand when he is shown raising the dead, Lazarus, or Jairus's daughter (fig. 71). When he is shown as healer, Jesus generally has his right hand upon the suppliant, a gesture also associated with baptism and the reconciliation of sinners.[33]

The predominance of this Jesus type in the earliest iconography suggests that visual art, at least, emphasized Jesus' role as healer and wonderworker during his earthly ministry, which, according to early theologians, showed forth the power and glory of God as well as Christ's role of savior. At the same time, certain key events of Jesus' earthly life, which were equally important for revealing his divinity, appear to be missing. For example, almost no visual representations of the transfiguration, Last Supper, crucifixion, resurrection, or ascension appear in Christian iconography prior to the fifth century. Pictorial references to Jesus' nativity do occur with some frequency but seem more focused on the adoration of the three magi than on the incarnation (compare figs. 56 and 99, pp. 128 and 192). Toward the end of the fourth century, iconography of the passion begins to appear, but extant examples omit the actual crucifixion, which rarely appears before the sixth and seventh centuries. Instead, they focus on Jesus' arrest and trial. An empty cross appears as a triumphant symbol, surmounted with a wreath of victory and the *chi rho* monogram (fig. 96, p. 188). Arguably, one exception to this surprising (to us) lack of dogmatic images is the relatively frequent appearance of Jesus' baptism by John, where he is represented as a small nude child instead of a thirty-year old adult (compare Luke 3:23; fig. 72). In most examples, the dove descends into the picture, thus joining a narrative scene with a theological statement about the identity of the one being baptized.

The lack of artistic portrayals of the key creedal professions of Jesus' virginal birth, salvific death, and resurrection in the early period could suggest that the doctrinal emphasis on the human incarnation, suffering, and passion of Christ, so central in the literature of the first three centuries, was bypassed in the art altogether, or that the visual tradition balanced (or challenged) the literary with images that represented Jesus' earthly works—his teaching, wonders, and miracles—rather than attending solely to his nature(s) or divine status. However, a conclusion that the evidence of visual art emphasizes his humanity rather than divinity is challenged by the lack of artistic representations of Jesus engaged in more mundane human activities (for example, eating a meal or fishing with his companions). Rather, artworks portray him performing wonders and healings and raising the dead—activities that still show aspects of his divine character and power. Such images may have been modeled on imagery of other gods performing great deeds (especially Hercules), which was available and familiar to third-century artisans during a time when the visual vocabulary needed to represent the distinct doctrinal aspects of the Christian religion was still undeveloped. In other words, the earliest artistic compositions borrowed from and adapted the art of the surrounding culture, and they conveyed the message about the work and the person of Jesus through the established and available savior types.

For this reason, Jesus' image looks very much like one of the youthful gods, and the iconographic focus on certain aspects of the story—Jesus' signs, wonders, and miracles—was a way of establishing him as a savior god, who could have a personal relationship with an individual or intervene in a particular historical circumstance. Such gods were more accessible and immediate, present to their devotees in times of need or stress, and certainly relevant to the hopes for a blessed life after death. Many of them were said to have died, descended to the underworld, and risen into heaven, and so the analogy is that much more apparent.[34] Certainly, hope for a similar resurrection from death (promised through faith in Jesus Christ) was especially relevant for the art, most of it created for a funerary context.

Fig. 72. Baptism of Jesus, detail from a 4th cen. C.E. sarcophagus, Museo Pio Cristiano, Vatican City (Photo: Author).

Jesus as Teacher, Philosopher, and Ruler: The Bearded Type

Despite the preponderance of early narrative portrayals of Jesus as a beardless and beautiful youth, in at least some rare early examples, including the fourth-century plaque in Rome's Museo Nazionale alle Terme (fig. 61), Christ also appears in the guise of the philosopher, with full beard and bare chest (he has no tunic or undergarment, but only the *pallium* draped over his left shoulder—the garb of an itinerant intellectual) and holding a scroll. His right hand makes a gesture of speech, and at his feet is a row of small figures meant to represent his disciples. Paul Zanker would identify this as a classic representation of "Christ the teacher of the true philosophy."[35] However, to either side of this group is a portrayal of Christ healing. Here again he is shown with a full beard and in one case (the cure of the woman with the hemorrhage) with a bare chest. The two proximate healing scenes prompted Thomas Mathews to point out the similarities between Jesus' portrayal here and that of the god Asclepius, who also is represented with a full beard and bare chest, his outer garment carefully draped, but with no undertunic.[36]

Early representations of Christ among his disciples clearly present him as a teacher, although usually as a young and beardless pedagogue, without the traditional facial features given to Socrates or other philosophers (compare figs. 73 and 74). Although some scholars have compared a similar image of Christ among his disciples from the Catacomb of the Via Anapo in Rome with a roughly contemporary representation of Socrates with his disciples from Syria, the primary similarity between the two lies only in their general composition.[37] The first image shows Jesus and his disciples as relatively young, and, although some of the disciples wear short beards, Christ is beardless. The second image of Socrates and his followers presents them all as bearded and balding elders. The only similarity is the clothing of both groups (a *pallium* draped over a tunic). Another such image of Christ appears in mosaic in the apse in Milan's Chapel of San Aquilino, attached to the Basilica of San Lorenzo (fig. 75). Here

Fig. 73. Portrait head of Socrates, Greco-Roman, Imperial, Later Antonine Period, ca. 170–195, based on Greek original. Found in Attica, Athens (said to be from), Museum of Fine Arts, Boston (Photograph ©2004 Museum of Fine Arts, Boston).

Fig. 74. Jesus as teacher from the Catacomb of Domitilla, Rome (© The International Catacomb Society. Photo: Estelle Brettman).

we again see a youthful beardless Christ seated among his apostles, making a gesture of speech, with a basket of scrolls at his feet, and relatively youthful-looking disciples.

In several clearly Christian sarcophagi, a figure appears in profile who looks rather like the seated reader/intellectual/poet on some non-Christian monuments (fig. 27, p. 44). While on most of the non-Christian sarcophagi and even some of the Christian ones (for example, the sarcophagus of Santa Maria Antiqua, fig. 29, p. 48), these may have been meant to be portraits of the deceased or at least references to his learning and intellectual pursuits (in Christian contexts, perhaps a reader of Scripture). In some cases, however, the identification of this figure is less clear. For example, on a mid-fourth-century sarcophagus in the Musée de l'Arles Antique, we see Jesus presented with a youthful face standing near to a seated and bearded reader (fig. 76). Because Jesus already appears in the composition as youthful and beardless, we might identify this figure as God the Father. An enigmatic diminutive figure bends

Fig. 75. Jesus as teacher, 4th cen. C.E. mosaic from the Chapel of San Aquilino, Basilica of San Lorenzo Maggiore, Milan (Photo: Michael Flecky, S.J.).

down to kiss the feet of this reader, in very much the same posture as the sister of Lazarus in scenes of Jesus' raising him from the tomb.

By the middle to late fourth century, a new iconographic type appeared that quickly became popular in relief sculpture, painting, and mosaic right through the fifth century—the image of Jesus as giving the "new" law (or gospel) to his apostles (*traditio legis*). In most of these compositions, a transcendent Christ stands, facing front and between Peter and Paul (one of whom is receiving the scroll of the law), usually upon the rock of Golgotha/Eden from which spring the four rivers of Paradise. In some instances, instead of standing, Christ sits, his feet upon a footstool that is actually the mantle of Caelus, the god of the heavens (his head, shoulders, and arms showing below—compare figs. 14 and 67, pp. 34 and 148). These compositions usually show Jesus as beardless, but there are significant exceptions in which Jesus also has a beard and a full head of hair (figs. 63 and 77, pp. 144 and 157). Thus, the figures of Jesus as teacher, philosopher, or lawgiver are varied with regard to the facial type (bearded or beardless). This may indicate that the images are transitional, borrowing from different prototypes in order to express distinct messages.

However, while certain of the bearded Jesus types conform to the traditional philosopher image, others seem more closely aligned with the presentation of the older, mature, and overtly masculine gods of the classical world, especially Jupiter, Serapis, Asclepius, and Neptune, as well as some of the youthful gods who also appear in "mature guise" (for example, Hercules and Dionysus, who can be seen with beards and more mature body types). Heavily bearded and majestic, they were shown enthroned as rulers, usually draped and almost never fully nude. These were the regal "father gods" of the pantheon who held authority and passed judgment on mortals. Certain early bearded depictions of Jesus emphasize this type over the others, and the philosophical association is diminished in favor of an emphasis on royalty, dignity, and transcendent power. And, as Mathews has convincingly argued, to the extent that such an image is allied to the portrayal of the emperor, it is because the emperor himself wanted to be seen with the attributes of these ruling or supreme Roman gods.[38]

The apse of Rome's Santa Pudenziana Basilica (ca. 400; fig. 78) is a superb example of this. Here Christ is majestic in royal purple and gold—the very image of the ruler god. Sitting in his high-backed throne with thick beard and long hair, Jesus' depiction looks very much like the sculptural or painted images of Jupiter or Serapis.[39] For purposes of comparison, we might consider the contemporary apse of Hosios David in Thessalonica, which shows another version of the transcendent Christ, but here enthroned upon a rainbow and appearing as a beardless youth, even though he is similarly dressed in purple and gold. The Santa Pudenziana iconography of Christ emphasizes his role as mature lord and judge; the Son who, according to the church's creed, has now ascended to heaven, where he sits on the right hand of the Father to judge the living and the dead; and the One whose kingdom will have no end. The image in Thessalonica points more to the one who is the Begotten Son and Pre-existent One—a prince and savior instead of a sovereign magistrate.

That this similarity to the iconography of the Greco-Roman gods was acknowledged at the time might be argued from the witness of an ancient text. According to a story contained in the *Ecclesiastical History* of Theodorus Lector (and repeated by John of Damascus), the Patriarch

Fig. 77. Jesus giving the law, detail from a 4th cen. C.E. sarcophagus in the Museo Pio Cristiano, Vatican City (Photo: Author).

Fig. 78. Jesus enthroned, ca. 400 C.E. Church of Santa Pudenziana, Rome (Photo: Author). See also fig. 97, p. 189.

Gennadius of Constantinople healed the withered hand (or hands) of a painter who had dared to paint an image of Christ in the likeness of Zeus. The pagan who had commissioned the painting *wanted* the image to be ambiguous (showing the hair parted and combed back off the face like Zeus's). In this way he could continue to worship as a pagan, while appearing to venerate Christ. The bishop, after healing the artist, admonished him to refrain from portraying Christ in any other form than the "authentic one," with "short, frizzy, hair."[40] Although we should not place too much weight on this single (and perhaps doubtful) text, it yet offers some slender evidence that in this era traditional polytheists needed to keep their religious loyalties a secret by disguising them as Christian and that people (including church authorities) were aware of visual representations of Christ in the guise of the regal Jupiter.

The presentation of Jesus Christ in the guise of a youthful savior, philosopher, or ruling elder god may have been more than a matter of borrowing and transforming familiar visual prototypes in order to explain his divinity in the familiar iconographic "language" of the culture. Augustine, commenting on the line in Psalm 133 in which the unity of brothers is compared to oil running down Aaron's beard (Ps 133:2), says that the beard signifies the courageous and distinguishes the mature man, the earnest, active, and vigorous.[41] This imagery also sent a message regarding the kind of god and teacher that Jesus was, including savior, true philosopher, worker of great wonders, human hero, ruling and transcendent lord, and judge. His many "faces" confirmed his duality of natures as well as his divine adaptability. The language of visual metaphor was a matter of both available models and effective communication. It was also a language that had been taken over from the iconography of the Greco-Roman gods and even emperors. Both youth and age carry particular connotations in portraits, and each of them in some sense was an ideal type. For example, Marcus Aurelius was represented first as a youthful and beautiful prince, then in time as a bearded and vigorous middle-aged ruler, and finally as an aging and introspective elder.[42]

Christology and the Image of Christ in Ravenna

The variations of Jesus iconography within a single building or iconographic program continued in the next centuries, particularly in Ravenna, which for a short time was capital of the Roman Empire in the West. From the mid-fifth to the early sixth centuries, persons with different political and theological affiliations constructed a group of important buildings in three subsequent stages. The first was the era from 402 to 493 C.E., when the city became the Western capital under the Catholic orthodox rulers Honorius and his stepsister Galla Placidia, acquired metropolitan standing, and was served by bishops Ursus and Neon. From this era survive the so-called Orthodox Baptistery and the mausoleum of Galla Placidia, begun around 425 when Galla Placidia acted as regent for her son, Valentinian III.[43]

In 493, the Arian Ostrogoth Theodoric captured the city and constructed a palace, a cathedral, a church with a baptistery, and a mausoleum for himself. Still remaining from this second era are the palace chapel (or "Arian Cathedral," originally dedicated to Christ the Savior, but now known as San Apollinare Nuovo and probably finished after Theodoric's death in 526), the Arian Baptistery, some of the mosaic decoration of the archbishop's chapel, and the mausoleum. The third phase of Ravenna's building was after the reconquest of the city by the Byzantine general Belisarius in 540 and its return to the orthodox faith in the reign of Justinian (and the bishops Maximian and Agnellus). New construction in this era included the Basilica of San Apollinare in Classe and the exquisite Basilica of San Vitale (both of which may have been begun during the second period and intended to serve the orthodox community living under Gothic rule). In 555–556, during the time of Bishop Agnellus, the Arian cathedral was rededicated to San Martin (an orthodox foe of Arians) and was renovated, removing some of its mosaics and replacing them with new iconographic themes.[44]

Among all these buildings, three offer some insight into the matter of the variable visual portrayal of Christ. The first, the Arian church begun by Theodoric in the early sixth century (probably finished by his daughter after his death), has an interior mosaic program that might well reflect the theological stance of Theodoric or his Arian bishop, perhaps deliberately meant to contrast with that of the orthodox citizens and leaders of the city who were allowed to continue to practice their own form of Christianity. Although much of the original decoration of the church has been lost—at first altered after the Byzantine reconquest and subsequent rededication of the church to the orthodox faith, then by an earthquake in the eighth century (which damaged the apse), and finally by renovation and expansion in the sixteenth century (which destroyed any remaining mosaics in the apse)—some original decorations, in particular an upper register of mosaics along the nave above the clerestory windows that shows narrative images from the life of Christ, may reflect an aspect of Gothic Arian Christology.[45]

The series of twenty-six images (thirteen on each longitudinal wall) may be the earliest extant examples of such a narrative series in monumental art, and they seem particularly appropriate for a church that had been dedicated to Christ the Savior. We might speculate that the defaced mosaics on the lower register (replaced by the two processions of martyrs—women on one side, men on the other) were either portrayals of Theodoric's court or—less likely—additional images from the life of Christ that were more doctrinally offensive to the orthodox powers than the smaller images of the upper register, since the former were removed while the latter were allowed to remain. On the left side of the nave (as one looks toward the apse and above the processing women) is a series

Fig. 79. Jesus calling the disciples, mosaic, early 6th cen. C.E., San Apollinare Nuovo, Ravenna (Photo: Author).

of panels depicting Christ's ministry of healing, teaching, and wonder-working, while on the right (above the processing men) is a series of scenes from his passion and resurrection.

Looking at these two sets of panels, a viewer will notice that the face of Jesus on the left side of the nave is markedly different from the appearance of Jesus on the right side of the nave. On the left, in scenes in which he raises Lazarus, meets the woman at the well, heals the man born blind, heals the woman with the issue of blood, heals the paralytic (showing both versions), multiplies loaves and fishes, and changes water to wine, Jesus has no beard and his hair is light in color (fig. 79). Along the right side of the nave, we see scenes of the Last Supper, Jesus in the garden, his arrest, the trial before Pilate, the trial before Caiaphas, the procession toward Golgotha, the empty tomb, and finally some postresurrection scenes (there is no scene of the crucifixion itself). Jesus is shown with long dark hair and a beard that appears to grow longer as the narrative progresses toward the crucifixion (figs. 80–81).

In other ways, the consistency among all these images is striking. Jesus always wears the same purple tunic and *pallium* with gold *clavi*, while his disciples or other characters are in traditional white garments, sometimes with colored mantles or capes. His cruciform (and jeweled) halo is exactly the same from panel to panel. The style of the work (folds on the garments, proportions of the figures) and overall compositional details of the panels (gold backgrounds, decorative borders) also are the same throughout. Such consistency argues for a deliberate and meaningful choice of these two representations, rather than their being the result of employing two different workshops with two different perceptions of how Jesus should appear.

Fig. 80. Jesus before Pilate, mosaic, early 6th cen. C.E., San Apollinare Nuovo, Ravenna (Photo: Author).

An obvious explanation for these two different types of Jesus figures is that artisans deliberately portrayed Jesus in scenes from his earthly ministry as youthful. Once the narrative picks up his fulfillment of his destiny through suffering, death, and resurrection, Jesus is cast in the role of a mature god, one who is entering into his inheritance and becoming both King and Lord. This might reflect an otherwise unknown aspect of late fourth- or early fifth-century Gothic Arian Christology that emphasizes the dual natures of Christ but that sees them as sequential, rather than simultaneous. Arguably, this might be a form of adoptionist theology that shows Jesus coming into his divinity, perhaps beginning at his baptism.[46] Or this iconography might also reflect a biblical Christology based on the narrative structure of the Gospel of John, which begins with a recounting of signs and wonders and transitions to a "gospel of glory" as Christ approaches his Passion. This transition commences with the washing of feet at the Last Supper in chapter 13, when "Jesus knew that his hour had come" (John 13:1), compared to his earlier proclamation, "my time has not yet come" (John 7:6). As we have noted, beginning with the image of the Last Supper at the apse end of San Apollinare Nuovo, Christ's beard actually seems to grow longer through the story of the passion and the postresurrection appearances. Jesus' growing in stature and more mature masculine presence in this case represents Jesus' manifest divinity, apparent more through his passion than in his miracles.

The same contrast of physical types for Jesus occurs in the iconography of baptism found in the two baptisteries of Ravenna, one designed for the orthodox (the Neonian Baptistery, ca. 475) and the other designed for the Arians. In some respects, the iconography of these two baptisteries is so similar that it is clear the later one (the Arian, ca. 525) was modeled on the earlier (the Neonian). Although much of the mosaic decoration of the Arian Baptistery has been lost, and significant restoration work has made details rather doubtful in both, we also see basic compositional parallels.[47] Processing apostles carrying wreaths of victory form an inner band around a central medallion at the apex of both domes. In both medallions, we see a scene of Jesus being baptized by John the Baptist (figs. 82–83). In addition to John and Jesus, the scenes include the descending Holy Spirit and the personification of the River Jordan (the river god). But although the two are similar, they also are very different. The two river gods are very different in their appearance; while the Jordan of the Orthodox Baptistery is partially submerged in the water and has veiled hands, the Jordan of the Arian Baptistery is more like traditional (classical) river gods: he sits to the side, draped but bare-chested, holding his jug from which the river flows.[48]

Fig. 82. Dome mosaic, mid-5th cen. C.E., Orthodox Baptistery, Ravenna (Photo: Author).

The most intriguing and perhaps most significant difference between these two works of art is the way Jesus is portrayed. The Jesus of the Orthodox Baptistery has a more mature appearance, with beard and a gaunt body, while the Jesus of the Arian Baptistery has no beard and a youthful, almost pubescent body. At least one scholar has suggested that later restorers have added the beard to an original beardless and youth-

Fig. 83. Dome mosaic, early 6th cen. C.E., Arian Baptistery, Ravenna (Photo: Author).

ful figure of Christ in the Orthodox Baptistery in order to make it conform to later portraits of Christ.[49] This explanation, however, fails to explain the marked differences in all aspects of the compositions of both medallions, including the placement of John (right versus left) and the obvious differences in representation of the River Jordan, aspects that could not have been

Fig. 84. Apse mosaic, mid-6th cen. C.E., San Vitale, Ravenna (Photo: Author).

easily changed in later centuries. But, even assuming that the bearded Christ of the Orthodox Baptistery could be original, whether or how these two different images correspond to the different Christologies of orthodox and Arian believers is difficult to say since we know very little about Ostrogothic Arianism (or its Christology). Thus we cannot be certain that a non-orthodox theology was consciously proclaimed on the ceiling of the Arian Baptistery, as a clear and direct challenge to the Christology of the Orthodox Baptistery even though we may assert that the Arian representation of Jesus' baptism clearly differed from the orthodox model. Furthermore, following the Byzantine conquest of Justinian, the Arian Baptistery was transferred to the orthodox (just as was the church of San Apollinare in Nuovo) and converted into a small oratory (Santa Maria in Cosmedin). If the iconography was in any sense overtly heretical to orthodox eyes, it could have been removed or replaced (just as the lower register mosaics in San Apollinare Nuovo was obliterated by the Byzantines).

But, as we can see in another important monument, a beardless Christ was not perceived as problematic by the orthodox community. In fact, two distinct images of Jesus, one bearded and the other beardless, appear in the Basilica of San Vitale, probably begun in 526, but not consecrated until 547 or 548. The striking apse mosaic—the focal point of a complex mosaic program—shows a beardless and transcendent Christ, along with the orthodox Bishop Ecclesius (who founded the church while the city was still under Gothic rule), Saint Vitalis, and two archangels (fig. 84). This Christ sits enthroned on a blue orb and has short hair and a youthful face. On the inside of the arch over the presbyterium, however, we see the bearded portrait type, complete with

Fig. 85. Medallion portrait of Christ from arch of presbyterium, San Vitale, Ravenna (Photo: Author).

darker complexion and long hair parted in the middle (fig. 85). The bearded Christ may have been added at a later date, perhaps during the time of Bishop Maximian, who appears in the lower apse with the Emperor Justinian. In this case, the difference between the beardless Christ in the apse and the bearded Christ in the medallion portrait of the soffit of the arch is so pronounced that they imply the distinct styles of two different eras—unlike the consistency of the mosaics in the upper register of San Apollinare Nuovo.

The Transfigured Christ and the Two Natures Controversy

In addition to seeing the variations in Jesus' image based on his different roles (savior and teacher versus judge and king), a key text of Scripture also points to a variation in the appearance of Jesus at the crucial moment of his transfiguration. Up on a high mountain, Jesus appeared to Peter, James, and John as transfigured, his face shining like the sun and his clothes dazzling white (Matt 17:1-8 and parallels). Origen pointed to this text as the proof that all persons were not equally able to look upon this sight in its full glory. Peter, James, and John were singled out from the others as alone capable of this vision, and in this way these three parallel Moses and Elijah who were both allowed a divine theophany upon a mountain. As if this were his cue, Moses also appears, suddenly, with Elijah, talking to Jesus. And a bright cloud overshadowed them all from which a voice said: "This is my Son, the Beloved; with him I am well pleased; listen to him!" (Matt 17:5; compare the voice at Jesus' baptism, Matt 3:17).

Fig. 86. Transfiguration mosaic, mid-6th cen. C.E., apse of San Apollinare in Classe, Ravenna (Photo: Author).

Based upon this passage in the Gospels, Origen argued that Jesus had two modes of appearance: one for his daily appearance in his earthly life as a human (which would not cause comment or raise issues) and the other that only shone forth on one (known) occasion prior to his death on the cross. Origen uses this as a reason why those who came to arrest Jesus in the garden did not recognize him, because he was already "transfigured."[50] Thus Christ's outward figure or form was capable of visible change during his life and also after his resurrection (according to the Gospel narratives), when he was not necessarily immediately recognizable and might be mistaken for the gardener (John 20:15) or for an ordinary traveler (Luke 24:13-35) or even just a person standing on the beach (John 21:4), until he caused his followers to "open their eyes" (Luke 24:31). Later exegetes also saw the transfiguration as a vision of future glory granted to certain disciples. John Chrysostom, for example, surmised that the ultimate purpose of the vision was to reassure and give hope to the disciples, who had heard Christ talking much about dangers and death, even of impending slaughter of the disciples themselves. At the same time, it revealed who Christ really was and anticipated the glory of his second coming.[51]

The artistic portrayal of the transfigured Christ in particular required that the artist find a distinct way to show the change in his appearance as the three disciples saw it. The oldest known portrayals of the transfiguration both date to the mid-sixth century, and then almost no images occur again until the high Middle Ages. The first, found in the apse of the Basilica of San Apollinare in Classe just outside of Ravenna, shows the transfiguration made up of symbols rather than a realistic narrative image. Half-figures of Moses and Elijah float amid clouds on either side of a starry medallion containing a jeweled cross that has a bust of Christ (with beard) fixed to the crossing of the arms. Below the cross are the words *Salvus Mundi*. Beneath the medallion and to either side on the ground (a green field dotted with flowers) we see the three disciples James, Peter, and John, but here portrayed as sheep. The hand of God issues from heaven just over the medallion. The starry medallion is centered in the apse in such a way as to give the impression of an oculus window, opening into the night sky (fig. 86).

Dated a little later (only a decade or so) is a more narrative-based apse mosaic at Saint Catherine's monastery in Sinai. In this image, Jesus appears in gleaming white garments with gold bands. He stands within an almond-shaped aureole around his entire body (*mandorla*), made up of shimmering bands of blue and radiating beams of light. The rest of the ground is shimmering gold. The three disciples (Peter, James, and John) kneel in amazement at the sight (Peter, in the center, actually prostrate) and are identified by the names over their heads. The two prophets stand to either side, also named for our convenience.

This image is a better illustration of the story of the transfiguration as it appears in the text, especially since the figure of Jesus is clad in white garments, as it says in the Gospel of Mark: "glistening, intensely white, as no fuller on earth could bleach them" (9:3) The Saint Catherine's composition may have served as a model, since later Eastern icons share many of these same features— the aureole of light fractured by rays, three amazed disciples (the one in the center falling completely to his face). Elijah and Moses stand to either side of the spectacle[52] (fig. 87).

Fig. 87. Byzantine transportable icon depicting the transfiguration, mosaic from the Louvre Museum, Paris (Photo: Bridgeman Art Library).

The transfiguration images, rare as they were, were a way of reflecting the two distinct natures of Christ, both human and divine, and gave an indication of what was to come, after the resurrection, when he ascended into heaven. This was seen in some mode by three of his disciples while he was still alive. Earlier than the sixth century, however, there may have been other ways for artists to reveal the divine nature of Christ. For instance, the use of gold as background or giving Jesus a halo were simple ways of indicating that he possessed a divine nature as well as a human form. But at least one example, a late fourth-century lunette mosaic from a chamber of the Catacomb of Domitilla, addressed the matter of his earthly transcendence in a different way. This composition showed Christ seated on a high-backed throne within a bright green aureole. Seated to either side are Peter and Paul and at Christ's feet (beneath the aureole) is a leather container (*capsa*) containing scrolls, perhaps a reference to his role as the teacher of true philosophy. In large green mosaic letters that make a border for the mosaic is the legend: "You are called the Son and found to be the Father" (*Qui filius diceris et pater inveneris*).

Such a legend seems to come right out of the late fourth-century controversies over the relationship between the Father and the Son, and it addresses the specific question of whether they are of equal nature yet distinct persons (the orthodox formula) or of different natures, the Son being created by the Father (the Arian position). This mosaic seems to take a third position, rather like the Sabellian, or modalist, one—the Son, despite his earthly appearance, *is* the Father, one and the same being (one person with one nature).

The arguments on all sides of this question are too vast to summarize here. However, one text that summarizes many of the issues also addresses the matter of the distinct appearance of Jesus, who by virtue of his divine nature must have had some apparent glory, even in his human appearance. Gregory of Nazianzus, quoting Phil 2:7-8, argued that Christ voluntarily stripped away his visible glory so as to be comprehensible to human vision:

> If he had dwelled within his own eminence, if he had not condescended to infirmity, if he had remained what he was, keeping himself unapproachable and incomprehensible, a few perhaps would have followed him—perhaps not even a few, possibly only Moses—and he only so far as to see with difficulty the back parts of God. For he penetrated the cloud, either being placed outside the weight of the body or being withdrawn from his senses; for how could he have gazed upon the subtlety, or the incorporeity, or I know not how one should call it, of God, being incorporate and using material eyes? But inasmuch as he strips himself for us, inasmuch as he comes down (and I speak of an abasement, as it were, a laying aside and a diminution of his glory), he becomes by this comprehensible.[53]

Thus the artisans might want to represent that glory, and yet also its diminution, in compositions that placed Christ within an halo of light, either as transcendent and enthroned (as in the mosaic from Hosios David described above, p. 157) or by showing him at the moment of the transfiguration, when he did in fact appear to some human eyes in his full divine glory. Only certain persons could have barely glimpsed such glory, and then only at certain moments, for as Gregory says, in most circumstances Christ had to lower himself to base human form or be otherwise incomprehensible. Thus, when the three disciples looked upon the transfigured Jesus, they had a visual intimation of his full divine glory, and their vision was itself a sign that such seeing was actually possible to those who were spiritually aware or open.[54]

But even so, these images are arguments for the possibility of depicting Jesus not only in his humanity but also in his divinity, a feat that Eusebius had denied was possible in that letter to Constantia where he purportedly claimed that no image could represent both natures. In his argument, he also cited the transfiguration as his example, a sight almost unbearably glorious:

> Indeed, it is not surprising that after his ascent to heaven he should have appeared as such, when, while he—the God Logos—was yet living among mortals he changed [from] the form of a servant and indicating in advance to a chosen band of his disciples the aspect of his kingdom, he showed on the mount that nature which surpasses the human one—when his face shone like the sun and his garments like light. Who then would be able to represent by means of dead colors and inanimate delineations the glistening, flashing radiance of such dignity and glory, when even his superhuman disciples could not bear to behold him in this guise and fell on their faces, thus admitting that they could not withstand the sight? . . . How can one paint an image of so wondrous and unattainable a form—if the term "form" is at all applicable to the divine and spiritual essence—unless, like the unbelieving pagans, one is to represent things that bear no possible resemblance to anything?[55]

The way this text frames the issue puts it directly within the controversy surrounding the matter of Christ's natures, and, if genuine, the letter anticipates the christological controversy of the late fourth and early fifth centuries. The issue at stake was now no longer the equality of the divinity of Father and Son, but the ways in which Christ's dual natures (human and divine) were united (or kept distinct) in one Person after the incarnation. Eusebius's point was that, even though the human Jesus had a physical appearance, that appearance was thoroughly and necessarily altered by its being mingled with the divine nature so as to render it beyond the capability of any human artist to represent. This new appearance was seen in the transfiguration, but it certainly could not be reproduced by a painted portrait, because it was unique. It had no possible resemblance to anything on earth.

Christology, Salvation, and the Role of the Image

Eusebius's letter to Constantia was found (as noted above) in the iconoclastic *florilegium* dated to 754. Its appearance there required its refutation during the sixth session of the Seventh Ecumenical Council (787), when the definition (*horos*) of the prior iconoclastic council was refuted point by point. When they came to Eusebius's letter, they introduced it as a product of "a defender of Arius," an "opponent of the holy Council of Nicaea," someone "having given himself up to a base mind," and "a double-minded man, unstable in all his ways, who must not suppose that he will receive anything from the Lord" (James 1:8).[56] Thus the iconophiles dismissed Eusebius's letter not on the grounds that it was inauthentic, or even on the grounds that his Christology was incorrect, but on the grounds that he, himself, was a known Arian.

But Eusebius's objections to images of Jesus as recounted in his letter (authentic or not) arguably have more in common with the Christology of Athanasius than of Arius, and certainly more in common with Cyril than Nestorius. His assertion—that the mortal nature was "swallowed up" by the divine (citing 2 Cor 5:4), and that the mingling of flesh with the glory of divinity made it so changed as to be no longer ordinary, but wondrous, unimaginable, and as such beyond representation—has the ring of Alexandrian arguments, in which the purpose of the incarnation was to take the human body, transform it, and thus extend that possibility of transformation to all human beings (and bodies). Death and corruption are thereby banished by human appropriation of his body and by the "grace of the resurrection."[57] We recall Athanasius's vivid comparison of the transformation of human life to the work of an art restorer:

> For as, when the likeness painted on a panel has been effaced by stains from without, the one whose likeness it is must needs come once more to enable the portrait to be renewed on the same wood since, for the sake of the picture, even the mere wood on which it is painted is not thrown away, but the outline is renewed upon it; in the same way also the most holy Son of the Father, being the image of the Father, came to our region to renew humanity once made in his likeness, and restore the one lost, through the remission of sins . . . and created anew in God's image.[58]

And the incarnation was necessary, according to Athanasius, because humans had ceased to recognize the divine image in creation through their own perversity and carelessness. Thus, the Image itself had to make an appearance in order to renew the human "image after the image." But, he adds, the incarnation did not circumscribe the divine nature within a body but, while in the body, quickened it (and all creation thereby); the Image did not suffer any change or dulling of glory, but rather sanctified and glorified the body itself, since he was the maker and Lord of his as well as of all other bodies.[59] Returning to his central theme, Athanasius insists that salvation for the human means becoming a more perfect image. The restoration of Adam is, in effect, the work of a divine artist on a human canvas, an image perhaps suggested in some of the sarcophagus images of Adam and Eve with Christ.

The parallel of salvation to the work of the artist occurs in other late fourth-century writings, which contain no condemnation or even criticism of the work of the artist, only an assertion that the making of art might be an object lesson. For instance, John Chrysostom, in his instructions to candidates for baptism, compares the artist painting an image to the ways these new Christians ought to be preparing their souls. The outlines may be erased and redrawn, but, once the colors are applied, the image has been set:

> Let the same thing happen now which occurs in the case of painters. They set forth their wooden tablets, draw white lines around them, and trace in outline the royal images before they daub on the true colors. They are perfectly free to erase the sketch and to substitute another instead, correcting mistakes and changing what turned out badly. But after they go ahead and daub on the pigments, they can no longer erase again and substitute, since they injure the beauty of the image by doing so, and it becomes a matter for reproach. You do the same thing. Consider that your soul is an image. Before daubing on the true color of the Spirit, erase the bad habits which have become implanted in you. . . . The bath takes away the sins, but you must correct the habit, so that after the pigments have been daubed on and the royal image shines forth, you may never thereafter blot it out or cause wounds or scars on the beauty which God has given you.[60]

The comparison that both Athanasius and John Chrysostom draw between the salvation of souls and the work of an artist suggests that they (unlike Eusebius) see a value in the making and appreciation of images. If anything, Athanasius's argument insists that all of creation reveals the nature of its divine creator, although the incarnation makes it present in a unique and dramatic way. But the artist, of course, cannot reproduce this divine glory, which infinitely transcends its own image in its full glory and is fundamentally distinct from it, and the artist must be content with representing it in some kind of symbolic fashion that can speak to the heart and mind as well as to the eye. Or, the artist might choose to represent a breakthrough such as the transfiguration, in order to show that such vision is fully possible in certain circumstances. So, the art is not meant to be itself the truth but only a means of revealing a truth that cannot be contained by it, any more than the body of Jesus could circumscribe the divine nature. And yet, these texts suggest that portraits were not deemed to be idols any longer.

The coincidence of the appearance of portrait images of Christ and the saints at the end of the fourth and through the early fifth centuries with the controversy over the natures of Christ is significant. These images began to appear just at the same time that the debate over the union and distinction of the divine and human natures in the incarnate Logos really emerged with its full intensity. The *Tome* of Leo I, for example, which was approved at the Council of Chalcedon in 451 and contributed much to the creed promulgated there, asserts that the distinctiveness of both natures and substances is preserved in the incarnation, "whereby the Invisible made himself visible."[61] Certainly then, the radical cultural and theological developments that affected the church from the mid-fourth to the mid-fifth century had a profound influence on the subject and style of Christian art. The shift from a dominance of symbolic and narrative art to the emergence of and emphasis on the portrait or iconic images must be explained by theological as well as cultural and political forces that shaped the nature and future of Christianity as an established religion of the Empire. The fear of pagan idolatry and religion was no longer so pronounced in a world that was rapidly becoming dominantly Christian, while the language of two natures uniquely and permanently joined into one Person (with one external form) supplied the theological justification, even the need, for such fashioning of the portrait of Christ. But what form or model, finally, could be chosen? As Augustine said, the "face of the Lord is pictured with infinite variety by countless imaginations, though whatever it was like he certainly only had one."[62] And so, although the bearded image came to the fore and remained a standard for subsequent centuries, the variations continued (and still do, even in modern times), while nonetheless, and in an almost mysterious way, yielding still recognizable images of Christ.

SIX

Early Portraits of the Saints
and the Question of Likeness

AS THE CHURCH grew and became securely established, the threat of idolatry from the outside (polytheism) diminished along with Christian reticence about making portraits of holy persons. By the beginning of the fifth century, portraiture was becoming a dominant type of iconography and, while narrative art continued to be produced for illuminated books or for decorative programs on church walls, saints' likenesses were everywhere, often as relatively inexpensive items that might be mass produced. The portrait frescoes in the catacombs were joined by etchings in glass, carvings in stone or metal, and the insides of bowls or plates with images of martyrs and saints. As portraits, these images usually lacked a larger narrative frame that would "tell a story." Instead, the physical representation of the saint, sometimes with simple props or specific attributes that assisted in identification, provided an aid to devotion and inspired veneration. Saints, of course, were not divine beings, so their images could not be attacked for trying to circumscribe an infinite nature or divine glory. At the same time, the saints were exceptional persons, thought to be filled with the Holy Spirit in a special way and sanctified in both body and spirit, so that their images were still different from portraits of ordinary individuals.[1]

Almost as soon as saints' portraits appeared, they began to play a significant role in the devotional practices of the faithful. Portraits were not seen as edifying alternatives to written texts or lessons from Scripture, but rather a means of focusing the viewer's attention on an individual whose life was particularly holy and who, though no longer alive on earth, was still spiritually present. These images achieved this by representing physical appearance of a saint's or martyr's face and body, often with few definitive background or associated narrative elements apart from the helpful inclusion of the saint's name over his or her head.

However, these images were regarded as more than mere records of physical appearance, and as such they began to receive veneration or homage, very much like pagan portraits of the gods or the emperor had. People understood the concept of offering signs of respect, love, and reverence to an image as a means of showing those same tokens to its model. Soon such images became a central aspect of the developing cult of the Christian saints and martyrs.

The account of Lycomedes' devotion to his portrait of the apostle John is an early example of how such behavior would have seemed idolatrous to an earlier generation.[2] Lycomedes had obtained a portrait of John and set it up in his bedroom, hung it with garlands, and placed lamps on an altar before it—as he said "crowning, loving, and offering reverence to it." John's reaction was to repudiate first the practice of veneration and then the portrait itself (he objected that portraits could not be "true" and suggested that good works made a better paint box than an artist's actual colors).[3] This story offers some indication that earlier Christians both practiced and criticized such veneration, which may mean that its reemergence in the late fourth and early fifth centuries was not wholly unprecedented. Showing reverence to portraits almost certainly started with the late fourth-century funerary portraits, which soon led to the decoration of shrines that held the relics of saints to which pilgrims came to pray.

For example, the early fifth-century fresco from the Catacomb of San Gennaro in Naples that portrays a bust of the deceased Proculus is surrounded, like Lycomedes' image of John, by garlands and candles. Whether the presence of such honors indicates that Proculus was deemed a saint or whether his was a simple memorial portrait is difficult to determine. The difference between an ordinary funeral portrait and an official saint's image was not clear at this early stage, although the inclusion of saints' images in the catacombs as a part of the general decoration of an ordinary person's tomb was becoming more common. In Proculus's case, the image itself tells us that his remains were near his portrait. Later on, the portraits of saints might appear anywhere, with or without being proximate to relics. In that same Naples catacomb, in a different arcosolium, we can see the image of Saint Januarius himself, standing between two lit candles in the orans position. His halo shows the christogram (with *alpha* and *omega*), and, over his head, additional *tau-rho* crosses appear, along with the dedicatory inscription "*Sancto Martyri Ianuario*" (fig. 33, see p. 50). Although Januarius's relics were brought to Naples and deposited in this catacomb in the early fifth century, the bodies actually buried in this tomb are of the two females shown to either side of the saint, a child named Nicatiola and identified as an "*infans*" and the woman Cominia, both of them *in pace*.[4]

A slightly earlier example, a fresco beneath a tomb in the confessio adjacent to the church of Santi Giovanni e Paolo in Rome, shows two individuals bowing low before a standing figure who appears behind two drawn curtains, his hands outstretched in prayer (fig. 88). Since the posture of the two kneelers is one of veneration, the orant cannot be an ordinary person or deceased family member, as in earlier catacomb paintings. Above this image is a small opening, which may have given access to the tomb or served as a means of communication with the remains of martyrs buried inside. On either side of this opening are the partially preserved paintings of two additional standing figures (with missing heads). On the two side walls are rare and unusual scenes that have been identified as the arrest of three holy persons (two men and a woman) and their beheading. This latter image shows the three figures with their hands tied behind their backs and their eyes blindfolded. Below these scenes are standing portraits of four additional figures (two on each side).[5] One other rare, early representation of martyrdom by beheading was carved in relief on a ciborium column found in the subterranean basilica of Saints Nereus and Achilleus, built over the Catacomb of Domitilla in the late fourth century, which shows the beheading of Achilleus.

According to one legend, prior to becoming a church the site of the confessio described above was the dwelling of saints John and Paul, who were martyred under the Emperor Julian in the year 362 c.e. and buried

Fig. 88. Fresco of Saint from the Confessio of Ss. Giovanni and Paolo, Rome (Photo: Graydon Snyder).

inside their own home (or, according to a different version, in the house of a Christian named Byzans). In addition to the remains of John and Paul, however, tradition claims that the bodies of three other martyrs were deposited at this place, at a later time and by a lady named Ruffina, a sister-in-law of Pammachius, who built the first basilica on the site. The identity of all the figures in the iconography is therefore somewhat problematic. The two "headless" saints might be John and Paul, while the two kneeling figures have been identified as Pammachius and his wife Paulina. The standing orant has been identified as Christ (without a halo), as one of the saints associated with the place, or some other saint altogether. The three martyrs are variously identified as Crispin, Crispianus, and Benedicta; or as Cyprian, Justina, and Theoctistus, depending somewhat on the dating of the different martyr accounts as well as the dating of the painting itself.[6]

As we noted earlier, in the third century, a section of the Catacomb of Callistus was set aside for burial of the bishops of Rome. The remains of as many as nine Roman bishops were either buried at this place or translated at a later time (identified by their epitaphs as Pontian, Anterus, Fabian, Lucius I, Stephen I, Sixtus II, Dionysus, Felix, and Eutychian). In addition to these popes, three African bishops (Urban, Numidian, and Octatus) are interred here. Adjacent to this "crypt of the popes" is the tomb of Saint Cecelia, which may have originally contained the martyr's relics (prior to their ninth-century translation to the basilica named for her in Trastevere), as well as the remains of those who wanted to be buried near her. This chamber was adorned with mosaics and paintings in the fifth and sixth centuries, including fresco portraits of the martyrs Polycamus, Sebastianus, and Quirinus (their names appear above their portraits). Just to the left of a modern copy of Maderno's statue of Saint Cecelia (ca. 1600), a small niche contains a painted portrait of Christ with a short dark beard and long dark hair, probably dating to the late eighth century. He has a jeweled, cruciform halo and holds a Gospel book in his left hand. With his right hand, he makes the traditional gesture of speech or blessing. Just next to the portrait of Christ is an even later portrait of Saint Urban (identified by name), and above is a restored figure that shows Saint Cecelia herself, in the orans position.

Farther on in the Callistus catacomb is a chamber built by the Deacon Severus for himself and his family, apparently with the permission of Pope Marcellinus at the beginning of the fourth century. Adjacent to Severus's chamber is a small cubiculum with a fresco of five figures, traditionally thought to have been martyrs, each standing in the orans position and surrounded with birds and garlands, and each identified by name (Dionysia, Nemesius, Procopius, Eliodora, and Zoe), with the addition of the epithet "*in pace*." A sixth epitaph, "*Arcadia in pace*," appears below the figure of Dionysia and just above the image of a peacock. The five figures are all clearly intended to be recognizable portraits, and their hairstyles, clothing, and body size vary according to their gender and age. Almost nothing is known about these individuals, and their customary identification as saints is difficult to substantiate from any documentary evidence. Perhaps the only reason to assume that these were five martyrs rather than members of a single family is that their portraits were all apparently painted at the same time, suggesting that they also died together, perhaps in the Great Persecution at the beginning of the fourth century.

The cult of saints was stimulated in Rome at the end of the fourth century, largely through the efforts of Pope Damasus (366–384) to identify and restore the burial places of the saints and to provide itineraries for pilgrims' visits (along with verses written by the Pope himself, engraved and inserted along the route). Portraits of the saints began to replace biblical figures and scenes, particularly as ordinary burials in the catacombs began to end and these places became destinations for pilgrims who came to visit the shrines of the special dead (fig. 89). As early

Fig. 89. Ss. Cyprian and Stephen from the Catacomb of Callistus, Rome (© The International Catacomb Society. Photo: Estelle Brettman).

as the late fourth or early fifth century, relics were even brought to the catacombs from elsewhere, despite the attempts by secular powers to prohibit the transference of such remains.[7] Chapels soon were built into the catacombs with altars for the celebration of masses at martyrs' tombs, and decorated with portraits that displayed both the saints' images and names. Since ancient Christians desired to have their own remains buried near a martyr's tomb, those sites were in high demand and probably only granted to individuals of wealth, power, position, or influence. One example is the crypt of Veneranda in the Catacomb of Domitilla, which contains the only existing material evidence for the cult of the Saint Petronilla. Veneranda's tomb, probably built at the end of the fourth century, lies in the area behind the altar of the basilica of Saints Nereus and Achilleus that was filled with tombs of those who wished to be buried near the saint's relics. In a lunette fresco in a small cubiculum is the figure of Veneranda, identified by name and date of burial. The deceased is shown as an orans figure, being led into the garden of paradise by Saint Petronilla herself (also identified by name: "Petronilla martyr"; fig. 90).

Another painting of a distinguished person with patron saints is in a crypt at the bottom of the main stair of the Catacomb of Commodilla, in which lie the relics of Saints Felix, Merita, Nemesius, and Adauctus. In the early fifth century, a fresco was added portraying Christ, enthroned on a globe and holding the book in his left hand, handing the keys to Peter with his right. To Christ's left is Paul, holding scrolls of the law. Both Peter and Paul are identified by name, and on either side are the martyrs Felix, Stephen, and Merita. A larger sixth-century fresco decorates the rear of the crypt and shows the Virgin seated on a throne with the child Jesus on her lap. To her right and left are Saints Felix and Adauctus, the latter with his right hand on the shoulder of a rather simply dressed woman who is merely identified as "Turtura" ("turtle dove") in the accompanying inscription and who probably was a patron of the shrine and perhaps also buried nearby in order to be close to the saints' holy relics. She holds an open scroll in her hands, perhaps an offering either to Mary or Jesus.

Fig. 90. Veneranda with Saint Petronilla, Catacomb of Domitilla, Rome (© The International Catacomb Society. Photo: Estelle Brettman).

As this example demonstrates, in addition to portraits of saints whose relics were nearby, fifth-century catacomb frescoes also showed Mary or even Christ with his apostles. An example of the latter was found on the ceiling of a chamber in the Catacomb of Peter and Marcellinus, where Christ is presented enthroned between Peter and Paul. Directly below Christ is a small lamb, standing on a rock from which spring the four rivers of Paradise. To each side of the lamb are two saints, altogether the four martyrs who are especially connected with this catacomb and identified by name —Gorgonius, Peter, Marcellinus, and Tiburtius. A similar composition, in the Catacomb of Callistus, shows five saints (fig. 91). Like

the saints' portraits in Commodilla, the style and composition of these images easily distinguish them from earlier paintings in the catacomb and mark them off as later additions for the purpose of enlivening a place of pilgrimage, rather than recording an ordinary place of burial.

Fig. 91. Five saints from the Catacomb of Callistus, Rome (© The International Catacomb Society. Photo: Estelle Brettman).

Descriptions of Saints' Portraits in Literary Documents

At the beginning of the fifth century, Paulinus of Nola, who had commissioned artists to decorate his basilica dedicated to Felix, commended the value of paintings on the walls of churches—sacred scenes as well as portraits of Christ and the saints. He did not believe that the images themselves contained some kind of sanctity and, in fact, called them "empty figures." All the same, he thought that contemplating things would "nurture the believing mind with representations by no means empty." According to his description, his art program included narrative scenes from the hero stories of the Old Testament, as well as portrayals of the saints' deeds "performed in Christ's name." Over these paintings, he noted, were captions that identified them. Paulinus admitted that some might think his decoration "unusual," but he defended his artistic program both as a means of competing with the continuing attractions of pagan idols and as a way to draw pilgrims into the church and away from the martyr's tomb, where the customary feasting and drinking might get a little unruly:

> This was why we thought it useful to enliven all the houses of Felix with
> paintings on sacred themes, in the hope that they would excite the interests
> of the rustics by their attractive appearance, for the sketches are painted in

various colors. Over them are explanatory inscriptions, the written word revealing the theme outlined by the painter's hand. So when all the country folk point out and read over to each other the subjects painted, they turn more slowly to thoughts of food, since the feast of fasting is so pleasant to the eye. In this way, as the paintings beguile their hunger, their astonishment may allow better behavior to develop in them . . . as they gape, their drink is sobriety, and they forget the longing for excessive wine.[8]

In a letter written to his friend Severus, Paulinus discusses another case of interior church decoration that presented a different problem—the appropriateness of including the portrait of a living individual. He has learned that Severus adorned the baptistery he had constructed at Primulacum with portraits of Saint Martin of Tours (died 397) as well as of Paulinus himself. Although, Paulinus argues, *Martin's* portrait is acceptable for such a space, since "he bore the image of the heavenly man by his perfect imitation of Christ so when men lay aside the old age of their earthly image in the baptismal font, the portrait of a heavenly soul worthy of imitation would strike their eyes," he is not so sure about the suitability of his own likeness being there. He declines to believe that his own image is worthy of being included in the décor:

Indeed, if I did not know that you had had this portrait done through great zeal of your excessive love for me, I would charge you with devious malice. I would have said that by depicting me close on the opposite wall, you had contrasted my lowly figure shrouded in mental darkness with Martin's holy person; and that by doing so, you had painted only him and done a caricature of me, exposing me to merited contempt once Martin's countenance is sighted, and demonstrating the heinousness of this absurd comparison.[9]

Acknowledging that Severus's gesture was inspired by true affection, Paulinus graciously offers a few verses to go along with the twin portraits that demonstrate their function—to give a "healthy formation" to all those baptized in that font. Since they look up to see both Martin, the model of saintly courage and nobility, as well as Paulinus, the model of one who merited forgiveness by means of his profligate charity, they have before them two distinct models, one of virtue and the other of well-deserved humility. Or, according to Paulinus, whereas Martin's portrait "catches the eye of the blessed," his own face is there for the comfort of wretched sinners.[10]

Numerous descriptions of visual representations of saints exist in ancient literary sources and provide evidence for a pictorial tradition that has no counterpart in the existing material remains, apart from the confessio at Saints Giovanni and Paolo that shows an act of martyrdom as well as an act of veneration. Rather than only recounting the stories of the martyrs' passions, these interesting texts also describe the portrayals of these passions as they appeared on art objects. A textual description of a pictorial subject (*ekphrasis*) had a rhetorical purpose of its own, of course; it may have been intended not only to describe an actual visual image but, even more, to recreate the visual experience and emotional reaction of a viewer who may have been simultaneously hearing the story.[11] The audience (or reader) of this description is thus invited to imagine what it felt like to see the artwork and experience its emotional impact. However, in almost all cases, the works described in these documents have disappeared (or never existed), and so we have no basis for comparing a verbal description with an actual object. At the very least, we may assume that authors elaborated or enhanced the images they described in order to achieve a particular literary purpose, even if they did not make them up entirely.[12]

The value of these images lay not only in their accurate and edifying illustration of particular individuals' courageous deeds but also in their ability to instruct viewers on the nature of sanctity itself, something that might be attained by gazing upon the image of the saint, while calling to mind the fortitude and transcendent aims of the hero. In time, the face alone could serve as an emblem of holiness, and gazing on a portrait would offer some direct knowledge or awareness of the character of its model and would thereby edify, inspire, or influence the viewer to imitation. This was the case made by Paulinus, at least with respect to Martin's portrait as it was seen by those being baptized in the font at Primulacum. In that instance, the image, although a simple portrait, revealed far more than a mere external likeness since it bore witness to Martin's entire character and called to mind his many wonderful deeds. Another example comes from a homily of John Chrystostom's in honor of Saint Meletius, Bishop of Antioch (360–361). He pointed out that parents both named their children after Meletius and reproduced his likeness in painted portraits that were etched on rings, seals, and bowls. Thus, Chrysostom notes, the faithful not only hear his name repeated frequently in their community but can take additional consolation in seeing his "physical traits" on an almost daily basis.[13]

In many of these literary descriptions of martyrs' images, the artworks described seem to focus on the acts of the hero, more than on his or her external appearance, and so are not portraits in the strict sense. Many of them supposedly presented several scenes in sequence and with extensive narrative detail, perhaps somewhat embellished by the writer in order to give a dramatic, pictorially oriented presentation, characteristic of much rhetoric of Late Antiquity. Still, the vividness of these written descriptions provide important data about the significance of saints' images in the devotional life of the era.

One such example comes from a homily that was apparently delivered at the martyrium of Saint Barlaam in Antioch, which has been attributed to Basil of Caesarea. According to tradition, Barlaam died at the beginning of the fourth century during the persecutions of Galarius and Maximinus Daia. He refused to drop incense into the sacrificial fire, allowing his hand to be burnt instead. The author (perhaps John Chrysostom, since the homily was delivered at Antioch) describes a visual depiction of this scene (and includes Christ as the presider over the "contest"), possibly in the shrine itself, and praises the work of the artists who skillfully presented it:

> Arise now, O splendid painter of the feats of martyrs! Magnify with your art the general's mutilated appearance. Adorn with your cunning colors the crowned athlete whom I have but dimly described. . . . May I behold the struggle between the hand and the fire, depicted more accurately by you; may I behold the wrestler as he is represented more splendidly on your image. . . . Let the burnt yet victorious hand be shown to them once again. Let Christ, too, who presides over the contest be depicted on the panel.[14]

The inclusion of Christ in the picture, as the judge or presider over the contest, is similar to a text ascribed to Basil's friend and contemporary, Gregory of Nyssa, which describes an extremely complex scene of martyrdom in Saint Theodore's shrine at Euchaita (near Amaseia in Pontus). Gregory praises the artist for including the deeds of the saint, his resistance, torments, the "ferocious faces of the tyrants," the insults, and the death of the martyr himself. He goes even further, making a comparison between the vivid portrayals of the martyr's passion as recorded in documents and the image as portrayed in visual art, crediting the painter with portraying by means of colors "as if it were a book that uttered speech . . . for painting, even if it is silent, is capable of speaking from the wall and being of the greatest benefit."[15] Given the many aspects of the artwork described, it apparently had many sequential scenes, showing the trial, mocking, and finally the death of the saint.

The powerful relationship we see here between storytelling and visual portrayal as lauded by Gregory of Nyssa above is also affirmed by Basil, in a feast-day homily he delivered in the Caesarea church that housed the relics of the Forty Martyrs who died under Liciniüs, frozen to death on a lake near Sebaste. Proclaiming that the words of orators, like the visual images of artists, are equally able to make dead heroes vividly present and excite both courage and commitment in listeners and observers alike, Basil observes: "Those parts of the story that a sermon presents through the hearing, the silent picture sets before the eyes for the sake of imitation."[16] Here Basil, like Gregory, parallels the benefits of rhetoric and image and claims an equal value of seeing and hearing or reading for the inspiration of the faithful.

A more detailed description of pictorial imagery in a martyr's shrine comes to us from Asterius of Amaseia, who claims to have been captivated by a painting on canvas of Saint Euphemia on a visit to her tomb. Asterius provides a brief account of Euphemia's story and the establishment of her cult and then goes on at great length to describe the visual portrayal of her passion—a vast narrative image that included a huge cast of characters (government guard, soldiers, secretaries, magistrate, and executioners), as well as the saint herself in a number of episodic scenes including her torture, imprisonment, and death by fire. Throughout this description, Asterius comments on his own reaction to the imagery. For instance, Euphemia's expression at her trial showed a mixture of modesty and courage. Asterius praises the artist for being able to combine both these affections in a single expression and adds that, although the virgin was portrayed as quite beautiful, he (Asterius) also perceived the "virtue that adorns her soul." Asterius even compares this image with a famous first-century painting of Medea and announces that, based on his viewing of Euphemia's passion, he has transferred his admiration from those painters of classical myths to the artist of this Christian story, who "blended so well the bloom of his colors, combining modesty with courage, two affections that are so contradictory in nature."[17]

Perhaps the most impressive of these descriptions of martyr's images, combined with a verbal retelling of their stories, comes from the poetry of Prudentius, a Spanish ascetic who was a slightly older contemporary of Paulinus of Nola. In his cycle of martyr poems known as the *Peristephanon* (meaning "wreaths" or "crowns"), he tells the stories of fourteen renowned saints, including Peter, Paul, Lawrence, Cyprian, Hippolytus, and Agens, as well as more local Spanish saints from Cahahorra, Tarragona, and Saragossa. In most cases, these poems are more than hagiographies presented in verse, since they also evoke the space and décor of the martyrs' shrines and even describe liturgies and pilgrims' activities at those places, making the work a valuable record of the cult of martyrs in the late fourth century.[18]

For example, in his poem dedicated to Saint Cassian of Imola, the speaker presents himself as a pilgrim on his way to Rome, stopping along the way at the shrine of Saint Cassian. Lying prostrate on the ground in front of the martyr's tomb, he tearfully looks up to the portrait of the saint, "depicted in colors and bearing a thousand wounds, his whole body lacerated and his skin torn by tiny punctures."[19] According to the image, the little puncture wounds were inflicted by schoolboys wielding sharp styluses. These schoolboys were once Cassian's pupils, who became his executioners when the judge handed the confessed Christian over to them for torture in revenge for his harsh lessons.

In a later poem, Prudentius describes a pictorial image—apparently a mural of some sort—that showed the sufferings of the third-century

Saint Hippolytus, torn apart by wild horses like his namesake in Greek mythology, in graphic and gory detail:

> A wall bears a representation of this horrid scene, on which varied colors set out the whole outrage, while over the tomb are pictures that show the vivid sight of the dragged man's bleeding limbs. I saw there the wet and pointed rocks, oh best of fathers, and the purple marks on the brambles. A hand skilled at reproducing the green thicket also portrayed the redness of the blood with vermillion paint. One could also make out the body parts and limbs, torn apart and randomly strewn about. The artist also showed the martyr's weeping and faithful devotees, following along his tortured path. Stunned with grief and searching with their eyes as they went along, they gathered the torn flesh in the folds of their garments.[20]

The poem goes on to describe the scene more fully, including the martyr's followers gathering up his relics (including his head with snowy white hair), and retrieving drops of his blood from the dust with a sponge. The scene of the finding of a cave in which to bury the remains allows the poet to relate the description to the actual shrine as it was in his day, complete with an altar next to the saint's tomb positioned in a special chapel adorned with worked marble and precious metals. The fantastic description of this vast painting, of course, has caused some scholars to doubt that the artwork actually existed, or could have been as complex as Prudentius's description would make it, but perhaps that is beside the point. The writer's aim was not to provide an accurate record of a pictorial composition, but rather to bring image and story together as a single aesthetic experience.[21] On the other hand, even if greatly elaborated in poetic or semonic exposition, we know that such paintings must have existed, given the number of written testimonies to them. Augustine, for example, referred to a picture of Saint Stephen's stoning in a sermon that he preached at Stephen's shrine in Hippo. He particularly pointed out Saul in this image, standing by and holding the cloaks of those throwing the stones, thus working this image into a lesson about the transformation of a persecutor into an apostle and saint.[22]

Seventh-century pilgrims arriving at Tours to visit the shrine of Saint Martin (as rebuilt at the turn of that century by Gregory of Tours) were likewise able to see wall paintings that depicted some of Martin's miracles, elaborated by poetic captions written by Fortunatus.[23] We may assume that a formal portrait of Saint Martin, perhaps like the one in Severus's baptistery at Primulacum, also appeared at the site. At about that same time, Gregory the Great, in his famous defense of images in churches, admonished another Gallican bishop, Serenus of Marseilles, for destroying pictures on the walls, since such things were useful for instructing the unlearned and inspiring them to imitate the courage and fortitude of both biblical heroes and Christian saints.[24]

Without any doubt, these visual martyrologies had their own pagan parallels in the first- and second-century wall paintings that showed mythological scenes of heroic suffering and death, such as the punishment of Dirce, the sacrifice of Iphigenia, or the flaying of Marsyas (fig. 92). As noted above, Asterius of Amaseia mentions having seen powerful images of Medea (probably copies of a first-century original) and compares them with representations of the martyr Euphemia. The close relationship between story and image was, in this case, far older than this Christian tradition and provided a still-recognized prototype for the figurative cycles of the Christian saints. As we have noted, in time the emphasis shifts away from narrative types, and the portrait becomes more prominent, with the saint's face rather than the saint's deeds as the focus of devotion. Thus *imago* begins to replace *historia* in Christian art, insofar as it invites veneration and prayer.

Fig. 92. Marsyas, 1st or 2nd cen. C.E., found in Rome, Louvre Museum, Paris (Photo: Author).

The narrative images do not disappear, but even as they continue to visually recount the stories of Christian heroes, their function is clearly different from the portraits, and their power more latent than active. The face, much like the relic of the saint or even the saint's name, is the point of attachment between devotee and object of devotion, while the story is necessary background to that point of contact. John Chrysostom, in his homily praising the sainted Bishop Meletius, comments on the importance of the holy person's physical appearance on small domestic items (rings, bowls, etc.) in the formation of personal piety and inspiring his flock. Also important, however, was the fact that many of their children bore Meletius's name, which gave them a "double consolation" after the saint's demise.[25]

But just as the tradition of honoring and even venerating saints by means of their portraits was being established, it was also being criticized (additional evidence that it was actually occurring). We have noted earlier that Epiphanius of Salamis condemns the making of images of the saints, which he says were meant as a memorial and even worshiped in their [the saints'] honor. In his criticism, however, he gives some information about the practices he abhors. For instance, he claims that some of his readers "dared to plaster walls inside the house of God and by means of different colors represented pictures of Peter and John and Paul, as I see by the inscription of each of these false images." Here, he may be referring to the practice of inscribing the names of the saints over their images. And then he adds: "But, you will say, we contemplate their images so as to be reminded of their appearance."[26] In response to what seems to him a useless claim, he reiterates the traditional argument that paintings of external appearances from life are dead and speechless, while the saints themselves, although now dead, are still living, conformed to the image of God and adorned with glory—like the angels. Like Lycomedes' John, he scolds those who would venerate a dead likeness of what is dead.

Specific Examples of Holy Portraits

PETER AND PAUL

Epiphanius's condemnation of them by name indicates that portraits of Peter, John, and Paul were the earliest recognizable saints' portraits to appear in Christian art. Eusebius likewise had mentioned seeing portraits of Peter and Paul, painted in colors, which were being accorded certain kinds of honors.[27] Augustine mentions portraits of Peter and Paul with Christ in a passing comment on misattribution of books to these apostles, based on such pictures.[28] And extant art historical data show that while iconographic representations of all twelve apostles, often seated to either side of Jesus, are relatively common in the mid-fourth century, those of Peter and Paul begin to show particular, recognizable facial features from that time. The other apostles are not easily recognizable at this early stage, and it will be some centuries before their facial likenesses are established according to tradition. Peter and Paul, however, are not only early to appear but frequent by the late fourth century, especially on Roman sarcophagi, where they often are placed on either side of Christ giving the law.

In addition to Peter and Paul being perceived as the representative leaders of the two "branches" of the church (Jews and Gentiles, respectively), another obvious explanation for their particular popularity in Rome, as well as their being frequently shown in double portraits, is the Roman church's claim to have a double apostolic foundation and to be the site of the martyrdom and burial of both saints. Rome's Christian identity is associated with these two in particular, and their portraits are widespread by the beginning of the fifth century. Moreover, in addition to painting and sculpture, their likenesses appear on ivories, gold-glass (fig. 93), metalwork, and pottery, as well as mosaic (fig. 94).[29]

Fig. 93. Gold-glass portrait of Peter and Paul, Vatican Museum, Vatican City (© The International Catacomb Society. Photo: Estelle Brettman).

An interesting iconographic transformation of the mid-fourth century is the assimilation of Peter and Moses into what were formerly representations of Moses' striking the rock to provide water for the Israelites in the wilderness (Exod 17:1-6; Num 20:2-12). In these scenes, the Israelites are similarly changed into Roman soldiers, wearing short tunics and fur caps. Although the transformation of the imagery may be based on a play on Peter's name (*petros* = rock), or—more likely—an earlier (no longer

Fig. 94. Portrait of Jesus with Peter and Paul, late 5th or early 6th cen. C.E. mosaic in the chapel of the Archiepiscopal Museum, Ravenna (Photo: William Tabbernee).

existing) version of a later (perhaps sixth-century) insertion into the apocryphal *Acts of Peter* that describes his striking the walls of his prison in order to baptize his Roman jailers, the typology of Peter as new Moses was also known in the literature. Augustine, elaborating on the text of 1 Cor 10:4 (which cites the rock-striking story and makes Christ the rock), continues Paul's typology by making Moses the figure for Peter. Moses doubted the Lord's good will, just as Peter denied Christ during the trial and doubted that he would be resurrected as he promised.[30] Such a typology makes sense out of the frequently combined sarcophagus images of Peter's arrest, the rooster, and the striking of the rock (fig. 95). The iconography also confirms that Peter, particularly in Rome, is the new leader of God's people, taking the place of Moses in the "old dispensation."

Fig. 95. Peter striking the rock, 4th cen. C.E. sarcophagus, Museo Pio Cristiano, Vatican City (Photo: Author).

Fig. 96. Cain and Abel, with the arrest of Peter and the empty cross, from a 4th cen C.E. "Passion" sarcophagus, Museo Pio Cristiano, Vatican City (Photo: Author).

Elsewhere, as on the Junius Bassus sarcophagus, Peter's arrest is juxtaposed with that of Christ's, since it is in a parallel niche on the upper register (fig. 14, p. 34). Paul's arrest appears in the lower register in the far right with a Roman soldier drawing his sword to suggest his beheading. In the center of the upper register, a youthful Christ is enthroned with his feet on the head of the god Caelus. On either side of Christ stand Peter and Paul. On another, single-register, sarcophagus from Rome of approximately the same date (ca. 360), the composition shows the arrest of Peter to the left of a centered triumphal cross surmounted by a christogram within a wreath and, to the right, the arrest of Paul (fig. 96). On the far left, Cain and Abel present their sacrifices to God, and on the far right Job appears with his wife. The parallels with the Junius Bassus sarcophagus are marked even though the latter is of superior quality. However, on the single-register sarcophagus, the facial types of Peter and Paul are more clearly delineated, perhaps because they are not as likely to have been restored by later artisans. In the second sarcophagus, Peter has thick hair that comes down over his forehead and a trimmed beard, while Paul is balding and his face is longer.

A similar presentation of the two apostles' facial types appears on a tomb carving from the late fourth century. In this case, both apostles are identified by name. Peter's hair is curly and thicker and comes down over his broad brow, and his jaw is quite square. Paul's forehead is more prominent, his hairline receding, and his beard slightly longer, making his face appear more narrow and his features finer. Between their two heads the christogram appears again. The two apostles also appear with Christ in the apse mosaic of Rome's Basilica of Santa Pudenziana, dated to the turn of the fifth century. The majestic Christ sits on a jeweled throne in the center of the composition, flanked by the apostles. Immediately to Christ's right and left are Paul and Peter, identifiable by their facial types. Two female figures, offering crowns to these two "chief" apostles are usually identified as personifications of the Church of the Gentiles and the Church of the Jews. Although the mosaic has been much changed by restorations over the centuries, the central figures in the composition appear to be more or less original (fig. 97).[31]

In addition to the tomb carving described above, possibly the earliest known example of a double portrait of Peter and Paul is found on a mid-fourth-century terracotta bowl, now in New York's Metropolitan Museum. The exterior of the bowl has four circular stamps of a christogram enclosed in a wreath. The inside floor of the bowl is also stamped, but with an image of Peter and Paul, each identified by name. The two are seated facing one another as if having a conversation, and Peter extends his right arm, pointing at Paul, while Paul's own right hand is raised in the traditional gesture of speech. Here, both Peter and Paul are beardless, and Peter's hair appears to be shorter than Paul's, which curls and covers the back of his neck. Between their two heads is another christogram inside a wreath.[32] Other examples of the paired portraits of Peter and Paul appear on gold-glass, as well as one on a fresco in the Cemetery of Severo in Naples (ca. 350–450).[33] In most of

Fig. 97. Christ with Peter and Paul, detail of apse mosaic, Basilica of Santa Pudenziana, Rome (Photo: Author).

these cases, the christogram is placed between the heads of the two apostles, or Christ appears to offer them both wreaths of victory.

The traditional facial features given to Peter and Paul become even consistent and pronounced through the next century. Peter's face is broader, his hair thicker and curling over his brow. Paul, on the other hand has a narrower face, somewhat pointed beard, and balding head. Their appearances are so marked that identification does not depend on the inclusion of their names, as in most sarcophagus presentations as well as others in ivory, bronze, or mosaic: for example, the late fourth-century dome mosaic of the baptistery of the Naples cathedral; a late fourth-century lamp in the shape of a ship (that is, the church), with Paul in the stern and Peter at the helm; a fifth-century ivory belt buckle showing the meeting of Peter and Paul in Rome; or the sixth-century portrait medallions of Peter and Paul flanking Jesus in the main arch of the basilica of San Vitale in Ravenna.[34]

Such conventions may come from oral tradition or brief references in apocryphal texts, since there is no extant canonical description of either man. For example, the *Acts of Paul and Thecla* (3.3) describes Paul as "small in stature, bald-headed, with crooked legs, in a good state of body, with eyebrows meeting and nose somewhat hooked, full of friendliness; for now he appeared like a man, and now he had the face of an angel."[35] This description apparently influenced only the common iconographic presentation of Paul with a receding hairline. No written description of Peter exists, apart from a thirteenth-century history of the church written by Nicephorus Callistus that describes Peter as being of moderate stature, with a pale face and thick, wooly, yellow hair. It goes on to add that he had dark, bloodshot eyes, raised eyebrows, and a long flat nose. This same author describes Paul as having a small frame, curved shoulders, high forehead, narrow nose, and long face.[36] A different theory, however, proposes that the portraits of Peter and Paul, as recognizable as they were, were based on conventions that revealed the model as a philosopher or teacher.[37] According to Paul Zanker, Paul's face is modeled on Socrates', while Peter's is based on the typical appearance of a Cynic or itinerant philosopher.[38]

The compositional pairing of Peter and Paul with Jesus giving the law and/or the keys (*traditio legis et clavium*) varies somewhat according to geographical region. Those images that come from Rome tend to show Peter receiving the law from Christ's left hand, while Paul stands in the place of honor to Christ's right (see figs. 14, 62–63, 67, 77), whereas artworks from outside of Rome (for example, a number of sarcophagi found in Ravenna) often show Paul receiving the law from Christ's right hand. This variation of placement and of which apostle is given the law may reflect a tradition of rivalry between the two apostles or the churches claiming their foundation, or it may be nothing more than a variance of traditions between Rome and other regions.[39] In some of the images, Peter and Paul are given equal stature and, moreover, appear facing one another in a composition often identified by art historians as the *concordia apostolorum*.[40] In the two dome mosaics of the Orthodox and Arian baptisteries in Ravenna, Baptistery of the Arians—Peter and Paul both show up at the head of circling procession of apostles, each identified by name. In the earlier mosaic, both apostles approach one another holding their crown of martyrdom. In the later, Arian, baptistery however, Peter and Paul face each other across an empty throne surmounted by a jeweled cross, Peter to the left of the throne, holding the keys, and Paul to the right, holding a scroll (fig. 49, p. 124).

MARY, THE MOTHER OF JESUS

Prior to the Council of Ephesus in 431, which officially declared Mary to be the Mother of God (*Theotokos*), little evidence exists to suggest that the Madonna had a specific iconographic tradition or standard portrait type. Given her centrality to the art of both East and West in subsequent centuries, it may be surprising to discover that Mary did not play a prominent role in early Christian art. Several mother and child images from the catacombs have been identified as Mary with Jesus, but lacking any clear evidence, they are more likely portraits of a deceased mother holding her child (compare fig. 31, p. 49). Similarly, a scene of marriage, sometimes identified as the wedding of Joseph and Mary, almost certainly portrays only a traditional Roman wedding.[41] Mary's earliest and most certain appearances in Christian art are in scenes of the adoration of the magi, dating from the late third or early fourth century, in both catacomb painting and relief carving (fig. 98). Other images of a woman seated with a visitor have sometimes been identified as early representa-

Fig. 98. Adoration of the Magi from a 4th cen. C.E. sarcophagus, Museo Pio Cristiano, Vatican City (Photo: Author).

Fig. 99. Annunciation, from the Catacomb of Priscilla, Rome (© The International Catacomb Society. Photo: Estelle Brettman).

tions of the annunciation or of the Virgin and child with the prophet Balaam (figs. 99–100).

Shortly after the Council's declaration in 431, however, Marian iconography blossomed and incorporated images from both the canonical Gospels and the Apocrypha. Empress Pulcheria dedicated three churches in her honor, one of which was later said to possess an image of the Virgin painted from life by Saint Luke, reportedly sent to her from Jerusalem by her sister-in-law, Eudocia. Luke, of course, had provided the fullest picture of Mary in his infancy narrative, and, according to the legend, Luke included this painting (blessed by Mary herself) with the text of his Gospel, which he sent to the "most excellent Theophilus" (Luke 1:3). The prototype, like the image of the *Mandylion* of Abgar, had been reproduced and known under the name of *Hodegitria* ("she who shows the way"), to which miraculous powers were attributed.[42]

Christian iconography soon begins to present Mary in narrative sequences, beginning with her youth and marriage to Joseph, continuing through the annunciation, visitation, and birth of Jesus, placing her at the foot of the cross, and—by the sixth century—at the center of the apostles at Pentecost. A late fifth-century ivory Gospel cover in the treasury of the Milan Cathedral portrays the apocryphal stories of

Mary as a girl in the temple and the annunciation to Mary at a spring, as well as scenes from the birth and childhood of Jesus.[43] Around the same time, the nativity and the flight into Egypt also began to appear with some frequency in Christian art. Perhaps the earliest and most monumental program of Marian narrative imagery were the mosaics in the apse and on the triumphal arch of Santa Maria Maggiore in Rome, often dated as early as 432 C.E. and dedicated by Pope Sixtus III (432–440). These mosaics must have been already underway some time prior to the Council of Ephesus's affirmation of Mary's status. The original apse mosaic of the church portrayed the enthroned Madonna with the child on her lap, among a group of saints presenting their crowns. (The present apse mosaic, showing the coronation of the Virgin, dates from the thirteenth century.) The three registers of the triumphal arch in front of the apse depict scenes of Jesus' advent, birth, and infancy, in which Mary appears, perhaps along with her prototype or precursor, Sarah.[44]

The now-lost apse image of Mary enthroned with the child on her lap was undoubtedly widely copied, and its parallel appeared in later works as reconstructed nave mosaics of the Basilica of San Apollinare Nuovo in Ravenna. Set here after the reconsecration of that formerly Arian basilica, the Virgin is shown seated on the red cushion of a high-backed jeweled throne, her feet upon a similarly jeweled footstool. She wears a dark bluish-purple hooded tunic (*maphorion*) with gold bands, and her head covering is adorned with a single white star over her brow. Her

Fig. 100. Virgin and Child with Balaam, Catacomb of Priscilla, Rome (© The International Catacomb Society. Photo: Estelle Brettman).

child wears a white tunic and *pallium* with similar gold bands. The mother has a simple halo, while the son's is cruciform. Both mother and child make the sign of blessing with their right hand. To the right and left stand archangels with green haloes that match the green ground on which they stand (fig. 101). A similar composition can be seen on a sixth-century Coptic tapestry, now in the Cleveland Museum, in which Mary sits upon a very similar high-backed and jeweled throne, her feet upon a large jeweled footstool. Her mantle and veil are the same dark bluish-purple. In this artwork, however, the mother has a golden halo, while the child has none. Her hand is on his right shoulder and he holds a scroll in his right hand (fig. 102). Her name and the names of the archangels, Michael and Gabriel, are woven into the border above her, which creates an upper panel that shows a smaller figure of the enthroned (and nimbed) Christ within a blue orb, held by two angels. Surrounding both scenes is a floral border that contains medallion portraits of the twelve apostles, also identified by name.[45]

The transition from narrative image to icon is clear here, and one of the traditional modes of presenting the Mother of Christ is established in these compositions. A sixth-century ivory diptych from Constantinople also shows Mary with the child on her lap, flanked by the two archangels, and a seventh-century encaustic icon from Saint Catherine's monastery in Sinai portrays Mary and her child between the saints Theodore and George, while the archangels stand behind the group of four. As in the other images, the central figures all face forward, and, except for Mary whose eyes look to her left, all gaze out at the viewer. The two angels, by contrast, are gazing upwards as if at God (whose hand descends into the composition). As before, Mary is garbed in a dark purple *maphorion*. This icon is one of the three important early pre-iconoclasm panel icons at Sinai, along with the famous icon of Christ the Teacher (fig. 59, p. 138), and one of Saint Peter.[46]

Fig. 101. Madonna and child, 6th century C.E. mosaic, San Apollinare Nuovo, Ravenna (Photo: Author).

The early image of the Virgin enthroned became, in time, only one of the traditional presentations of Mary in art. Sometimes she is shown cheek-to-cheek with her child expressing compassion and tenderness; sometimes she is shown standing, with her child in her arms or in the orans position with a medallion containing the child over her breast or womb, indicating the incarnation. Although Mary almost never appears without the child in portrait icons, she (of course) does in the narrative icons (showing the annunciation, the crucifixion, the ascension, and her dormition). She almost always wears the dark bluish-purple robe that appears in the earliest images, usually with a star over her forehead and one on each shoulder.

Her centrality in post-fourth-century art, of course, has much to do with the defense of art in general, since the incarnation of God in visible human form formed the essential argument in defense of Christian devotional images. The declaration that she be properly called "Mother of God" was a key part of the Orthodox christological position (proclaimed by the Council of Ephesus in 431 C.E.) ratified by the Council of Chalcedon in 451. For these reasons, her image is key to the theology of images in the Eastern church. The traditional liturgical hymn (*kontakion*) in the Orthodox church for the Sunday that celebrates the restoration of the icons after iconoclasm (the Sunday of the Triumph of Orthodoxy) is addressed to Mary, Mother of God, and asserts the association between the icon and orthodox Christology: "The indefinable word of the Father made himself definable, having taken flesh of thee, O Mother of God, and having refashioned the soiled image to its former estate, has suffused it with divine beauty. But confessing salvation, we show it forth in deed and word."[47] The invisible God became visible by means of the flesh of this woman, and so her visible image is as essential as Christ's.

Fig. 102. Icon of the Virgin, Egypt, Byzantine period, 6th century C.E., slit and dove tailed-tapestry weave, wool, 178 x 110 cm. (©The Cleveland Museum of Art, 2003. Leonard C. Hanna Jr. Bequest, 1967.144).

The Question of Likeness: Conclusion

The question of actual physical likeness in all these portraits is a thorny one, particularly since actual "from life" portraits do not exist (even including any that may have been painted by Luke). Moreover, in the absence of contemporary written descriptions of most of the saints (with the possible exception of Paul's description in the *Acts of Paul and Thecla*), we have no way of comparing descriptions with portraits. Yet portraits of Peter, Paul, or Mary are clearly recognizable, and they in turn contribute to the established tradition of how these individuals "looked," at least in their artistic representations. Through time, subsequent artists drew upon the early traditions, and so, in time, their images became even more standardized. Even so, names were still placed above or near the faces of most other saints, and particular attributes or objects were included to aid in their identification (like Saint Lawrence's griddle or Saint Catherine's wheel).

However, if the "truth" of the portrait is based at some level on its purported likeness to its subject, then a likeness based merely on tradition might be challenged, and the basis for an image's legitimacy would then be open to question. At least one early critic, opposed to all kinds of religious images, may have used this problem of "likeness" as a way to discredit them. Epiphanius, the renowned opponent of heresy, wrote a letter to Emperor Theodosius I, urging him to tear down curtains that bore images of the saints in churches, martyria, baptisteries, and even private homes, to whitewash over walls with fresco portraits, and—as much as possible—to remove mosaics with such figures. He claims that such things have no authority from antiquity and accuses those who crafted them of inventing falsehoods and thereby dishonoring the saints:

> Furthermore, they lie by representing the appearance of saints in different forms according to their whim, sometimes delineating the same persons as old men, sometimes as youths, [and so] intruding into things which they have not seen. . . . These imposters represent the holy apostle Peter as an old man with hair and beard cut short; some represent St. Paul as a man with receding hair, others as being bald and bearded, and the other apostles as being closely cropped.[48]

Clearly, Epiphanius doubted the validity of anything created out of the imagination of artists, and he would have dismissed any claims of inspiration as mere "whim." However, he was not so much worried that the artists got the likeness "wrong" as that they dared to make portraits at all.

But imagination was not always seen as a mere whim of an artist, since images created from the mind might also be seen as improvements over those seen with the eye. Since external physical images were ever-changing in any case, they could never be an ultimate truth. This was an old idea, elaborated by the Greeks as far back as Aristotle, when he argued that the imaginative work of the artist had intrinsic value and was not merely a mimetic activity, trying to reproduce an exact "likeness." The artist's vision, according to Aristotle, was guided by divine reason and reflected an ideal image known by the mind. When this guidance was incorporated into the final product, the outcome was an improvement upon the original, eliminating natural defects and enhancing beauty. Likeness was not lost in this process, but rather more closely achieved.[49]

Nearly six hundred years later, the portrait-shy Neoplatonist philosopher Plotinus elaborated on this aspect of artistic "invention," contending much like Aristotle that true artists do not simply imitate what they see, but instead transform their bodily vision through the work of the mind or soul. Thus, the product is made more perfect than the model (in nature) because of their inspired awareness of the perfect form. In this case, a work of art is no mere imitative by-product of a skilled or unskilled imitator or a mere physical appearance, but the result of an aim to achieve the perfect likeness as it exists in an ideal realm. For example, when he discusses the figure that the sculptor Pheidias made of Zeus, Plotinus regards the artist's imposition of a form seen in the intellect but not in the senses with approval: "Thus Pheidias wrought the Zeus upon no model among things of sense, but by apprehending what form Zeus must take if he chose to become manifest to sight."[50] Such a statement recalls Apollonius of Tyana's defense of the manner by which Greek artists fashioned images of their gods:

> Imagination wrought these works, a wiser and subtler artist by far than imitation; for imitation can only create as its handiwork what it has seen, but imagination equally what it has not seen; for it will conceive of its ideal with reference to the reality, and imitation is often baffled by terror, but imagination by nothing; for it marches undismayed to the goal which it has itself laid down.[51]

Although Plotinus's positive regard for some kinds of artistic production may seem almost ironic given his general suspicion of the material world and external appearances, he is joined in this by another unlikely advocate. Augustine, although not a well-recognized defender of the value of visual images, took a similar line in his distinction between sense-knowledge and art. For him, art is judged as truthful through the faculty of reason, although the senses are the intermediaries in this process. The standard of truth is perceptible by the mind and absolutely unchangeable. Because of this, the human mind is also able to recognize error, and even to suffer it to some degree, but yet to distinguish the discrepancy between the ideal and the actual as well as the degree to which the image represents the world. For Augustine, however, good judgment is even better than artistic skill.[52]

Religious portraits were also held to incorporate this element of artistic skill and stamp, but, eventually, they would be seen less as a product of imagination than of inspiration and devotion, since they were intended to be careful reproductions. Basil of Caesarea described painters as painting from other pictures, constantly looking at the model, and doing their best to transfer its lineaments to their own work.[53] Theodore the Studite, defending the icons against the second wave of iconoclasm in the ninth century, called on Basil as an ancient authority, and quoted him as saying:

> In general the artificial image, modeled after its prototype, brings the likeness of the prototype into matter and acquires a share in its form by means of the thought of the artist and the impress of his hands. This is true of the painter, the stone carver, and the one who makes statues from gold and bronze: each takes matter, looks at the prototype, receives the imprint of that which he contemplates, and presses it like a seal on to his material.[54]

The artist is here a kind of visionary, one who receives an image and moreover is granted the ability to transfer the idea into visible form.

Thus, the likeness of the saint is a reality that exists apart from the pure imagination of the artist, which would not have been deemed a positive or even adequate means of attaining a "likeness" by itself. The claim for likeness lies either in a miraculously received prototype (for example, the *Mandylion* of Abgar), in the tradition (which may make a claim for an original "from life" prototype or an eyewitness descrip- tion), or in the simple recognition of the devout beholder. In the end, the truth lies in the acceptance of the image and in its efficacy as an object of veneration, which may have nothing in the end to do with absolute claims to accurately represent the physical appearance of the saint—or even of Christ. After all, the representations of the same saint do show a marked variety, just as a set of contemporary photographs of the same person might, without necessarily raising doubts about the "truth" of the image. Recognition is based not only on external details but, finally, on a whole complex of almost inexplicable signs that add up to identity and allow the viewer to claim: "I'd know her/him anywhere."[55]

Despite this general truism, the tradition of saints' portraits preserves a strongly held belief that saints' images were faithful representations of their actual physical appearance. Later saints' lives often mention their sitting for their portraits, as in the case of Saint Theodore of Sykeon in the seventh century, who (like Plotinus) resisted and had to be painted surreptitiously.[56] Those saints who had died without having left such records, however, presented a challenge. In time, however, those saints' appearances began to conform, helpfully, to their portraits. For exam- ple, those awarded apparitions of the Blessed Virgin generally describe her in terms that match her representation in popular portraiture, which only makes sense. How else would they identify her? Epiphany depends, after all, on recognition. Gilbert Dagron cites many cases where the saint's appearance to a visionary was authenticated by reference to its conformity to that saint's portrait and concludes: "I recognize the saint from his image, but this image prefigures the vision I shall have of him. This is more or less the vicious circle in which we are caught and which gives the world of the icon its perfect autonomy."[57] And this autonomy, as Dagron points out, is based in the same claims that the ancient philosophers made about the portrait—that the "truth" of an image never lies in its external accuracy, but rather in its ability to inspire the viewer to see more than the surface image and to recognize the transcendent ideal to which it points. On a more practical level, the saints were recognizable according to the way that tradition had defined them, which might have very little to do with the definition of likeness in the purely external or mundane sense, and, when traditions differed, as they did later from the East to the West, the portraits might not be universally recognizable.[58]

And this point returns us to the one that Augustine articulated in his treatise on the Trinity, that the faith of the viewer was not shaken, nor the quality of devotion affected, in the end, by the external likeness of any portrait:

> Anyone, surely, who has read or heard what the apostle Paul wrote or what was written about him, will fabricate a face for the apostle in his imagination and for everybody else whose name is mentioned in these texts. And every one of the vast number of people to whom these writings are known will think of their physical features and lineaments in a different way, and it will be quite impossible to tell whose thoughts are nearest the mark in this respect. . . . Even the physical face of the Lord is pictured with infinite variety by countless imaginations, though whatever it was like he certainly only had one. Nor as regards the faith we have in the Lord Jesus Christ is it in the least relevant to salvation what our imaginations picture him like, which is probably quite different from the reality. . . . What does matter is that we think of him as a man; for we have embedded in us as it were a standard notion of the nature of man. . . . Nor do we know what the virgin Mary looked like, from whom he was marvelously born . . . nor have we seen Lazarus and what kind of figure he had. . . . And so without prejudice to faith it is permissible to say "Perhaps she had a face like this, perhaps she did not."[59]

Notes

1. Ronald Leeuw, ed., *The Letters of Vincent van Gogh,* trans. A. Pomerans (London: Penguin, 1996), 394–95. I previously published a portion of this preface in a slightly different form: "Image, Sanctity, and Truth: The Place of the Portrait in Christian Tradition," *ARTS* 13.2 (2001): 26–31.

1. Visual Art, Portraits, and Idolatry

1. Hippolytus, *Ref.* 9.12; *Liber Pont.* 17.

2. The term "catacomb" comes from an ancient reference to the topography of the land near the site of a shrine for Peter and Paul near the Basilica of San Sebastiano, not far from the area of the Callistus cemetery, containing abandoned possolana or tufo quarries that may have made it easier to construct the subterranean shafts and tunnels of the catacombs (*ad catacumbas* is derived from the Greek *kata kumbas* and roughly means "near the hollows").

3. Although Christians were among the first groups to construct catacombs, the practice of tomb decoration was not invented by Christians or practiced uniquely by them. Wall paintings also adorned the burial chambers and catacombs of non-Christian Romans, both pagans and Jews, and are known far back into antiquity. Bibliography on catacombs and non-Christian Roman tomb decoration (including Jewish tomb catacombs) is now vast. Introductory works include Graydon F. Snyder, *Ante Pacem: Archaeological Evidence of Church Life before Constantine,* rev. ed. (Macon, Ga.: Mercer Univ. Press, 2003); Vincenzo Nicolai, Fabrizio Bisconti, and Danilo Mazzoleni, *The Christian Catacombs of Rome: History Decoration, Inscriptions,* 2nd ed., trans. Cristina Carol Stella and Lori Ann Touchette (Regensburg: Schnell and Steiner, 2002); Paul Corby Finney, *The Invisible God: The Earliest Christians on Art* (New York: Oxford Univ. Press, 1994), 146–275; Fabrizio Mancinelli, *The Catacombs of Rome and the Origins of Christianity* (Florence: Scala, 1981); James Stevenson, *The Catacombs Rediscovered: Monuments of Early Christianity* (London: Thames and Hudson, 1978); Ludwig Hertling and Engelbert Kirschbaum, *The Roman Catacombs and Their Martyrs* (Milwaukee: Bruce, 1956).

4. The assumption that Christians were reticent about art because of Jewish proscriptions comes up widely in the older literature, and Mary Charles Murray summarizes many of these arguments in her seminal article, "Art and the Early Church," *JTS* 28 (1977): 303–6. With regard to the matter of social class, gender, education, or authority see, for example, Snyder, *Ante Pacem,* 164–68, where he distinguishes between rural "cemetery" Christians and the urban elite, but I note that in his revised edition, Snyder takes a more cautious approach to these distinctions and notes the problem of evidence and chronology. Also see Margaret Miles, *Image as Insight* (Boston: Beacon, 1985), 38, where the author argues that "religious imagery delights in themes specific to the stages of women's life experience" and that the "universality

of physical existence, articulated by images, is different from universality of the subjective consciousness, articulated by language." Here, language users include theologians who are antagonistic to visual images and demonstrate a "fundamental disdain for the vast majority of human beings, women and men, whose perspective was based on the exigencies of physical existence, in other words for the educationally underprivileged who had not been trained to identify themselves with intellectual activity."

5. This argument was cogently made by Mary Charles Murray, "Art and the Early Church," but also in more recent texts including Finney, *The Invisible God,* 106–8.

6. For a list of these works, see Charles Murray, "Art and the Early Church," 303 n. 2. See also Finney, *The Invisible God,* 99–104. A fairly recent example can be found in an introduction by Margaret Frazer in Kurt Weitzmann, ed., *The Age of Spirituality: Catalogue of the Exhibition at the Metropolitan Museum of Art, November 19, 1977–February 12, 1978* (New York: Metropolitan Museum of Art, 1979), 513: "In the first centuries following Christ's death, Christians, in accordance with their Jewish heritage, did not use religious images as a means of proselytizing their young religion."

7. Ernst Kitzinger, *Byzantine Art in the Making* (Cambridge: Harvard Univ. Press, 1980), 19.

8. Henry Chadwick, *The Early Church* (Harmondsworth: Penguin, 1967), 277. See Thomas F. Mathews, *The Clash of Gods: A Reinterpretation of Early Christian Art,* rev. ed. (Princeton: Princeton Univ. Press, 1999), 138–41, where he suggests that some Christian art may have come from Gnostic communities or reflected a "woman's vision of Christ" in order to explain the apparent androgyny of the iconography.

9. Tertullian, *Pud.* 10 (see also 7).

10. Irenaeus, *Haer.* 1.25.6 (trans. ANF 1:351). See Paul Corby Finney, "Alcune note à proposito delle imagini Carpocrazione di Gesú," *RAC* 57 (1981): 35–41.

11. Tertullian, *Idol.* 8 (trans. ANF 3:65).

12. Clement, *Prot.* 4 (trans. LCL, 140–43). Here Clement refers to the prohibition of idols as found in Deut 4:19: "and beware lest you lift up your eyes to heaven, and when you see the sun and the moon and the stars, all the host of heaven, you be drawn away and worship them and serve them, things that the Lord your God has allotted to all the peoples under the earth." See also Clement, *Strom.* 6.16.

13. Clement, *Paed.* 3.11. See Paul Corby Finney, "Image on Finger Rings and Early Christian Art," *DOP* 41 (1987): 181–86.

14. Clement, *Strom.* 5.5 (trans. ANF 2:451).

15. Ibid., 6.16.12. This passage is discussed by Mary Charles Murray, "Art in the Early Church," 320–21.

16. Pliny, *Nat.* 35.36.66–67.

17. Origen, *C. Cels.* 4.31 (trans. ANF 4:510).

18. Ibid., See also *C. Cels.* 3.76, where Origen attacks those who "hasten to temples and worship images or animals as divinities" as "insane" and those who fashion such images as being persons of worthless and wicked character.

19. Origen, *Hom. Exod.* 8.3–4.

20. See, for instance, Tertullian, *Idol.* 15; and *Spect.* 11.

21. Hippolytus, *Trad. Ap.* 2.16.

22. For a good discussion of this subject , see Robert M. Grant, *Gods and the One God* (Philadelphia: Westminster, 1986), chaps. 3 and 4, pp. 45–61. A rich presentation of the visual culture of the time is found in Jaš Elsner, *Imperial Rome and Christian Triumph: The Art of the Roman Empire AD 100–450* (Oxford: Oxford Univ. Press, 1998).

23. Minucius Felix, *Oct.* 8.4; Tertullian, *Idol.* 11.7. See G. Clarke's helpful footnote in his translation and edition, *The Octavius of Marcus Minucius Felix,* ACW 39 (New York: Newman, 1974), 211 n. 110. Compare the rabbis' similar instruction to Jews described below, n. 39.

24. Tertullian, *Mart.* 2.

25. Cyprian, *Laps.* 28; *Ep.* 31.7.1; and *Ep.* 58.9.2. G. Clarke (trans. and annotator, *The Letters of St. Cyprian,* vol. 2, ACW 44 [New York: Newman, 1984], 139 n. 31) also calls the reader's attention to the Council of Elvira, canon 59, which prohibits Christians from attending pagan sacrifices.

26. Athanasius, *C. Gent.* 8–24.

27. In addition to the examples cited above (Clement, *Prot.* 4; Origen, *C. Cels.* 4.31; Tertullian *Idol.* 4.2), see also Tertullian, *Marc.* 2.22; 4.22; and *Spect.* 20.3. Also see Finney, *The Invisible God,* 101–3.

28. See Robert M. Grant, "The Decalogue in Early Christianity," *HTR* 40 (1947): 1–17, and summary discussion in Mary Charles Murray, "Art in the Early Church," 307–8, on the use of the Decalogue in early Christian teaching and theology.

29. On the Deuteronomic reform and aniconism see Joseph Gutmann, "Deuteronomy: Religious Reformation or Iconoclastic Revolution?" in *The Image and the Word,* ed. J. Gutmann (Missoula, Mont.: Scholars, 1977), 5–25.

30. On Jewish aniconism and Decalogue proscription, see T. N. D. Mettinger, *No Graven Image? Israelite Aniconism in Its Ancient Near Eastern Context* (Stockholm: Almquist and Wiksell, 1995), especially his last chapter, "From West Semitic Aniconism to Israelite Iconoclasm," where he concludes that Israelite aniconism emerges from a long cultural history of West Semitic aniconism and is not unique to Israel itself, nor is it based on particularly Jewish theological reflection or teaching, 191–97. See the older work of Joseph Gutmann, "Deuteronomy: Religious Reformation"; and idem, "The Second Commandment and the Image in Judaism," in *No Graven Images: Studies n Art and the Hebrew Bible,* ed. J. Gutmann (New York: Ktav, 1971), 3–14, where he says that Deuteronomy, more than any other book in the Bible, stresses the exclusive worship of an invisible deity, and he cites scholarship that claims that Israelite aniconism cannot be dated before the eighth century B.C.E. Also, C. H. T. Fletcher-Louis, "The Worship of Divine Humanity as God's Image," in *The Jewish Roots of Christological Monotheism,* ed. C. Newman et al. (Leiden: Brill, 1999), 120–25. Regarding the matter of the invisibility of God, see discussion below, chaps. 3 and 4.

31. See Josephus, *Ant.* 8.195 (on Solomon); and *C. Ap.* 2.71–78 (on the Roman imperial cult). Compare Tacitus, *Hist.* 5.5, which says that Jews set up no statues in their cities—either of their kings or to the Roman emperor.

32. The conflict between Jews and Romans is discussed in chap. 2, with fuller textual citations (*Ant.* 17.3–4; 18.3.1; and *B.J.* 2.9.2).

33. Philo, *Decal.* 14.65–66, trans. C. D. Yonge, *The Works of Philo: New Updated Edition* (Peabody, Mass.: Hendrickson, 1993), 524.

34. Philo, *Contempl.* 1.7.

35. Philo, *Giants* 13.58–59, trans. Yonge, *The Works of Philo,* 156.

36. "The assumption that Judaism was an entirely aniconic religion was shattered with the discovery of the Dura Europos Synagogue and then further undermined by the finding of decorative pavement mosaics in the remains of ancient synagogues in Israel, figurative paintings in the Jewish catacombs of Rome and the like." Among the earliest to discuss these matters were Erwin R. Goodenough, *Jewish Symbols in the Greco-Roman Period,* 13 vols. (New York: Pantheon, 1953–68); and J. Gutmann, ed., *No Graven Images.* About general assumptions that Judaism was a consistently aniconic religion see the summary chapter in Margaret Olin, *The Nation without Art: Examining Modern Discourses on Jewish Art* (Lincoln: Univ. of Nebraska Press, 2001), 5–31. See Steven Fine's very helpful work on Jewish art and aniconism in Late Antiquity, including "Iconoclasm and the Art of Late Antique Palestinian Synagogues," in *From Dura to Sepphoris: Studies in Jewish Art and Society in Late Antiquity,* ed. Lee I. Levine and Ze'ev Weiss, Journal of Roman Archaeology Supplementary Series 40 (Portsmouth: R.I.: Journal of Roman Archaeology, 2001), 183–94.

37. R. Akiba allowed Jewish artisans to continue in their craft, even making idols for the Gentile trade, so long as they did not practice idolatry themselves: Jerusalem Talmud, *'Abodah Zarah* 4:4. See Rachel Hachlili, "Synagogues in the Land of Israel," in *Sacred Realm: The Emergence of the Synagogue in the Ancient World,* ed. S. Fine (New York: Oxford Univ. Press; Yeshiva University Museum, 1996), 111–29, for a helpful discussion of Jewish art and attitudes toward visual art in Late Antiquity.

38. Jerusalem Talmud, *'Abodah Zarah* 3:3, 42d. See the much later redaction of the *Targum Pseudo-Jonathan,* which is an Aramaic paraphrase of Lev 26:1. This restates the prohibition of idols but allows pavements with images and likeness so long as they are not objects of worship.

39. Compare Jerusalem Talmud, *'Abodah Zarah* 3.1; 42b-c: Rabbi Yohanan explains that one should avoid looking at the idols except when they fall to the ground, citing Ps 37:34, while Rabbi Judah says that one should not look at them at all.

40. See discussion in Grant, *Gods and the One God,* chap. 6, pp. 75–83; also Finney, *The Invisible God,* 26–31.

41. This last identification can be found in David Cartlidge and Keith Elliott, *Art and the Christian Apocrypha* (London: Routledge, 2001), 36.

42. See, for example, Lactantius's description of the church at Nicomedia, destroyed on orders of Diocletian and Galerius, and described as a "lofty edifice," *Mort.* 12.

43. See Kurt Weitzmann and Herbert L. Kessler, *The Frescoes of the Dura Synagogue and Christian Art* (Washington, D.C.: Dumbarton Oaks, 1990), for a thorough presentation of Weitzmann's influential argument.

44. Council of Elvira, canon 36. Latin text and translation in Karl Joseph Hefele, *History of the Christian Councils*, trans. W. Clark (London: T. & T. Clark, 1894), 151; see also José Vives, *Concilios Visigóticos e Hispano-Romanos*, España cristiania, Textos 1 (Barcelona: Conseio Superiod de Investigaciones Cientificar, 1963), 8. Translation variants are discussed by Edwyn Bevan, *Holy Images* (London: George Allen & Unwin, 1940), 114–15; and Mary Charles Murray, "Art and the Early Church," 317 n. 2.

45. Paulinus, *Carm.* 27.542.

46. Gregory the Great to Serenus Ep. 9.105 (trans. *NPNF²* 13, 23). (See also Ep. 11.13 *NPNF²* 13.53-54.) (For other testimonies to the use of images in churches, see Gregory of Nyssa, *Hom.* 19.2 (*Laudatio S. Theodori*), where he describes the painting of martyrs' images: "for painting, even if it is silent, is capable of speaking from the wall and being of the greatest benefit" (trans. in Cyril Mango, *Art of the Byzantine Empire, 312–1453, Sources and Documents* [Toronto: Univ. of Toronto Press, 1986], 36–37), and discussion in chap. 6.

47. Gregory to Serenus *Ep.* 11.13 (trans. *NPNF²* 13.53, translation adapted slightly). See Celia Chazelle, "Pictures, Books, and the Illiterate: Pope Gregory I's Letters to Serenus of Marseilles," *Word and Image* 6 (1990): 138–53.

48. See Herbert Kessler, "Pictures as Scripture in Fifth-Century Churches," in *Studies in Pictorial Narrative* (London: Pindar, 1994), 357–79.

49. The oldest existing icons are found at Saint Catherine's Monastery on Mount Sinai; see Kurt Weitzmann, *The Monastery of Saint Catherine at Mount Sinai, The Icons*, vol. 1 (Princeton: Princeton Univ. Press, 1976), 5–6; and David Talbot Rice and Tamara Talbot Rice, *Icons and Their Dating* (London: Thames and Hudson, 1976). The icon of Christ Pantocrator certainly is one of the oldest and dates to the mid-sixth century.

50. See discussion of these funerary images in chap. 2.

51. Trans. taken from Daniel Sahas, *Icon and Logos: Sources in Eighth-Century Iconoclasm* (Toronto: Univ. of Toronto Press, 1986), 134, based on an edition of the Acts of the Council of 787, originally published by G. D. Mansi in 1867 (*Sacrorum Conciliorum nova et amplissima Collectio*, vol. 13).

52. From Mango, *The Art of the Byzantine Empire,* 17, which provides a longer version of the letter, taken from J. B. Pitra's collection of fragments, *Spicilegium Solesmense*, I (Paris, 1852). See PG 20:1545–49, which reproduces the work of F. Boivin (ca. 1700). For a brief, helpful discussion of the textual tradition, see Stephen Gero, "The True Image of Christ: Eusebius' Letter to Constantia Reconsidered," *JTS* 32 (1981): 460–61 n. 2.

53. Mango, *The Art of the Byzantine Empire,* 18.

54. Eusebius, *Hist.* 7.18 (trans. *NPNF²* 1.304); also *Vit. Const.* 3.48, where Eusebius describes colossal statues of Daniel and the Good Shepherd that Constantine set up to adorn fountains in Constantinople. According to *NPNF²* (1, p. 304, col., 2 fn.1), both Sozomon, HE 5.21 and Philostorgius *HE* 7.3, also refer to this statue, which (according to J. K. L. Gieseler's, *Ecles. Hist.*) might have been originally erected to honor an emperor and then re-identified by Christians because of the possible Greek inscription including either the word *soteri* or *theo*.

55. Irenaeus, *Haer.* 1.25.6.

56. Mary Charles Murray's arguments are most persuasive but rarely have been considered since her 1977 "Art and the Early Church," 335–36, and the 1981 response of Gero, "The True Image." Scholars have mainly repeated the text of Eusebius without noting the questions raised about its authenticity or that it is found only in the Acts of the Seventh Ecumenical Council and the *florilegium* of Nicephorus of Constantinople, who copied out a portion into a work known as "Contra Eusebium et Epiphanidem." See sources for text of Nicephorus as listed and briefly discussed in Gero, "True Image," n. 2.

57. Epiphanius, *Test.*, text and trans. in Mango, *The Art of the Byzantine Empire*, 41, from Georgije Ostrogorsky, ed., *Studien zur Geschichte des byzantinische Bilderstreites* (Breslau: Marcus, 1929), 67. See discussion regarding the authenticity of this and the other fragments of Epiphanius in chap. 6, n. 48.

58. Ibid.

59. See general discussion in chap. 2.

60. Gnostics are still associated with early Christian image-making by historians. See Mathews, *Clash of Gods,* 138–39, or the older and problematic work of Walter Lowrie, *Art in the Early Church* (New York: Norton, 1947), 12–13.

61. *Acts of John* 27.

62. *Acts of John* 28–29, slightly adapted from Edgar Hennecke, *New Testament Apocrypha*, ed. Wilhelm Schneemelcher, trans. Robert McL. Wilson (Philadelphia: Westminster, 1959),

2:220–21. The association of a painter's colors with certain virtues appears also in later Christian literature, for example, in Gregory of Nyssa, *Anima et res.*, and John Chrysostom, *Hom. 1 Cor.* 13.3.

63. Lampridius, *Hist. Aug. Sev. Alex.* 29.2.

64. See discussion in chap. 3.

65. Lampridius, *Hist. Aug. Sev. Alex.* 29.2.

66. Porphyry, *Vit. Plot.*, found in Stephen Mackenna, trans., *Plotinus, The Enneads*, revised by B. S. Page (New York: Faber and Faber, 1956), 1.

67. Frg. D, in Bentley Layton, *The Gnostic Scriptures* (Garden City, N.Y.: Doubleday, 1987), 237.

68. See the exemptions for artists conferred by legal decrees of Constantine, *Codex Theo.* 13.4.1 and 13.4.2.

69. Eusebius, *Vit. Const.* 3.49.

70. *Liber Ponf.* 34.9 and 13 (Sylvester), ed. Louis Duchesne, *Le Liber Pontificalis* 1 (Paris: Boccard, 1955), 172, 174. See English trans. by Louise Ropes Loomis, *Liber Pontificalis* (New York: Octagon, 1965), 47–50.

71. Jerome, *Comm. Ezech.* 40.5–13.

72. See much more detailed discussion of these developments in chap. 6.

73. A full discussion of the portrait of Christ follows in chap. 5.

74. Discussed by George M. A. Hanfmann, "The Continuity of Classical Art: Culture, Myth, and Faith," in *Age of Spirituality: A Symposium,* ed. Kurt Weitzmann (New York: Metropolitan Museum of Art, 1980), 85–86.

75. For seated Christ statuette, see Mathews, *Clash of Gods,* 128; Johannes K. Kollwitz, "Probleme der theodosianischen Kunst Roms," *RivAC* 39 (1963): 222; and Beat Brenk, "Zwei Reliefs des späten 4. Jarhunderts," *Acta* 4 (1969): 54–55. Lowrie claims that this was likely a Gnostic production, implying that its feminine attributes would help identify it as such, in *Art in the Early Church,* 12–13.

76. See the discussion of bearded and beardless Christ in chap. 4

77. Augustine, *Serm.* 198.17, trans. Edmund Hill, *The Works of St. Augustine,* pt. 1, vol. 3, *Sermons* (Newly Discovered Sermons), ed. J. E. Rotelle (Brooklyn: New City, 1997), 193–94; see chap. 4, pp. 109–10, for more discussion.

2. Image and Portrait in Roman Culture and Religion

1. Pliny, *Nat.* 35.2.1–7 (trans. LCL 9:263–65). Almost the whole of Book 35 is dedicated to the visual arts and a listing of famous artists, including the earliest Greek portrait painters. See, for instance, 35–36, especially 98–99 on the painter Aristides, who was the "first to depict the mind and express the feelings" of his model.

2. Ibid., 35.2.11.

3. Plutarch, *Alex.* 1 (trans. LCL 7:225). For another example of language portraiture, with comparison to classical statuary, see Lucian, *Pro imag.* and *Imag.*

4. James Breckenridge, *Likeness: A Conceptual History of Ancient Portraiture* (Evanston, Ill.: Northwestern Univ. Press, 1968), 153–56.

5. Reproduced in Breckenridge, *Likeness,* 166, fig. 84. See discussion in Susan Walker, *Greek and Roman Portraits* (London: British Museum Press, 1995), chap. 7, "The Roman Image," 72–82.

6. On the Julio-Claudian portraits in general see Charles Brian Rose, *Dynastic Commemoration and Imperial Portraiture in the Julio-Claudian Period* (Cambridge: Cambridge Univ. Press, 1997). On the images of Augustus, see Paul Zanker, *The Power of Images in the Age of Augustus,* trans. A. Shapiro (Ann Arbor: Univ. of Michigan Press, 1988); and Jaš Elsner, "Inventing Imperium: Texts and the Propaganda of Monuments in Augustan Rome," in Jaš Elsner, ed., *Art and Text in Roman Culture* (Cambridge: Cambridge Univ. Press, 1996), 32–53. For a more general study of Roman sculpture (and portraits) during the Empire, see Diana E. E. Kleiner, *Roman Sculpture* (New Haven: Yale Univ. Press, 1992), with full bibliography.

7. On portraits of women in Roman art see Dianna E. E. Kleiner and Susan B. Matheson, eds., *I Claudia II: Women in Roman Art and Society* (Austin: Univ. of Texas Press, 2000).

8. See Richard Brilliant, *Roman Art from the Republic to Constantine* (London: Phaidon, 1974), 179–80.

9. See Walker, *Greek and Roman Portraits*, chap. 8, "Bearded and Beardless Men," 83–93.

10. H. P. L'Orange, "The Origin of Medieval Portraiture," in his *Likeness and Icon: Selected Studies in Classical and Early Mediaeval Art* (Odense: Odense Univ. Press, 1973), 93. On third-century Roman portraiture in general, see Susan Wood, *Roman Portrait Sculpture 217–260 AD* (Leiden: Brill, 1986); and Eve D'Ambra, *Art and Identity in the Roman World* (London: Calmann and King, 1998).

11. On the Plotinus portrait from Ostia, see L'Orange, *Likeness and Icon*, 32–42.

12. Kleiner, *Roman Sculpture*, 4.

13. Ibid., 95–102. Note the quotation from Plutarch above. See also Pliny *Nat.* 11.145.

14. Kleiner, *Roman Sculpture*, 343–435.

15. Ibid., 441.

16. On this particular point, see Paul Zanker, *The Mask of Socrates: The Image of the Intellectual in Antiquity,* trans. A. Shapiro (Berkeley: Univ. of California Press, 1995).

17. H. P. L'Orange, *Apotheosis in Ancient Portraiture* (Cambridge: Harvard Univ. Press, 1947), 19. This seminal study discusses the image at length and includes examples from ancient literature that underscore this aspect of Alexander's reputation.

18. Ibid., 28–29.

19. L'Orange has much to say about the hair of these figures, 30–42. See also Dorothea Michel, *Alexander als Vorbild für Pompeius, Caesar, und Marcus Antonius, archäologische Untersuchungen,* Collection Latomus 94 (Brussels: Latomus, Revue d'études latines, 1967).

20. See discussion below of the imperial portraits and the relationship of these images to the youthful gods.

21. Zanker, *Mask of Socrates*, 202.

22. Ibid., 66–86.

23. Ibid., chap. 5, "Hadrian's Beard."

24. Pliny, *Nat.* 35.2.7–9 (trans. LCL 9:265–7).

25. Polybius, *Hist.* 6.53 (trans. LCL 3:389). Compare Ovid, *Her.* 13.153, and Sallust, *Bell. Jug.* 4.5–6, "eminent men of our country had the habit of saying that whenever they contemplated the *imagines* of their ancestors, their souls burned with the most vehement desire for virtue." These texts are cited and translated by Michael Koortbojian, *Myth, Meaning, and Memory on Roman Sarcophagi* (Berkeley: Univ. of California Press, 1995), 122–26. See also Heinrich Drerup, "Totenmaske und Ahnenbild bei den Römern," *MDAI (R)* 87 (1980): 81, 120–29; and Annie Nicolette Zadoks-Josephus Jitta, *Ancestral Portraiture in Rome and the Art of the Last Century of the Republic* (Amsterdam: Noord Hollandsche, 1932).

26. See Nancy Ramage and Arthur Ramage, *Roman Art: Romulus to Constantine*, 3d ed. (Upper Saddle River, N.J.: Prentice Hall, 2001), 142–43 and figs. 4.14–16 of the columbarium of Vigna Codini.

27. Pliny, *Nat.* 35.3–4.

28. See J. M. C. Toynbee, *Death and Burial in the Roman World* (Baltimore: Johns Hopkins Univ. Press, 1971), 51–52.

29. Augustine, *Mor. eccl.* 34.75. See discussion of saints' portraits in chap. 6.

30. Richard Brilliant, "'What Is Death, That I Should Fear It?' Aspects of the Roman Response," in *Imago Antiquitatis: Religions et iconographie du monde romain, mélanges offerts à Robert Turcan,* ed. Nicole Blanc and André Buisson (Paris: De Boccard, 1999), 145.

31. See, for example, the sarcophagus of Titus Aelius Euangelus in Guntram Koch, *Roman Funerary Sculpture: Catalogue of the Collections* (Malibu, Calif.: J. Paul Getty Museum, 1988), 24–27, fig. 9; Robert Turcan, *L'art romain dans l'histoire* (Paris: Flammarion, 1995), chap. 1, "L'hommage des images aux morts," 17–31; Hans Belting, *Likeness and Presence: A History of the Image before the Era of Art*, trans. E. Jephcott (Chicago: Univ. of Chicago Press, 1994), 78–101.

32. A general summary in Toynbee, *Death and Burial in the Roman World*, chap. 6, "Gravestones and Tomb Furniture," 244–81; Jaš Elsner, *Imperial Rome and Christian Triumph: The Art of the Roman Empire AD 100–450* (Oxford: Oxford Univ. Press, 1998), chap. 6, "Art and Death," 145–65.

33. See Eve D'Ambra, "Mourning and the Making of Ancestors on the Testamentum Relief," *AJA* 99 (1995): 667–81.

34. See Susan Wood, "Alcestis on Roman Sarcophagi," *AJA* 82 (1978): 499–510.

35. Koortbojian, *Myth, Meaning*, 124–25. On Dionysian themes, see Friedrich Matz, *Die dionysischen Sarkophage* 4 (Berlin: Mann, 1968); Robert Turcan, *Les sarcophages romains à représentations dionysiaques* (Paris: Boccard, 1966); and Karl Lehmann-Hartleben and Erling C. Olsen, *Dionysiac Sarcophagi in Baltimore* (Baltimore: Walters Art Gallery, 1942).

36. The tomb of Proculus in Naples, catacomb of San Gennaro, is a noteworthy exception, although it dated to the fifth century and was probably a pilgrimage site; see discussion p 174.

37. The portraits of saints in the catacombs and other burials are more fully discussed in chap. 5.

38. Regarding the gold-glass portraits, which are some of the earliest images of the Christian saints, see brief discussion by Elsner, *Imperial Rome*, 232–33, and the older work by Charles Rufus Morey, *The Gold-Glass Collection of the Vatican Library*, ed. G. Ferrari (Vatican City: Biblioteca Apostolica Vaticana, 1959).

39. See Belting, *Likeness and Presence*, 78–88, esp. 82 and fig. 32; also Hans Achelis, *Die Katakomben von Neapel* (Leipzig: Hiersemann, 1936), 48, 62–63, and plate 27. Proculus's image is discussed again in chap. 6.

40. On the imperial cult in general, see Simon R. F. Price, *Rituals and Power: The Roman Imperial Cult in Asia Minor* (Cambridge Univ. Press, Cambridge, 1984); Glen W. Bowersock, "The Imperial Cult: Perceptions and Persistence," in *Jewish and Christian Self-Definition*, vol. 3, ed. B. F. Meyer and E. P. Sanders (Philadelphia: Fortress Press, 1982), 171–82; Paul Zanker, "The Power of Images," in *Paul and Empire: Religion and Power in Roman Imperial Society*, ed. R. A. Horsley (Harrisburg, Pa.: Trinity, 1997), 72–86; Robert Turcan, *The Gods of Ancient Rome: Religion in Everyday Life from Archaic to Imperial Times*, trans. A. Nevill (London: Routledge, 2001), 134–45 ("The Imperial Cult"); and Duncan Fishwick, *The Imperial Cult in the West* (Leiden: Brill, 1987).

41. On the apotheosis of Julius Caesar, see Suetonius, *Jul.* 84; Pliny, *Nat.* 2.94; and Dio Cassius 47.18.5.

42. Historians who view the ruler cult in terms of secular power politics include the following: Price, *Rituals and Power*; John H. W. G. Liebeschütz, *Continuity and Change in Roman Religion* (Oxford: Clarendon, 1979); Lilly Ross Taylor, *The Divinity of the Roman Emperor* (Middletown, Conn.: American Philological Association, 1931); and Duncan Fishwick, "The Development of Provincial Ruler Worship in the Western Roman Empire," in *ANRW* 2.16.2 (1978). On imperial portraits in general see Niels Hannestad, *Roman Art and Imperial Policy* (Aarhus: Aarhus Univ. Press, 1986); and Brilliant, *Roman Art*, 166–87.

43. See Bowersock, "The Imperial Cult," on this distinction.

44. An example of this is the riot in Antioch in 387 C.E. when citizens destroyed imperial images after Theodosius I tried to impose a new tax. The emperor executed all held responsible and punished the entire city by removing its metropolitan statue. See Libanius, *Or.* 19.60–61, a plea for clemency or reconsideration. See also Chrysostom, *Stat.* 2.1–3, where he said the whole city should feel like Job on his dunghill, lamenting what had befallen them. In addition, *Codex Theo.* 9.4, promulgated in 393 C.E., seems to make a distinction between maledictions of the emperor's name uttered in levity and those suggesting actual sedition or sacrilege. On the legal status of the emperor's image, see Thomas Pekary, *Das römische Kaiserbildnis in Staat, Kult, und Gesellschaft* (Berlin: Mann, 1985); Belting, *Likeness and Presence*, 105–7. For an illustration and short discussion of this leaf of the Rossano Gospels see Kurt Weitzmann, *Late Antique and Early Christian Book Illumination* (New York: George Braziller, 1977), 90–93, pls. 30–31.

45. Pliny, *Ep.* 10.96.5 (To Trajan). See Daniel Schowalter, *The Emperor and the Gods: Images from the Time of Trajan*, HDR 28 (Minneapolis: Fortress Press, 1993), esp. 4–6.

46. This quotation appears in Elsner, *Imperial Rome*, 54.

47. See Tacitus, *Hist.* 4.62 as an example (the defeat of the sixteenth Roman legion by the Gauls).

48. Paul Corby Finney, *The Invisible God: The Earliest Christians on Art* (New York: Oxford Univ. Press, 1994), 69–70; Meriwether Stuart, "How Were Imperial Portraits Distributed throughout the Roman Empire?" *AJA* 43 (1939): 601–17; Paul Zanker, *Provinzielle Kaiserporträts. Zur Rezeption der Selbstdarstellung des Princeps* (Munich: Bayerischen Akademie der Wissenschaften, 1983); and idem, *The Power of Images*, 297–333.

49. See Tacitus, *Hist.* 3.36 and 4.67. See also Suetonius, *Tib.* 58; and *Codex Theo.* 9.44, which gives those persons who flee for sanctuary to a statue of the emperor ten assured days of security.

50. Fronto, *Ad. M. Caes.* 4.12.4 (trans. LCL 207), cited both in Elsner, *Imperial Rome*, 54, and in Turcan, *The Gods of Ancient Rome*, 136. Note that later Christian emperors promulgated an edict that prohibited imperial images from being excessively beautiful, reserving such glory for representations of the divinity, *Codex Theo.* 15.4.1.

51. See *Codex Theo.* 9.40.17, which authorizes *damnatio* in the case of Eutropius so that such images may not pollute the vision of those who see them; and Elsner, *Imperial Rome*,

22–23. On the practice of *damnatio memoriae* in art and epigraphy see Eric Varner, ed., *From Caligula to Constantine: Tyranny and Transformation in Roman Portraiture* (Atlanta: Michael C. Carlos Museum, 2000).

52. Justin, *1 Apol.* 17 (trans. *ANF* 1:168). See Paul Corby Finney, "The Rabbi and the Coin Portrait (Mark 12.15b, 16): Rigorism Manqué," *JBL* 112 (1993): 629–44.

53. Tertullian, *Apol.* 28–35 passim.

54. Ibid., 33.

55. Minucius Felix, *Oct.* 29.5.

56. Josephus, *Ap.* 2.77–78.

57. Josephus, *B.J.* 2.9.2–3 (169–174); compare *Ant.* 33.32–26; 55–57. On the standards with images of the emperor see Cecil Roth, "An Ordinance against Images in Jerusalem," *HTR* 49 (1956): 169–76; and Carl H. Kraeling, "The Episode of the Roman Standards at Jerusalem," *HTR* 35 (1942), 263–89. Also see Tacitus, *Ann.* 3.36; and *Hist.* 4.62 as sources on the Roman standards.

58. Ibid. *B.J.* 2.10.1–5; compare *Ant.* 18.8.2–9. The text in *B.J.* speaks of more than one statue, while the account in *Ant.* mentions only one.

59. Josephus, *Ap.* 2.77–78, as cited above.

60. Tosefta, *'Abodah Zarah* 5.1; Palestinian Talmud, *'Abodah Zarah* 3.1 (42b); Babylonian Talmud, *'Abodah Zarah* 40b–41a. These texts are cited in Bowersock, "Imperial Cult," nn. 25–27, and referenced to Ephraim E. Urbach, "Rabbinical Laws of Idolatry in the Second and Third Centuries in Light of Archaeological and Historical Facts," *IEJ* 9 (1959): 149–65 and 229–45, esp. 152–53 and 238–39. Also see the more recent work of Gerald. J. Blidstein, "R. Yohanan, Idolatry and Public Privilege," *JSJ* 5 (1974): 154–61.

61. Hippolytus, *Ref.* 9.26.1. This text is noted by Finney, "Rabbi and Coin," 636.

62. Cyprian, *Ep.* 61.2.2, trans. Graeme Clarke, *The Letters of St. Cyprian,* vol. 2. ACW 46 (New York: Newman, 1984), 93. See also *1 Clement* 45:6–7; Tertullian, *Scorp.* 8.7; and *Idol.* 15.10; Cyprian, *Fort.* 2, 11; and *Ep.* 58.5.1; and 67.8.2 and *Laps.* 19; Jerome, *Expl. Dan.* 3.18; Chrysostom, *Stat.* 4.6 and 5.14; Gregory of Nazianzus, *Or. Bas.* 74.

63. See Eusebius, *Vit. Const.* 4.60 and 71; compare also the Arian historian Philostorgius, *Hist.* 3.1, GCS (1972), 28, who claimed that Christians prayed to Constantine as to a god. Philostorgius is noted in Bowersock, "Imperial Cult," 181.

64. Eusebius, *Vit. Const.* 4.15 (trans. *NPNF²* 1:544); compare 3.3. L'Orange doubts that Constantine's portraits actually were shown in this position, with arms upraised, based on the coin images, but rather only looking heavenward; *Apotheosis* 93–94.

65. On the cessation of sacrifices, see *Codex. Theo.* 16.10.2; Eusebius, *Vit. Const.* 4.25.

66. Bowersock, "Imperial Cult," 182.

67. Athanasius, *C. Ar.* 3.23.5 (*NPNF²* 4:396).

68. Basil, *Spir. Sanct.* 18.45 (trans. *NPNF²* 8:47). This text is discussed again in chap. 4. On the other hand, Cyril of Jerusalem, *Cat.* 12.5, argues that since the material image of the emperor is honored, why not so much more the rational image of God (the human being)?

69. Included in the Acts of the Seventh Ecumenical Council: Mansi, *Sacrorum conciliorum nova et amplissima collectio* (Florence, 1759–1798) 12.1013–15 (trans. *NPNF²* 14:535).

70. Theodore the Studite, *Ref.* 2.11, 13.

71. See Ernst Kitzinger, "The Cult of the Image before Iconoclasm," *DOP* 8 (1954): 116–18.

72. See more discussion of the visual portrayal of gods in chap. 3.

73. See discussion in chap. 1.

74. Thomas Mathews has argued that panel paintings of the gods were also produced, some with sliding doors, and were the forerunners of icons, particularly because of their composition (front facing and half or full length). See Thomas F. Mathews, *The Clash of Gods: A Reinterpretation of Early Christian Art,* rev. ed. (Princeton: Princeton Univ. Press, 1999), 178–82.

75. Dio Chrysostom, *Dei cogn.* 44–46. Compare this reticence about innovation to the later Christian icons of the saints (chap. 6).

76. Philosotratus, *Vit. Apoll.* 6.19.

77. Elsner discussed the conflict between omnipresence and spatially localized divinity in ancient polytheism, using the example of the Ephesian Artemis, *Imperial Rome,* 204–5.

78. Plutarch, *Mor.* 167 D (Superstition).

79. Julian, *Frag. Ep.*, 293–294 (trans. LCL 2:310–11).

80. Lucian, *Heracl.* 1.

81. See discussion of this image in Mathews, *Clash of Gods,* 182–83.

82. See discussion in chap. 6.

83. Augustine, *Civ.* 8.23–24, trans. Henry Bettenson (London: Penquin, 1984), 330–37. On the matter of the Hermetic tradition and the role of images in Neoplatonic theurgy, see the brief discussion in chap. 4.

84. Zanker, *The Power of Images*, 230–38.

85. See Turcan, *Gods of Rome*, 141–42.

86. Kleiner, *Roman Sculpture*, 243–44.

87. Ibid., 276–77.

88. Ibid., 280–83.

89. Zanker, *The Power of Images*; Kleiner, *Roman Sculpture,* 326–29.

90. See Mathews, *Clash of Gods*, 106, fig. 81, and 205 n. 16, which helpfully leads the reader to two useful sources on the halo in pre-Christian times and the halo as adopted by the Roman emperor: Marthe Collinet-Guérin, *Histoire du Nimbe, des origins aux temps moderns* (Paris: Nouvelles Éditions latines, 1961); and András Alföldi, "Insignien und Tracht der römischen Kaiser," *RM* 50 (1935): 19–22; 38–41.

91. See the discussion of the iconography of Christ in chap. 6.

92. Paul Orgels, "La premiere vision de Constantin (310) et le temple d'Apollon à Nimes," *Bull Roy Bel* (1948): 179ff., and the account in Lactantius, *Mort.* 55.5–6.

93. Julian, *Helios passim*.

3. The Invisible God and the Visible Image

1. Minucius Felix, *Oct.* 10.2–5, trans. Graeme Clarke, *The Octavius of Marcus Minucius Felix*, ACW 39 (New York: Newman, 1974), 66–67.

2. Ibid., 32.1–2 (trans. slightly adapted, 111–12).

3. Ibid. 18.8, where he seems to be relying on Tertullian's apology or on the writings of other (earlier) apologists who use only negative terms to describe God (Clarke, 260 n. 224).

4. Ibid., 19. See Clarke's annotations on this particular chapter, discussing the ways that Minucius Felix uses the various philosophers and teachers he lists here, 263–72, nn. 230–61.

5. Ibid., 24.10. Minucius Felix also allows Octavius to brand pagan deities as mere humans, only later made into gods (Euhemerism, after the fourth century B.C.E. philosopher who contended that the gods were merely deified kings and heroes); *Oct.* 20–21. Compare Clement, *Prot.* 2.20–21; Tertullian, *Apol.* 10–11; and Athanasius, *C. Gent.* 15. See discussion below, pp. 83–84.

6. Justin, *1 Apol.* 9–10. On the apologists' critique of Greco-Roman art and polytheistic idolatry, see Paul Corby Finney, *The Invisible God: The Earliest Christians on Art* (New York: Oxford Univ. Press, 1994), chaps. 2–3, pp. 15–68.

7. Ibid., 9 (trans. *ANF* 1:165).

8. Ibid., 20.

9. Ibid., 63.

10. Justin, *Dial.* 56 (trans. ANF, 1 223).

11. Since the text that Justin cites is the *Septuagint (*LXX*)*, he notes the use of the Greek words *kyrios* ("Lord") for God and *angeloi* ("angels") for the visitors.

12. Justin, *Dial.* 56.

13. Ibid., 56 cont. In Luke 20:43, Jesus cites this Psalm text. Acts 32:34-35 also does to the same purpose.

14. Ibid., 57–60.

15. Ibid., 127 (trans. *ANF* 1:263).

16. Irenaeus, *Haer.* 1.10.3.

17. Ibid., 4.20.5.

18. Ibid., 4.20.4.

19. Ibid., 4.20.5–12. See also 2.6.1 and 3.11.5.

20. Ibid., 4.20.4–7 (trans. *ANF* 1:488–90).

21. This fulfilled vision might be compared to the interpretation of Isaiah's vision as a fore-sight of Christ in the text of John 12:39-41, where Isaiah is quoted as saying "'he has blinded their eyes and hardened their heart, so that they might not look with their eyes…' because he saw his glory."

22. Irenaeus, *Haer.* 4.20.8–10 and following. Irenaeus continues with this theme, citing the visions of Daniel and the Book of Revelation. See also *Haer.* 4.32.10–11, where he again refers to Isaiah, Daniel, and Zechariah. Note: the belief that Moses' vision of Christ at the transfigu-

ration was the promised sight of God also appears in Tertullian, *Marc.* 22; and *Prax.* 14; as well as in Origen, *Hom. Exod.* 12; and *Comm. Cant.* 2.13.

23. Irenaeus, *Haer.* 4.20.11.

24. Irenaeus, *Epid.* 44–45.

25. Ibid., 47.

26. Irenaeus, *Haer.* 4.7.4 (*ANF* 1:470)

27. Ibid.

28. *Haer.* 4.22.2

29. Tertullian, *Apol.* 12–13 (trans. *ANF* 3:28–9).

30. Tertullian, *Idol.* 4.1–4, quoting Ps 115:3-8.

31. Tertullian, *Apol.* 17.

32. Tertullian, *Marc.* 2.27 (trans. *ANF* 3:318-19). This description of the Word rehearsing the part of human prior to the incarnation appears also in *Prax.* 16. He adds here that humans can more readily accept that God became human in the incarnation, since something similar had happened on these earlier occasions.

33. Tertullian, *Marc.* 3.9 (trans. *ANF* 3:328-9). In his treatise, *Carn. Chr.* (6.3), Tertullian argues against certain disciples of Marcion who taught that Christ might have human flesh without being born since angels have appeared in the flesh "without the intervention of the womb." Tertullian retorts that the difference between Christ and the angels is that Christ descended into flesh with the intention of dying. Angels did not have to die and therefore did not have to be born. But to be capable of death, Christ had to be born.

34. Tertullian, *Carn. Chr.* 3.

35. Tertullian, *Marc.* 5.19.

36. Tertullian, *Prax.* 1 (trans. *ANF* 3:597).

37. Ibid., 14 (trans. *ANF* 3:609).

38. Ibid.

39. Ibid. The translation of 1 Cor 13:12 that I have used here is not the traditional wording but is based on a more literal reading of the text, as suggested by my teacher, Richard Norris. Norris pointed out to me that the use of the term "enigma" or "riddle" was a fairly common trope in ancient rhetoric.

40. Ibid., 15 (trans. *ANF* 3:610).

41. Ibid., 14–15. Compare Clement of Alexandria, *Paed.* 1.7, in which the instructor is the "face that Jacob saw."

42. Clement, *Prot.* 4.1.

43. Ibid., 4.1, cont. (trans. *ANF* 2:184).

44. Ibid., 6. Quotation from Euripides, *Fr.* 1129. See Paul Corby Finney, *The Invisible God: The Earliest Christians on Art* (New York: Oxford Univ. Press, 1994), 44–47. Compare Clement, *Strom.* 5.12–13.

45. Clement, *Strom.* 5.1 (he also cites Exod 33:20; as well as 1 Cor 13:12; and Matt 5:8). See also *Strom.* 1.9.

46. Ibid., 5.11–14.

47. For Athenagoras's arguments regarding the teachings of the philosophers, see *Leg.* 6.

48. Ibid., 17.

49. Ibid., 18.

50. Ibid., 17.

51. Clement, *Strom.* 1.15 (trans. *ANF* 2:315–16). This is quoted later by Eusebius, *Praep. Ev.* 410.

52. Plutarch, *Num.* 8.8. The essential article by Lily Ross Taylor, "Aniconic Worship among the Early Romans," in *Classical Studies in Honor of John C. Rolfe,* ed. G. D. Hadzsits (Philadelphia: Univ. of Pennsylvania Press, 1931), 305–19, provides many of these primary sources.

53. Tertullian, *Apol.* 25.

54. Augustine, *Civ.* 4.31, trans. Henry Bettenson, *The City of God* (London: Penguin, 1972), 175. The treatise of Varro in which this was argued, *Antiquitatem rerum humanarum et divinarum libri* has been lost; see *Civ.* 6.3. Both Numa and Varro are mentioned by Arnobius, but in his treatise Numa is credited with introducing new forms of worship to the Romans with no mention of its lack of images, *Adv. Nat.* 2.12; 7.26; on the aniconism of Varro see *Adv. Nat.* 7.1.

55. Augustine, *Civ.* 7.5, in Bettenson, *City of God*, 261.

56. Taylor, "Aniconic Worship," claims that the earliest temples on the Capitol that had cult images date to the first Etruscan kings, Tarquinius Priscus and Servius Tullius, 306–7.

57. Cicero, *Nat. d.* 1.36.101–2, cited by D. Balch, "The Areopagus Speech: An Appeal to the Stoic Historian Posidonius against Later Stoics and the Epicureans," in *Greeks, Romans, and Christians: Essays in Honor of Abraham J. Malherbe,* ed. D. Balch et al. (Minneapolis: Fortress Press, 1990), 52–79.

58. Balch, "Areopagus Speech," 67–79.

59. Plutarch, *Stoic. rep.* 1034B (trans. LCL [*Moralia* 13.2] 423). Compare Clement, *Strom.* 5.11, and also see Balch, "Areopagus Speech," 67–68, for a discussion of the parallels with Paul's speech.

60. Plotinus, *Enn.* 5.8.1, trans. Stephen Mackenna, *Plotinus, The Enneads* (London: Faber and Faber, 1962), 422–23, translation included in Alain Besançon, *The Forbidden Image: An Intellectual History of Iconoclasm,* trans. J. M Todd (Chicago: Univ. of Chicago Press, 2000), 50–51.

61. Augustine, *Conf.* 11.5.7–11.6.8, trans. Henry Chadwick, *St. Augustine, Confessions* (Oxford: Oxford Univ. Press, 1991), 224.

62. Yochanan Lewy, *Chaldaean Oracles and Theurgy: Mysticism, Magic and Platonism in the Later Roman Empire* (Cairo: Institut français d'archéologie oriental, 1956); and see brief discussion in Besançon, *The Forbidden Image,* 54–56 with good notes.

63. See Joseph Bidez, *Vie de Porphyre: le philosophe néo-platonicien* (Hildesheim: Olms, 1964), appendix I, 143–57. On the care of statues and images, see Porphyry, *Marc.* 14, 16–19.

64. Augustine, *Civ.* 8.23, trans. Bettenson, *City of God,* 331, and cited in chap. 2. Regarding treatises of Hermes Trismegistus, esp. *Asclepius* 23–24, see discussion of sources in André Jean Festugière, *La révélation d'Hermès,* vol. 1: *L'astrologie et les sciences occultes,* (Paris: Lecoffre, 1950);

65. For example, see Clement, *Strom.* 5.5, 12, and 14. Also see Justin, *1 Apol.* 59, and the anonymous writer of the treatise formerly assigned to Justin, known as the "Address to the Greeks." This claim was also made by Tatian and Theophilus and can be found in Jewish apologetic writing as well (see below), which presents Plato as either a student of Moses (having visited Egypt) or merely derivative from him, based on his (Plato's) reading of sources.

66. Justin, *1 Apol.* 63. See the discussion above, pp. 72–73.

67. Justin, *Dial.* 114 (trans. *ANF* 1:256).

68. Josephus, *C. Ap.*, 2.191–192.

69. Tacitus, *Hist.* 5.5.

70. Philo, *Decal.* 66–72. Compare Justin Martyr, *1 Apol.* 20.

71. Philo, *Post.* 4. See also *Fug.* 141.

72. Philo, *Conf.* 134–140.

73. Philo, *Opif.* 23.69.

74. Elliot R. Wolfson, *Through a Speculum that Shines: Vision and Imagination in Medieval Jewish Mysticism* (Princeton: Princeton Univ. Press, 1994), 33.

75. *Mekhilta de-Rabbi Ishmael,* Shirata, 4, quoted in Wolfson, *Speculum,* 33–34.

76. Wolfson, *Speculum,* 39–40.

77. Theophilus, *Auto.* 1.2.

78. Ibid., 1.3 (trans. *ANF* 2:89–90).

79. Ibid., 2.22.

80. Novatian, *Trin.* 6–7.

81. Ibid., 18 (trans. *ANF* 5:628).

82. Ibid., 18–19.

83. Ibid., 18 (trans. *ANF* 5:628).

84. Origen, *Princ.* 1.1.4–5; compare with Minucius Felix, who proclaims that God is "nothing but mind, reason, and spirit," *Oct.* 19.

85. Origen, *Princ.*, 1.2.7–8.

86. In *C. Cels.* 6.4, Origen offers a critique of the theory that contemplation of sensible things leads to the transcendence of them to those things that are comprehended by the intellect alone.

87. Ibid.

88. Origen, *Princ.* 1.2.8, trans George William Butterworth, *Origen: On First Principles* (Glouster, Mass.: Peter Smith, 1973), 21–22. The editor points out that Jerome later refers to this passage in *Ep. ad Avitum* 2.

89. Ibid., 1.2.8, cont.

90. Ibid.

91. Ibid., 2.4.3.

92. Ibid., 2.4.3, cont., trans. Butterworth, *Origen,* 98–99 (emphasis mine).

93. Ibid.

94. The Greek verbs for "knowing" in these lines are not exactly the same. John 1:18 has the verbs for see (*horaē*) and interpret or narrate (*exēgeomai*), while in John 14:9 the pair is see (*horaō*) and know (*ginōskō*).

95. Origen, *Princ.* 2.4.3, trans. Butterworth *Origen,* 99.

96. Origen, *Hom Gen.* 4. In regard to his interpretation of the place name "Mambre" meaning "vision," see Ronald E. Heine, *Origen, Homilies on Genesis and Exodus* (Washington, D.C.: Catholic Univ. Press, 1982), appendix 2, 390–91.

97. Origen, *Comm. Cant.* 2.4.

98. Ibid., 2.13.

99. Origen, *Hom. Gen.* 1.13.

100. Origen, *C. Cels.* 6.4.

101. Origen, *Hom. Gen..* 13.4.

102. Origen, *Princ.* 1.6.4.

103. Origen, *Hom. Gen.*13.4.

104. Origen, *Princ.* 1.6.4, trans. Butterworth, *Origen,* 57.

4. Seeing the Divine in the Fourth and Early Fifth Centuries

1. Athanasius, *Inc.* 14 (trans. *NPNF²* 4:43).

2. Athanasius, *C. Gent.* 2.34 (trans. *NPNF²* 4:22). Other Christian writers compare the work of the artist to the gradual perfecting of the soul or the colors of an artist's palette as being made up of virtues; see Gregory of Nyssa, *Anima et res.*, and John Chrysostom, *Hom. 1 Cor.* 13.3; *Catech. illum.* 2.3.; *Hom. Heb.* 17.2; as well as the *Acts of John* 28–29 quoted above. Margaret Mitchell provided many of these references in her article, "The Archetypal Image: John Chrysostom's Portraits of Paul," *JR* 75 (1995): 15–43, esp. 28–29 and nn. 55–57.

3. Origen, *Prin.* 1.2.8.

4. Athanasius, *Inc.* 14.4, cont.

5. Ibid., 15.

6. Ibid., 16 (trans. *NPNF²* 4:43–44).

7. See Augustine's nuanced analysis of the visible works of Christ as showing forth the invisible nature of God, however: *Tract. Ev. Jo.* 24.1–2. In this same homily, Augustine contrasts seeing pictures with reading texts.

8. Arnobius, *Adv. nat.* 6.16 (trans. *ANF* 6:512).

9. Basil of Caesarea, *Spir. Sanc.* 18.45 (trans. *NPNF²* 8:47).

10. Ibid., 18.47.

11. Basil, *Adv. Eun.* 1.14. Epiphanius, in his refutation, quotes Eunomius as saying that he knew God in complete clarity and in fact did not know himself better than he knew God; *Pan.* 76.4.1.

12. Gregory of Nyssa, *Ad Eun. Lib.* 2 (trans. *NPNF²* 5:308–9).

13. Gregory Nazianzus, *Theo. Or.* 2.4 (trans. *NPNF²* 7:289–90).

14. Ibid., 4.20 (trans. *NPNF²* 7:316–17).

15. Gregory of Nyssa, *Vita Moses* 230–36, trans. Abraham Malherbe and Everett Ferguson, *Gregory of Nyssa: The Life of Moses*, CWS (New York: Paulist, 1978), 114–15.

16. John Chrysostom, *Incom.* 3. See the introduction of Jean Daniélou to the *Sources chrétiennes* edition of these homilies (Anne Marie Malingrey and Robert Flacelière, *Jean Chrysostome sur l'incompréhensibilité de Dieu*, vol.1: Homélies 1-V, SC 28 bis (Paris:Éditions du Cerf, 1970), as well as a helpful analysis of these sermons in Thomas Kopecek, *A History of Neo-Arianism* (Cambridge: Philadelphia Patristic Foundation, 1979), 541–42. See also the excellent (forthcoming) work of Angela Russell Christman, *"What Did Ezekiel See?" Christian Exegesis of Ezekiel's Vision of the Chariot from Irenaeus to Gregory the Great* (Boston: Brill USA, 2005). Christman's work, still an unpublished manuscript at the time of this writing, provides a detailed examination of patristic exegesis of the theophanies and visions of God in the third and fourth centuries.

17. John Chrysostom, *Incom.* 3.78–83.

18. Evagrius, *Or.* 66, trans. John E. Bamberger, *Evagrius Ponticus, The Praktikos and Chapters on Prayer* (Kalamazoo, Mich.: Cistercian, 1981), 66.

19. See Christman, *"What Did Ezekiel See?"* for a discussion of Theodoret's writing on this subject.

20. See Andrew Louth, *The Origins of the Christian Mystical Tradition: From Plato to Denys* (Oxford: Oxford Univ. Press, 1981), chap. 8, "Denys the Areopagite," 159–78. Note also that John of Damascus cites Pseudo-Dionysius as a source, summarizing a passage from the *Cel. hier.* to say that visible things are corporeal models that offer a vague apprehension of invisible and incorporeal things, *1 Apol.* 10-11 and *3 Apol.* 21. Compare Theodore the Studite, *Ref.* 2.11, who quotes Pseudo-Dionysius, *Ecc. hier.* 4.3.1: "Truth is in the likeness, the archetype in the image; each in the other except for the difference of essence."

21. Pseudo-Dionysus, *Myst. Theo.* 1.1000 C–1001 A. In general, but especially on this use of the Moses paradigm, see Paul Rorem, "The Uplifting Spirituality of Pseudo-Dionysius," in *Christian Spirituality: Origins to the Twelfth Century*, ed. B. McGinn et al. (New York: Crossroad, 1987), 132–51 (esp. 143–44).

22. Pseudo-Dionysius, *Div. nom.* 8.3.869 C–872 B , trans. Louth, *Origins of the Christian Mystical Tradition*, 168.

23. Socrates, *Hist.* 6.7. See Mark Delcogliano, "Situating Arapion's Sorrow: The Anthropomorphite Controversy as the Historical and Theological Context of Cassian's Tenth Conference on Pure Prayer," *CisSt* 38.4 (2003): 377–421, for an excellent discussion of this topic.

24. Ibid.; also, Epiphanius, *Pan.* 70; and Jerome, *Pamm.* 11, which refers to the anthropomorphite position as "that foolish heresy."

25. John Cassian, *Coll.* 10.3, trans. Colm Luibheid, *John Cassian, Conferences*, CWS (New York: Paulist, 1985), 127.

26. See discussion above, p. 85.

27. Augustine, *Serm.* 198.17, trans. Edmund Hill, *The Works of St. Augustine*, I.3, *Sermons* (Newly Discovered Sermons), ed. J. E. Rotelle (Brooklyn: New City, 1997), 193–94. The columns to which Augustine refers are a bit mysterious. Hill suggests that Christians may have been kissing the columns as they entered the church.

28. Ibid., 31.

29. Augustine, *Tract. Ev. Jo.* 24.2.

30. Augustine, *Ep.* 92.

31. Augustine, *Ep.* 120.7 (an answer to *Ep.* 119).

32. Ibid., 11–13.

33. Augustine, *Ep.* 147.20, trans. Roland J. Teske, S.J., *The Works of Saint Augustine* II.2, *Letters 100–155*, ed. B. Ramsey (Hyde Park, N.Y.: New City, 2003), 329.

34. Ibid. 18, Teske trans., 327–28.

35. Ibid., 20.

36. Ibid., 23–25.

37. Ibid., 37, Teske trans., 339. The paragraph contains a summary of previous chapters. Augustine also credits Ambrose for some of this teaching. He refers indirectly to the anthropomorphite controversy in chap. 49.

38. Augustine, *Tract. Ev. Jo.* 17–19.3. Compare *Fid. symb.* 7.14.

39. Eusebius, *Dem. Ev.* 5.9.

40. Eusebius, *Comm. Isa.* 41. See Michael Hollerich, *Eusebius of Caesarea's Commentary on Isaiah: Christian Exegesis in the Age of Constantine* (Oxford: Clarendon, 1999).

41. Eusebius, *Dem. Ev.* 5. 14 (the entire book, however, addresses this matter).

42. Augustine, *Trin.*, 2.4.20–22, trans. Edmund Hill, *The Works of St. Augustine*, I.5, *The Trinity*, ed. J. E. Rotelle (Brooklyn: New City, 1991), 111.

43. Ibid., 2.4.32, Hill trans., 120. In the next paragraphs, Augustine evaluates Daniel's vision of the Ancient of Days and the Son of Man.

44. Augustine, *Civ.* 22.29, trans. Henry Bettenson, *Augustine, City of God* (London: Penguin, 1972), 1087.

45. Athanasius, *Inc.* 18–19.

46. See Hans Belting, *Image and Presence: A History of the Image before the Era of Art*, trans. E. Jephcott (Chicago: Univ. of Chicago Press, 1994), 195.

47. Eusebius, *Dem. Ev.* 5.9, trans. William J. Ferrar, *Eusebius, The Proof of the Gospel*, vol. 1 (Grand Rapids: Baker, 1981), 253–54. The text certainly seems to contradict Eusebius's presumed condemnation of images (see chap. 1, pp. 23–25). In *3 Apol.* 26, John offers a distinctly different viewpoint from Eusebius, however: "Abraham did not see the divine nature, for no person has ever yet seen God, but he saw an image of God and fell down and worshiped."

48. Eusebius, *Dem. ev.* 5.9.

49. Suzanne Spain, "'The Promised Blessing': The Iconography of the Mosaics of S. Maria Maggiore," *AB* 61 (1979): 518–40. See discussion of this theory in chap. 6.

50. Ibid., 535–39. Spain thus identifies the woman in gold who appears four times on the triumphal arch mosaics (the adoration of the magi, the annunciation, the vision at the betrothal of Mary and Joseph, and the meeting of David, Isaiah, and Christ) with Sarah, rather than Mary in these programs, and argues that Abraham (his face badly restored) stands with her throughout.

51. See Herbert L. Kessler, *Spiritual Seeing: Picturing God's Invisibility in Medieval Art* (Philadelphia: Univ. of Pennsylvania Press, 2000), 3–6, for other examples of the hand of God in Christian and Jewish art.

52. Gregory of Nyssa, *Deit.*, trans. in C. Mango, *The Art of the Byzantine Empire 312–1453: Sources and Documents* (Toronto: Univ. of Toronto Press, 1972), 34.

53. Although the hand is usually interpreted as the hand of God, the biblical text actually says that an angel or messenger spoke to Abraham, telling him not to slay his son. Thus, if the iconography were (arguably) more closely based upon the text than Gregory's interpretation, the identification of the hand becomes more complicated.

54. Viewers often remark on the Trinitarian aspects of the scene of Jesus' baptism in the dome of the Arian Baptistery in Ravenna, where the imposing figure of the river god seems to suggest the presence of the Father.

55. Paulinus, *Ep.* 32.10, trans. P .G. Walsh, *Letters of Paulinus of Nola,* vol. 2, ACW 36 (Westminster, Md.: Newman, 1967), 145. Compare the description of the imagery in the basilica at Fundi, later in the letter 32.17: a lamb (for Christ), which is being "haloed" by a dove (Holy Spirit), and crowned by the "Father from a ruddy cloud."

56. Cain and Abel presenting their offerings to God appear on other early Christian sarcophagi, including one that shows the arrests of Peter and Paul (see fig. 96, p. 188).

57. See Robin Jensen, "The Trinity and the Economy of Salvation," *JECS* 7 (1999): 527–46, for arguments about different identities of these figures.

58. This is the interpretation of Irenaeus, *Haer.* 2.2.4–5 and 5.6.

59. See André Grabar, *Christian Iconography: A Study of Its Origins* (Princeton: Princeton Univ. Press, 1968), 113, who cites some ancient Semitic legends that I have been unable to locate. The identity of the person standing behind Mary is troublesome, but, based upon a similar image on a funerary plaque in the Museo Pio Cristiano, it seems reasonable to identify him as Balaam.

60. See the Armenian Infancy Gospel, chap. 11.19–20, French trans. Paul Peeters, *Évangiles Apocryphes II: L'Évangile de l'Enfance* (Paris: A. Picard, 1911–14), 143–44, cited in Thomas F. Mathews, *The Clash of Gods: A Reinterpretation of Early Christian Art,* rev. ed. (Princeton: Princeton Univ. Press, 1999), 139, and nn. 43, 208. Such a text is similar to the *Menologion*, which recounts a legend in which one of the magi saw Christ as a baby, the second as a thirty-year-old man, and the third as an old man (that is, the "three ages of man" tradition). This is similar to the traditional interpretation that the gifts of the magi (gold for royalty, incense for high priest or god, and myrrh for the suffering and dying one) project three aspects of Christ—see Irenaeus *Haer.* 3.9; Origen, *Hom. Num.* 13.5; Leo, *Serm.* 33.34, 36; and Fulgentius of Ruspe, *Ep. Ferrandus* 20. See also Robin Jensen, "Witnessing the Divine," *BR* 17.6 (2001): 24–31, 59.

61. John of Damascus, *2 Apol.* 5, trans. Andrew Louth, *John of Damascus, Three Treatises on the Divine Images* (Crestwood, N.Y.: St. Vladimir's Seminary Press, 2003), 61–62. Here John cites Gregory Nazianzen, *Hom.* 28.13.

62. Ibid., 2.7–8, trans. Louth, 64–65.

5. Portraits of the Incarnate One

1. Compare Matt 11:27 and Luke 10:22.

2. Note Paulinus of Nola's description of his apse mosaic, however, and the frequent use of the lamb as the symbol of Christ in the art of the fourth to sixth centuries. At the end of the seventh century (ca. 690), the eighty-second canon of the Council of Trullo (the Quinisext Council, Mansi 11.977–80) finally discourages the use of the lamb as a symbol for Christ since the human image of the savior was more effective in communicating the divine incarnation and expressing Christ's life in the flesh. See also Theodore the Studite, *2 Ref.* 38, which refers to this canon.

3. From Cyril Mango, *The Art of the Byzantine Empire 312–1453: Sources and Documents* (Toronto: Univ. of Toronto Press, 1986), 16–17; for discussion of this as a possible forgery from the eighth century see chap. 1.

4. Justin, *Dial.* 14.

5. Origen, *C. Cels.* 6.75–77 (trans. *ANF* 4:607). Compare the texts of Clement, *Paed.* 3.1 and Justin, *1 Apol.* 50, which also cite this passage from Isaiah. Clement also explains here that true beauty is not visible to the eye.

6. John Chrysostom, *Exp. Ps.* 44.3 (PG 55:185–86).

7. Text and discussion in Ernst von Dobschütz, *Christusbilder: Untersuchungen zur christlichen Legende* (Leipzig: Hinrichs, 1899), supplement 308–29, with critical discussion of the text (Latin text on 319), referring to J. A. Fabricio, *Codex Apocryphus* (Hamburg, 1703), 1st part, 301–2.

8. Epiphanius, *Test.*, text and trans. in Mango, *Art of the Byzantine Empire*, 41–42, from Georgije Ostrogorsky, ed., *Studien zur Geschichte des byzantinischen Bilderstreites* (Breslau: Marcus, 1929), 67, fragment 2. As Mango points out, the authenticity of the Epiphanius fragments has been questioned. See discussion in Mary Charles Murray, "Art and the Early Church," *JTS* 28 (1977): 336–38.

9. This is based on an early version of the story as recounted by Eusebius in *Hist.* 1.13, where one may also read a version of the letter from Abgar to Jesus itself. Eusebius claims to be translating from a Syriac document. Another mention of correspondence between Abgar and Christ comes from Egeria, *Pereg.* 19. Neither Eusebius nor Egeria mentions a portrait tradition, but Eusebius (or his source) does say that Abgar saw a "wonderful vision on the face of Thaddeus" (*Hist.* 1.13.12).

10. The earliest version of the legend that mentions a miraculous image (and describes a painted portrait) is contained in the apocryphal doctrine of Addai (ca. 400); text and trans. George Howard, *The Teaching of Addai* (Chico, Calif.: Scholars, 1991), 9–11; also as "The Abgar Legend" in Edgar Hennecke, *New Testament Apocrypha*, ed. Wilhelm Schneemelcher (Philadelphia: Westminster, 1964), 1:437–44. A later, sixth-century version, claims that Christ washed his face and left his facial likeness on the towel; see *The Acts of the Holy Apostle Thaddeus*, in *NPNF²* 8:558–59. John of Damascus records the detail of the difficulty of painting Jesus' face (*Fide orth.* 4.16), which is extended in Jacobus de Voragine's *Golden Legend*, to include the episode where Jesus then takes the painter's canvas and puts it to his face to leave the imprint of his appearance—having good eyes, a strong brow, and a long face with straight features indicating maturity; trans. Granger Ryan and Helmut Ripperger, *The Golden Legend of Jacobus de Voragine* (London: Longmans , Green, 1941), 634. See also Germanos, *Sermon before Leo the Isaurian* (PG 110:920), or an even later tradition (tenth century) from the court of Constantine Porphyrogenitos (PG 113:423–54); text and English trans. in Ian Wilson, *The Shroud of Turin* (Garden City, N.Y.: Doubleday, 1978), 238–39 (Appendix C).

11. The bibliography on the *Mandylion* and the Abgar legend is extensive. One may consult Dobschütz, *Christusbilder*, 120–96, as one of the earliest studies of the textual tradition and then Averil Cameron, "The History of the Image of Edessa: The Telling of a Story," in *Okeanos: Essays Presented to I. Sevcenko*, Harvard Ukrainian Studies 7 (Cambridge: Harvard Univ. Press, 1983), 80–94 ; see Hans Belting, *Likeness and Presence: A History of the Image before the Era of Art*, trans. E. Jephcott (Chicago: Univ. of Chicago Press, 1994), 208–24; Herbert L. Kessler, *Spiritual Seeing: Picturing God's Invisibility in Medieval Art* (Philadelphia: Univ. of Pennsylvania Press, 2000), 70–87; Stephen Runciman, "Some Remarks on the Image of Edessa," *Cambridge Historical Journal* 3 (1931): 238–52; Hans J. W. Drijvers, "The Image of Edessa in the Syriac Tradition," and Averil Cameron, "The Mandylion and Byzantine Iconoclasm," in *The Holy Face and the Paradox of Representation*, ed. Herbert Kessler and Gerhard Wolf (Bologna: Nuova Alfa, 1998), 13–54.

12. One rather interesting theory suggests that the actual *Mandylion* later turned up in Turin as the shroud—see Wilson, *The Shroud of Turin*; R. Drews, *In Search of the Shroud of Turin: New Light on Its History and Origins* (Totowa, N.J.: Rowman & Allanheld, 1984); and the critique of such a theory in Averil Cameron, "The Sceptic and the Shroud," Inaugural Lecture, King's College, London (1980), in *Continuity and Change in Sixth-Century Byzantium* (London: Variorum Reprints, 1981).

13. See Belting, *Likeness and Presence*, 218–24; J. Hamburger, *The Visual and the Visionary: Art and Female Spirituality in Late Medieval Germany* (New York: Zone, 1998), chap. 7, "Vision and the Veronica," 317–82; Gerhard Wolf, "From Mandylion to Veronica," in Kessler and Wolf, eds., *Holy Face and the Paradox of Representation*, 166–79.

14. Irenaeus, *Haer.* 1.25.6, see discussion in chap. 1. Note a parallel story regarding another miraculous image of Christ, the image of Camuliana in Mango, *Art of the Byzantine Empire*, 114–15.

15. These questions are examined in Kessler, *Spiritual Seeing*, chap. 4: "Configuring the Invisible by Copying the Holy Face," 64–87. See also Leonid Ouspensky and Vladimir Lossky, *The Meaning of Icons*, trans. G. E. H. Palmer and E. Kadloubovsky (Crestwood, N.Y.: St. Vladimir's Seminary Press, 1989), 37, where Ouspensky takes up the problem of variations in copies of the same prototype, claiming the "defect of resemblances does not cause a lack of connection with the prototype, or a lack of veneration towards him [the saint portrayed]." Ouspensky here quotes Theodore the Studite, *2 Ref.* 3, sec. 5: "Veneration is not shown to an icon inasmuch as it falls short of resembling the prototype, but inasmuch as it represents a likeness to it."

16. According to legend, this image was made by Nicodemus, whose sculpture of the crucified Christ was miraculously finished by angels. It washed up on the coast of Italy near Lucca after eighth-century Iconoclasts tossed it into the sea near Jerusalem. See short discussion and bibliography on this image in Belting, *Likeness and Presence,* 304–5 n. 37. See also Neil MacGregor, *Seeing Salvation: Images of Christ in Art* (New Haven: Yale Univ. Press, 2000), 96–98, and a reproduction of the Lucca images, fig. 30. MacGregor also discusses the *Mandylion* and Veronica images in his work.

17. Augustine, *Trin.* 8.4.7, trans. Edmund Hill, *The Works of St. Augustine,* pt. 1, vol. 5, *The Trinity,* ed. J. E. Rotelle (Brooklyn: New City, 1991), 246–47.

18. *Acts of Peter* 20, trans. from Hennecke and Schneemelcher, *New Testament Apocrypha,* 2:302–3.

19. *Acts of Thomas,* 153.

20. *Acts of John,* 87–89, trans. Hennecke and Schneemelcher, *New Testament Apocrypha,* 2:225–26.

21. Ibid.

22. *Apocryphon of John,* 2.4–8.

23. Origen, *C. Cels.* 2.64 (trans. *ANF* 4:457). Compare his arguments in 6.77: "But how can Celsus and the enemies of the divine Word, and those who have not examined the doctrines of Christianity in the spirit of truth, know the meaning of the different appearances of Jesus? And I refer also to the different stages of his life, and to any actions performed by him before his sufferings and after his resurrection from the dead."

24. Cyril of Jerusalem, *Cat.* 10.5, trans. Anthony A. Stephenson and Leo McCauley, *The Works of Saint Cyril of Jerusalem,* vol. 1, FOC (Washington, D.C.: Catholic Univ. Press, 1969), 198.

25. Henri Stern, "Les mosaiques de l'église de sainte-Constance à Rome," *DOP* 12 (1958): 157–218. See the recent reconstruction of this monument and its mosaics by R. Ross Holloway, *Constantine and Rome* (New Haven: Yale University Press, 2004), 103; and K.B. Rasmussen, "Tradition Legis," *Cah.Arch.* 47 (1999), 5–37.

26. Regarding the coexistence of both types (bearded and beardless), see Friedrich Deichmann, *Einführung in die christliche Archäologie* (Darmstadt: Wissenschaftliche Buchgesellschaft, 1983), 149 and 164; and Erich Dinkler, *Christus und Askelepios*, SHAW.PH (Heidelberg: Winter, 1980), 28–29.

27. This is the main thesis of Thomas F. Mathews, *The Clash of Gods: A Reinterpretation of Early Christian Art*, rev. ed. (Princeton: Princeton Univ. Press, 1999).

28. Clement, *Prot.* 11; and see Robin Jensen, *Understanding Early Christian Art* (London: Routledge, 2000), 42–44. Probably unrelated, but interestingly, the image of Sol also appears in the zodiac wheel of the synagaogue pavement at Hammath Tiberius.

29. Two prominent exceptions to this are the later mosaics in the two Ravenna baptisteries (see discussion below). By contrast, Christian art does show both Adam and Daniel as nude; Daniel especially appears as the classic hero-type. Against the association of Jesus with Apollo is Paul Zanker, *The Mask of Socrates: The Image of the Intellectual in Antiquity*, trans. A. Shapiro (Berkeley: Univ. of California Press, 1995), 299. Zanker argues that Apollo's beauty is best shown in his nude body (and Jesus is not shown nude). Zanker opts instead for "the tradition of romanticized portraits of young men with long hair of the second century A.D." and specifies the heroic images of Alexander, Achilles, and the image of the *Genius Populi Romani*. He also suggests (probably having Irenaeus's statement in mind, but mentioning no particular evidence for this unsupported statement) that the beautiful youth image was an invention of the Gnostics, 299.

30. Justin, *1 Apol.* 21–23 (trans. *ANF* 1:170–71); see also Justin, *Dial.* 69.3. For more discussion on the problem of parallels between Jesus and the "sons of Jupiter" in the early Christian period, see an important article by David Aune, "Heracles and Christ: Heracles Imagery in the Christology of Early Christianity," in *Greeks, Romans, and Christians, Essays in Honor of Abraham J. Malherbe,* ed. D. Balch et al. (Minneapolis: Fortress Press, 1990), 3–19.

31. See the discussion of Old Testament types in Jensen, *Understanding Early Christian Art,* 68–77.

32. See Justin, *1 Apol.* 26, and Mathews, *Clash of Gods,* chap. 3, "The Magician," 54–91 (with bibliography on this subject).

33. On this gesture, see Lucien DeBruyne, "L'imposition des mains dans l'art chrétien ancien," *RivAC* 20 (1943): 113–266.

34. These parallels are noted by Justin, *1 Apol.* 21.

35. See Zanker, *Mask of Socrates,* 289–92, although he seems to see this iconographic type (Christ as philosopher) as more extensive than I do, and he extends it to the nonbearded "teacher" types as well.

36. Mathews, *Clash of Gods,* 69–72.

37. Ibid., 109–11. See also Zanker, *Mask of Socrates,* 310–11.

38. This is the thesis of Mathews, *Clash of Gods,* see esp. chapter 3, "Larger than Life," 92–114. Note Zanker's objection to this identification, which he attributes to the work of Dinkler and others, *Mask of Socrates,* 300, n. 51 (392).

39. Well demonstrated by Mathews, *Clash of Gods,* 98–103.

40. Taken from Mango, *Art of the Byzantine Empire,* 40–41, who gives the source as Theodorus Lector, *Hist.* 1.15 (PG 86:173), and then as quoted by John of Damascus (PG 86:221). Also cited by Mathews, *Clash of Gods,* 186; and Gilbert Dagron, "Holy Images and Likeness," *DOP* 45 (1991): 29–30. J. Breckenridge defines this "authentic" type as the Semitic type, and shows its differences in early Byzantine coinage. See James Breckenridge, *The Numismatic Iconography of Justinian II (685–695) (705–711 A.D.),* Numismatic Notes and Monographs (New York: American Numismatic Society, 1959), 46–62.

41. Augustine, *Enarrat. Ps.* 133.6. Compare Clement of Alexandria, *Paed.* 3.11, which also cites this line from Ps 133, where he urges men not to shave, since beards give their faces dignity and "paternal respect." Also noted by Zanker, *Mask of Socrates,* 290.

42. See the discussion of this progression in Richard Brilliant, *Roman Art from the Republic to Constantine* (London: Phaidon, 1974), 179–82, and discussion in chap. 2, pp. 39–40.

43. An essential study of the Christian monuments of Ravenna was by Friedrich Deichmann, *Ravenna: Haupstade des spätantiken Abenlandes,* 3 vols. (Weisbaden: Steiner, 1969–1989).

44. For a general introduction to the political and religious context of Ravenna in this time, see Mark J. Johnson, "Towards a History of Theodoric's Building Program," *DOP* 42 (1988): 73–96; and Otto von Simpson's now classic work, *Sacred Fortress: Byzantine Art and Statecraft in Ravenna* (Princeton: Princeton Univ. Press, 1987); and Carl Otto Nordström, *Ravennastudien: Ideengeschichte und ikonographische Untersuchungen über die Mosaiken von Ravenna* (Stockholm: Almquist and Wiksell, 1953).

45. On this building see Giuseppe Bovini, *Sant'Apollinare Nuovo in Ravenna* (Milan: Silvana Editoriale d'arte, 1961).

46. Neil MacGregor's attempt to resolve this was unsatisfactory, since he cited Nestorian Christology rather than Arian Christology and argued that the beardless Christ represented more the divine nature (since he was working wonders and miracles), while the bearded Christ showed the human nature (since he suffered in his human nature according to Nestorius); *Seeing Salvation,* 79–83.

47. On the baptistery of the Orthodox, see the basic work of Spiro Kostof, *The Orthodox Baptistery of Ravenna* (New Haven: Yale Univ. Press, 1965).

48. See Robin Jensen, "What Are Pagan River Gods Doing at Scenes of Jesus' Baptism?" *BR* 9.1 (1993):35–41, 54–55.

49. Kostof, *The Orthodox Baptistery,* 87.

50. Origen, *Comm. Matt.* 100 (PG 13:756); see *Acts of John* 90; *Acts of Peter* 20 as well.

51. John Chrysostom, *Hom. Matt. 56.* This was also the moment when Moses finally "saw God," according to Irenaeus, Tertullian, and others; see discussion in chap. 3.

52. See the very interesting and helpful discussion of this mosaic and the motif of the transfiguration in Jaš Elsner, *Art and the Roman Viewer: The Transformation of Art from the Pagan World to Christianity* (Cambridge: Cambridge Univ. Press, 1995), 99–104, 111–23.

53. Gregory of Nazianzus, *Theo. Orat.* 37.3 (trans. NPNF² 7:339).

54. Elsner refers to this image as an "exemplum of the act of spiritual viewing" and a portrayal of mystical vision, *Art and the Roman Viewer,* 112–14.

55. Epistle of Eusebius to Constantia, trans. Mango, *Art of the Byzantine Empire,* 17.

56. See Daniel Sahas, *Icon and Logos: Sources in Eighth-Century Iconoclasm* (Toronto: Univ. of Toronto Press, 1986), 134–43.

57. Athanasius, *Inc.* 8.

58. Ibid., 14 (trans. *NPNF²* 4:43); also cited in chap. 4.

59. Ibid., 17–18.

60. John Chrysostom, *Catech. illum.* 12.23–24, trans. P. W. Harkins, *Baptismal Instructions*, ACW 31 (New York: Newman, 1963), 179–80. An interesting discussion on colors and the artist's work of mixing them and so forth appears in Gregory of Nyssa, *Anima et res.* (in *NPNF²* 5:445).

61. Leo, *Tome*, 3.

62. See note 17, p. 216.

6. Early Portraits of the Saints and the Question of Likeness

1. John of Damascus has an interesting defense of saints' portraits as added to images of Christ or Mary, *1 Apol.* 19. For an excellent and general introduction to this topic, see Cynthia Hahn, "Seeing and Believing: The Construction of Sanctity in Early-Medieval Saints' Shrines," *Speculum* 72 (1997):1079–106.

2. See chap. 1, pp. 27–28.

3. On the use of colors as symbols for virtues, see chap. 1, n. 60.

4. See Hans Achelis, *Die Katakomben von Neapel* (Leipzig: Hiersemann, 1936), 6, 48, 68, and pl. 38. The Proculus arcosolium is discussed here also, 48, 62–63, and pl. 27. See also Umberto Fasola, *Le catacombe di S. Gennaro a Capodimonte* (Rome: Editalia, 1975), 73 and 93; and discussion by Hans Belting, *Likeness and Presence: A History of the Image before the Era of Art*, trans. E. Jephcott (Chicago: Univ. of Chicago Press, 1994), 82.

5. The identities of all the figures in these frescoes are much disputed. See discussion of all these paintings, with helpful footnotes, in Belting, *Likeness and Presence*, 82.

6. The difficulties with identification of the figures in the paintings are matched by the controversy over the site itself. See the helpful summary of the problem in Lucy Grig's forthcoming work, *Making Martyrs in Late Antiquity* (London: Duckworth, 2004), chap. 6.

7. An edict of Gratian, Valentian, and Theodosius I forbade the transfer of a buried body to another place, along with the selling of a martyr's relics. The same edict encouraged the building or elaboration of a martyrium at the site of a saint's burial: *Codex Theo.* 9.17.7.

8. Paulinus, *Carm.* 27.542, trans. Patrick G. Walsh, *The Poems of Paulinus of Nola*, ACW 40 (New York: Newman, 1975), 290–91.

9. Paulinus, *Ep.* 32.2–3, trans. Patrick G. Walsh, *Letters of St. Paulinus of Nola*, ACW 36 (Westminster, N.Y.: Newman, 1967), 135–36.

10. Ibid., 3–4.

11. On the practice of *ekphrasis* in the ancient world, see Jaš Elsner, *Art and the Roman Viewer: The Transformation of Art from the Pagan World to Christianity* (Cambridge: Cambridge Univ. Press, 1995), 21–48, with bibliography.

12. See the forthcoming work of Grig, *Making Martyrs*, for an important discussion of this ancient practice.

13. John Chrysostom, *Hom. encom. in Melet.* (PG 50:516), also cited by Cyril Mango, *The Art of the Byzantine Empire 312–1453: Sources and Documents* (Toronto: Univ. of Toronto Press, 1986), 39–40.

14. Ps. Basil, *Hom.* 17 (PG 31:489), trans. Mango, *The Art of the Byzantine Empire*, 37. In another place, Basil urges one who is anxious to be perfect to gaze upon the lives of saints as if upon living and moving statues and imitate their virtue; *Ep.* 2.3.

15. Gregory of Nyssa, *Laud. Theod.* (PG 46:737), trans. Mango, *Art of the Byzantine Empire*, 36–37.

16. Basil, *Hom.* 19 (PG 31:507–8). An eighth- or ninth-century wall painting depicting these martyrs is in an oratory of the church of Santa Maria Antiqua in the Roman Forum.

17. Asterius, as cited by Mango, *Art of the Byzantine Empire*, 37–38.

18. Prudentius's *Peri.*, text and trans. in CCSL 126, ed. M. P. Cunningham (Turnhout, 1966), l. On Prudentius's work see these helpful books: Anne-Marie Palmer, *Prudentius on the Martyrs* (New York: Oxford Univ. Press, 1989); and Michael J. Roberts, *Poetry and the Cult of the Martyrs: The Liber Peristephanon of Prudentius* (Ann Arbor: Univ. of Michigan Press, 1993).

19. Prudentius, *Peri.* 9.9–12.

20. Ibid., 11.125–34.

21. See discussion in Roberts, *Poetry and the Cult of the Martyrs,* 138 n. 14; also see the discussion of Grig, *Making Martyrs,* chap. 6.

22. Augustine, *Serm.* 316.5, also noted by Roberts, *Poetry and the Cult of the Martyrs,* 138, n. 14.

23. Fortunatus, *Carm.* 10.6.92. See Raymond Van Dam, *Saints and Their Miracles in Late Antique Gaul* (Princeton: Princeton Univ. Press, 1993), 130–5; and Herbert L. Kessler, "Pictorial Narrative and Church Mission in Sixth-Century Gaul," in his *Studies in Pictorial Narrative* (London: Pindar, 1994), 1–32.

24. Gregory I, *Ep.* 9.105; 11.13.

25. As cited above, note 13: John Chrysostom, *Hom. encom. in Melet.*

26. Epiphanius, *Test.,* text and trans. in Mango, *Art of the Byzantine Empire,* 41, from Georgije Ostrogorsky, ed., *Studien zur Geschichte des byzantinischen Bilderstreites* (Breslau: Marcus, 1929), 67. See discussion below of the question of authenticity of the fragments of Epiphanius.

27. Eusebius, *Hist.* 7.18; see discussion in chap. 1, p. 25.

28. Augustine, *Cons. ev.* 1.10.16.

29. On the double apostolic foundation of Rome, see Irenaeus, *Haer.* 3.3.2. A fairly lengthy study of the iconography of Peter and Paul was published by J. M. Huskinson, *Concordia Apostolorum: Christian Propaganda at Rome in the Fourth and Fifth Centuries,* BAR International Series 148 (Oxford: B.A.R., 1982).

30. Augustine, *Serm.* 352.4. A study of this insertion into the *Acts of Peter* (text and its transmission), along with its various problems, may be found in *Acta Apostolorum Apocrypha* I, ed. R. A. Lipsius (Hildesheim: Olms, 1959), 1–22. See also Robin Jensen, "Moses Imagery in Jewish and Christian Art," in *SBL Seminar Papers* 31 (1992), 396–98.

31. The identification of the two women in the scene as the *Ecclesia ex Gentibus* and *Ecclesia ex Circumcisione* is supported by parallel mosaics in the Basilica of Santa Sabina in Rome, which can be dated to the early fifth century.

32. See Nancy Peterson Ševcenko, entry no. 506, in *The Age of Spirituality: Catalogue of the Exhibition at the Metropolitan Museum of Art, November 19, 1977–February 12, 1978,* ed. K. Weitzmann (New York: Metropolitan Museum of Art, 1979), 569.

33. On the gold-glass portraits, see Charles Rufus Morey, *The Gold-Glass Collection of the Vatican Library,* ed. G. Ferrari (Vatican City: Biblioteca Apostolica Vaticana, 1969), entries 49–76; and forthcoming, Lucy Grig, "Portraits, Pontiffs, and the Christianisation of Fourth-Century Rome," *PBSR* 59 (2004), where the author uses the fourth-century gold-glass portraits as a case study to examine the visual culture of Late Antiquity and compares the portraits of Christian saints to the efforts of Pope Damasus to establish the cult of Roman bishops and martyrs. A brief, recent discussion of these portraits is included in David Cartlidge and Keith Elliott, *Art and the Christian Apocrypha* (London: Routledge, 2001), 134–48. Also see F. Bisconti, "Pietro e Paolo: L'invenzione delle immagini, la rievocazione delle storie, la genesi delle teofani," in *Pietro e Paolo: la storia, il culto, la mamoria, nei primi secoli,* ed. Angela Donati (Milan: Electra, 2000), 43–53.

34. On the ivory buckle and the tradition of the meeting of Peter and Paul and its representation in iconography in general, see Kessler, "The Meeting of Peter and Paul in Rome," in his *Studies in Pictorial Narrative,* 529–48.

35. Trans. Hennecke and Schneemelcher, *New Testament Apocrypha* 2:239. For more on this description, see R. M. Grant, "The Description of Paul in the Acts of Paul and Thecla," *VC* 36 (1982): 1–4; and Abraham J. Malherbe, "A Physical Description of Paul," *HTR* 79 (1986): 170–75.

36. Nicephorus, *Hist.* 2.2.37. The description of Peter is quoted in Christopher Matthew, "Nicephorus Callistus' Physical Description of Peter: An Original Component of the Acts of Peter?" *Apocrypha* 7 (1996):143–45. Matthews argues that Nicephorus's description was based on a missing version of the *Acts of Peter,* mainly because he clearly based his description of Paul on a textual antecedent, the passage from the *Acts of Paul and Thecla* cited above, but also because a physical description was a "standard feature of Greco-Roman biography" (140). See a critical evaluation of earlier theories of Petrine portraiture in Cartlidge and Elliot, *Art and the Christian Apocrypha,* 142.

37. See Huskinson, *Concordia Apostolorum*; and E. Dassmann, *Paulus in frühchristliche Frömmigkeit und Kunst* (Opladen: Westdeutscher Verlag, 1982).

38. Paul Zanker, *The Mask of Socrates: The Image of the Intellectual in Antiquity,* trans. A. Shapiro (Berkeley: Univ. of California Press, 1995), 304.

39. See Ruth W. Sullivan, "Saints Peter and Paul: Some Ironic Aspects of Their Imaging," *AH* 17 (1994): 59–80, esp. 67–8; and Cartlidge and Elliott, *Art and the Christian Apocrypha*, 135–36.

40. See C. Pietri, "Concordia Apostolorum et Renovatio Urbis," *MEFR* 73 (1961): 275–322; Huskinson, *Concordia Apostolorum*; and Kessler, "The Meeting of Peter and Paul in Rome." A recent critique of this view is offered by Grig, "Portraits, Pontiffs, and the Christianisation of Fourth-Century Rome."

41. See the discussion of some of these images (including the procession of women from the Dura baptistery) and their interpretation as Marian in Cartlidge and Elliott, *Art and the Christian Apocrypha*, 36.

42. On this subject see Vladimir Lossky, "The Hodegitria," in L. Ouspensky and V. Lossky, *The Meaning of Icons*, trans. G. E. H. Palmer and E. Kadloubovsky (Crestwood, N.Y.: St. Vladimir's Seminary Press, 1989), 80–81; on the legend of St. Luke painting a portrait of Mary and the child Jesus, as well as a similar legend that the three magi produced one, see Belting, *Likeness and Presence*, 49–53, with bibliography. The historical account of Eudocia's sending the image to Pulcheria from Jerusalem, where she had been on pilgrimage, comes from Theodorus Lector's *History of the Church* as reported in Nicephorus Callistus Xanthopoulos (PG 86:165A), and trans. in Mango, *Art of the Byzantine Empire*, 40. Today, a tourist may see one such painting in the Basilica of Santa Maria Maggiore in Rome.

43. The apocryphal scenes mentioned here are found in the *Protevangelium of James*, 7–11. The mid-sixth-century ivory throne of Maximian in Ravenna also shows the annunciation, the trial of the water, Joseph's dream, the nativity, the Madonna with child (seated), and the flight into Egypt, thus combining Gospel accounts with the apocryphal stories.

44. See discussion (chap. 4) of the Mary/Sarah typologies in this program as argued by Suzanne Spain, "'The Promised Blessing': The Iconography of the Mosaics of S. Maria Maggiore," *AB* 61 (1979): 518–40. Jeanne Deane Sieger, in her article, "Visual Metaphor as Theology: Leo the Great's Sermons on the Incarnation and the Arch Mosaics of S. Maria Maggiore," *Gesta* 26 (1987): 83–91, disagrees, however, and bases her arguments on the centrality of the annunciation in Leo's sermons on the nativity. On Santa Maria Maggiore's decorative program in general, see Heinrich Karpp, *Die frühchristlichen und mittelalterlichen Mosaiken in Santa Maria Maggiore zu Rom* (Baden-Baden: Grimm, 1966); and Beat Brenk, *Die frühchristlichen Mosaiken in S. Marie Maggiore zu Rom* (Wiesbaden: Steiner, 1975).

45. See S. Boyd's entry no. 407 in Kurt Weitzmann, ed. *The Age of Spirituality,* 532, which includes some bibliography on this object.

46. Kurt Weitzmann, *The Monastery of Saint Catherine at Mount Sinai: The Icons* 1 (Princeton: Princeton Univ. Press, 1976), 18–21.

47. Translation taken from Ouspensky and Lossky, *The Meaning of Icons*, 31.

48. Epiphanius, *Test.*, text and trans. in Mango, *Art of the Byzantine Empire*, 41–42, from Ostrogorsky, ed., *Studien zur Geschichte*, 67. Partly because of their inclusion in the *florilegium* of the iconoclasts read at the Synod of Hieria in 754, these writings have doubtful authenticity for Ostrogorsky—both this letter and other fragments of Epiphanius's writings, including a portion of a letter to Bishop John of Jerusalem concerning another "saint" curtain in a church at the site of Bethel. However, since a version of this curtain episode was preserved in a chronologically contemporary letter of Jerome (*Ep.* 51.9), that document, as well as this one and the *Testament* quoted above, have now been generally accepted as authentic. For more discussion of this matter see Mary Charles Murray, "Art and the Early Church," *JTS* 282 (1977):303–45, esp. 336–39; and (more recently) Pierre Maraval, "Épiphane, docteur des iconoclasts," in *Nicée II. 787–1987, douze siècles d'images religieuses*, ed. François Boespflug and Nicolas Lossky (Paris: Cerf, 1987), 51–62.

49. Aristotle, *Poet.* 145b. This text is discussed by Alain Besançon, *The Forbidden Image: An Intellectual History of Iconoclasm*, trans. J. M. Todd (Chicago: Univ. of Chicago Press, 2000), 41.

50. Plotinus, *Enn.* 5.8.1., trans. S. McKenna, *Plotinus, The Enneads* (London: Faber and Faber, 1962), 422–23, and also discussed in Besançon, *The Forbidden Image,* 50–51.

51. Philostratus, *Vit. Apoll.* 6.19, LCL 2, 79. See previous discussion of Apollonius on the gods, chap. 2, p. 60.

52. Augustine, *Ver. rel.* 30.54–56.

53. Basil, *Ep.* 2.3.

54. Theodore the Studite, *Ref.* 2.1l, citing Ps. Basil, *C. Eun.* 5 (PG 29:724); trans. Catherine Roth, *St. Theodore the Studite on the Holy Images* (Crestwood, N.Y.: St. Vladimir's Seminary Press, 1981), 49.

55. See the work of Henry Maguire, *The Icons of Their Bodies: Saints and Their Images in Byzantium* (Princeton: Princeton Univ. Press, 1996), esp. chapter 1, "Likeness and Definition," 5–47. Maguire here discusses saints' portraits from the later period, but his discussion is most helpful, applies to much of the above, and is essential to any further study of saints' images in Byzantine art.

56. See Maguire, *The Icons of Their Bodies*, 7–8, for this and other examples.

57. Gilbert Dagron, "Holy Images and Likeness," *DOP* 45 (1991): 24–33, here 31–32.

58. The story of a young monk from Sinai, who recognized Saint Plato of Ancyra based on his appearance in portrait images, was recounted by Nilus of Sinai, PG 79:580–81; also in Mango, *Art of the Byzantine Empire*, 40.

59. Augustine, *Trin.* 8.4.7, trans. Edmund Hill, *The Works of St. Augustine*, pt. 1, vol. 5, *The Trinity*, ed. J. E. Rotelle (Brooklyn: New City, 1991), 246–47.

Glossary

aniconic. Having no visual images, especially no figurative images or portrayals of living beings (animals or humans).

apse. A semicircular or polygonal building recess, covered by a dome or vault and usually at the end of the chancel area of a church.

arcosolium. Burial niche within a chamber in a catacomb, marked by an arched opening, into which a container for the body is placed.

basilica. Rectangular building designed to house secular assemblies or Christian communities at worship. The interior space was usually divided into three or more aisles by rows of supporting columns, and an apse was often placed at one end.

beatific vision. The vision of God that is ultimately granted to the saved soul, or the direct knowledge or vision of God, which offers salvation to those who receive it.

catacomb. Underground burial place comprised of tunnels and chambers, accommodating different kinds of tombs, including narrow openings in the gallery walls, or group burials in separate small rooms.

christogram. The first two Greek letters of the name Christ (*chi* and *rho*), formed into a monogram, often within a circle or a wreath.

Council of Chalcedon. The Fourth Ecumenical Council (451 C.E.), especially significant for its definition of the ways that the two natures of Christ were to be understood by orthodox Christians—as distinct (not confused), but at the same time inseparable.

Council of Elvira. Local Spanish church council (305 C.E.), which resolved a series of disciplinary problems, including canon 36, which banned images on the walls of churches.

Council of Ephesus. Ecumenical council held in 431 C.E., which declared the Virgin Mary to be the *Theotokos* (God-bearer).

cruciform. Having the shape of a cross, usually with the cross bar above the center of the longer axis.

cubicula. Small chamber within an underground burial site or catacomb, probably used by a single family or group.

dormition. From the Latin *dormitio*, meaning "to sleep" and referring to the death and assumption of the Virgin Mary, often shown as recumbent on a bier while Christ receives her soul, which is depicted as an infant in swaddling clothes.

florilegium. A collection of passages from Christian dogmatic writings, in particular the documents of the early church, usually used to provide textual support on one or another side of a theological debate.

font. A basin holding water for the sacrament of baptism, in early times usually deep enough to accommodate adult immersion and inserted into the floor of a room built for the rite of baptism.

fresco. A type of wall painting, usually rapidly done with wet paint into fresh plaster, in order to produce a permanent mural.

hagiography. The writings of saints' lives and accounts of their miracles, as well as a description of their heroic deeds and deaths, often as martyrs.

hetoimasia. From the Greek word for "preparation," an image of an empty throne on which a cross or Gospel book is placed. In some cases a dove representing the Holy Spirit also appears.

himation. Long, loose tunic worn by both men and women in the eastern Roman Empire.

Hodegitria. An image of the Virgin Mary with the Christ child, believed to have been painted by Luke and subsequently copied and widely distributed.

icon. Any image, but usually used to refer to small panel portraits of a holy person, including Christ, the Virgin Mary, or the saints, produced for devotional purposes. Some icons also represent particular feasts of the church rather than portraits (for example, the nativity) and so are called "festal icons."

iconoclasm. The act of breaking or destroying icons, usually by those who accused those who used them for devotional purposes of practicing idolatry.

iconodule. From the Greek for "servant of images," referring to a person who offers veneration to the images and prayer to the saints represented in them.

iconography. The study of meaning in visual art, especially by looking for recurring symbols, motifs, or compositions and trying to interpret the meaning in the imagery, either intended by the artist or perceived by the viewer.

in pace. Traditional epitaph in the early Christian era, meaning "in peace."

labarum. A Roman military standard adapted by Constantine to include a christogram placed inside a wreath and sometimes also bearing the portraits of the emperor and his sons.

loculi. Small horizontal openings, cut into the walls of catacomb galleries, where shrouded bodies were placed and then covered with stone or pottery slabs.

maphorion. A large veil-like head covering worn by women in the East and usually shown in icons of the Virgin Mary.

martyrium. Shrine built to house the relics of a Christian saint or martyr, or at a holy site, usually having a centralized plan (for example, circular, octagonal, or cruciform).

nave. From the Latin word, *navis*, meaning ship, the center aisle of a basilica or main area of a church building, used for the gathering of the laity as opposed to the areas restricted to clergy.

nimbed. Having a halo or aureole of light behind the head indicating sanctity or power, as in the representations of Christ or the saints.

oculus. A circular opening or window, often placed in a dome or vault.

oratory. Small chapel, often private, set apart for prayer or devotional practice.

pallium. A wide mantle, usually worn by Roman men over an undertunic and loosely draped around the body and slung over the arm.

sarcophagus. From the Greek words for "flesh-eater," a rectangular or tub-shaped stone coffin used for inhumation (deposit of a body) and often elaborately carved with relief sculpture.

Seventh Ecumenical Council. Also known as the Second Council of Nicaea (787 c.e.), called by the iconophile Empress Irene, best known for affirming the orthodoxy of icons.

Synod of Hieria. Council supported by the iconoclasts in 754 c.e., which condemned the making or use of icons for devotional purposes. Overturned by the Seventh Ecumenical Council (Nicaea II) in 787 c.e.

tau-rho. Combination of the two Greek letters *tau* and *rho* into a sign that might be included in the word "stauros" (cross) and suggesting a human body on a cross.

theophany. The manifestation of the Divine to a human being, either as a natural appearance (sometimes in human form) or as a vision.

Theotokos. The title given the Virgin Mary in the councils of Ephesus (431) and Chalcedon (451), literally meaning "God Bearer," but usually translated "Mother of God."

theurgy. Summoning the Divine or divine power by means of magic, incantations, or rituals, especially in aid of individual salvation.

Traditio Legis. Latin term for "handing over the law," referring to the passing of authority or (alternately) the giving of the gospel to the apostles. Usually shown in art by Christ passing a scroll to either Peter or Paul.

Select Bibliography

Achelis, Hans. *Die Katakomben von Neapel.* Leipzig: Hiersemann, 1936.

Aune, David E. "Heracles and Christ: Heracles Imagery in the Christology of Early Christianity." In *Greeks, Romans, and Christians: Essays in Honor of Abraham J. Malherbe.* Edited by D. Balch et al., 3–19. Minneapolis: Fortress Press, 1990.

Barber, Charles. *Figure and Likeness: On the Limits of Representation in Byzantine Iconoclasm.* Princeton: Princeton Univ. Press, 2002.

Beard, Mary, John North, and Simon Price. *The Religions of Rome.* 2 vols. Cambridge: Cambridge Univ. Press, 1998.

Belting, Hans. *Likeness and Presence: A History of the Image before the Era of Art.* Translated by Edmund Jephcott. Chicago: Univ. of Chicago Press, 1994.

Besançon, Alain. *The Forbidden Image: An Intellectual History of Iconoclasm.* Translated by J. M. Todd. Chicago: Univ. of Chicago Press, 2000.

Bevan, Edwyn. *Holy Images.* London: George Allen & Unwin, 1940.

Bianchi Bandinelli, Ranuccio. *Rome, The Late Empire: Roman Art, A.D. 200–400.* Translated by Peter Green. New York: Braziller, 1971.

Bisconti, F. "Pietro e Paolo: L'invenzione delle immagini, la rievocazione delle storie, la genesi delle teofani." In *Pietro e Paolo: la storia, il culto, la mamoria, nei primi secoli.* Edited by A. Donati, 43–53. Milan: Electra, 2000.

Breckenridge, James D. *Likeness: A Conceptual History of Ancient Portraiture.* Evanston, Ill.: Northwestern Univ. Press, 1968.

———. *The Numismatic Iconography of Justinian II (685–695, 705–711 A.D.).* Numismatic Notes and Monographs 144. New York: American Numismatic Society, 1959.

Brenk, Beat. *Die frühchristlichen Mosaiken in S. Marie Maggiore zu Rom.* Wiesbaden: Steiner, 1975.

Brilliant, Richard. *Portraiture.* London: Reaktion, 1991.

———. *Roman Art from the Republic to Constantine.* London: Phaidon, 1974.

Cameron, Averil. *Christianity and the Rhetoric of Empire.* Berkeley: Univ. of California Press, 1991.

———. "The History of the Image of Edessa: The Telling of a Story." In *Okeanos: Essays Presented to I. Sevcenko,* 80–94. Harvard Ukrainian Studies 7. Cambridge: Harvard Univ. Press, 1983.

———. "The Sceptic and the Shroud." Inaugural Lecture, King's College, London (1980). In *Continuity and Change in Sixth-Century Byzantium.* London: Variorum Reprints, 1981.

Cartlidge, David R., and Keith J. Elliott. *Art and the Christian Apocrypha.* London: Routledge, 2001.

Chazelle, Celia. "Pictures, Books, and the Illiterate: Pope Gregory I's Letters to Serenus of Marseilles." *Word and Image* 6 (1990): 138–53.

Crook, John. *The Architectural Setting of the Cult of Saints in the Early Christian World, c. 300–1200*. New York: Oxford Univ. Press, 2000.

Dagron, Gilbert. "Holy Images and Likeness." *DOP* 45 (1991): 24–33.

D'Ambra, Eve. *Art and Identity in the Roman World*. London: Calmann and King, 1998.

———. "Mourning and the Making of Ancestors on the Testamentum Relief." *AJA* 99 (1995): 667–81.

Dassmann, Ernst. *Paulus in frühchristliche Frömmigkeit und Kunst*. Opladen: Westdeutscher Verlag, 1982.

Deichmann, Friedrich. *Einführung in die christliche Archäologie*. Darmstadt: Wissenschaftliche Buchgesellschaft, 1983.

———. *Ravenna: Haupstade des spätantiken Abenlandes*. 3 vols. Weisbaden: Steiner, 1969–1989.

Dinkler, Erich. *Christus und Askelepios zum Christustypus der polychromen Platten in Museo nazionale romano*, SHAW.PH. Heidelberg: Winter, 1980.

Dobschütz, Ernst von. *Christusbilder: Untersuchungen zur christlichen Legende*. Leipzig: J. C. Hinrichs, 1899.

Drerup, H. "Totenmaske und Ahnenbild bei den Römern." *MDAI (R)* 87 (1980): 81, 120–9.

Drews, Robert. *In Search of the Shroud of Turin: New Light on Its History and Origins*. Totowa, N.J.: Rowman & Allanheld, 1984.

Elsner, Jaš. *Art and the Roman Viewer: The Transformation of Art from the Pagan World to Christianity*. Cambridge: Cambridge Univ. Press, 1995.

———. *Imperial Rome and Christian Triumph: The Art of the Roman Empire* A.D. *100–450*. Oxford: Oxford Univ. Press, 1998.

Elsner, Jaš, ed., *Art and Text in Roman Culture*. Cambridge: Cambridge Univ. Press, 1996.

Fasola, Umberto. *Le catacombe di S. Gennaro a Capodimonte*. Rome: Editalia, 1975.

Fine, Steven. "Iconoclasm and the Art of Late Antique Palestinian Synagogues." In *From Dura to Sepphoris: Studies in Jewish Art and Society in Late Antiquity*. Edited by Lee I. Levine and Ze'ev Weiss, 183–94. *Journal of Roman Archaeology Supplementary Series* 40. Portsmouth: R.I.: Journal of Roman Archaeology, 2001).

Fine, Steven, ed. *Sacred Realm: The Emergence of the Synagogue in the Ancient World*. New York: Oxford Univ. Press; Yeshiva University Museum, 1996.

Finney, Paul Corby. "Alcune note à proposito delle imagini Carpocrazione di Gesú." *RAC* 57 (1981): 35–41.

——— "Image on Finger Rings and Early Christian Art." *DOP* 41 (1987): 181–86.

———. *The Invisible God: The Earliest Christians on Art*. New York: Oxford Univ. Press, 1994.

———. "The Rabbi and the Coin Portrait (Mark 12.15b, 16): Rigorism Manqué." *JBL* 112 (1993): 629–44.

Finney, Paul Corby, ed. *Art, Archaeology and Architecture of Early Christianity*. Studies in Early Christianity 18. New York: Garland, 1993.

Fishwick, Duncan. "The Development of Provincial Ruler Worship in the Western Roman Empire." In *ANRW* 2.16.2 (1978), 1201–53.

———. *The Imperial Cult in the West*. Leiden: Brill, 1987.

Fletcher-Louis, C. H. T. "The Worship of Divine Humanity as God's Image." In *The Jewish Roots of Christological Monotheism*. Edited by C. Newman et al., 120–25. JSJSup 63 Leiden: Brill, 1999.

Gero, Stephen. "The True Image of Christ: Eusebius' Letter to Constantia Reconsidered." *JTS* 32 (1981): 460–61.

Goodenough, Erwin R. *Jewish Symbols in the Greco-Roman Period*. 13 vols. Bollingen Series 37. New York: Pantheon, 1953–1968.

Grabar, André. *Christian Iconography: A Study of Its Origins*. Princeton: Princeton Univ. Press, 1968.

Grant, Robert M.," The Decalogue in Early Christianity." *HTR* 40 (1947): 1–17.

———. "The Description of Paul in the Acts of Paul and Thecla." *VC* 36 (1982): 1–4.

———. *Gods and the One God*. Philadelphia: Westminster, 1986.

Grig, Lucy. *Making Martyrs in Late Antiquity*. London: Duckworth, 2004.

———. "Portraits, Pontiffs, and the Christianisation of Fourth-Century Rome." *PBSR* 59 (2004). Forthcoming.

Gutmann, Joseph. "Deuteronomy: Religious Reformation or Iconoclastic Revolution?" In *The Image and the Word*. Edited by J. Gutmann, 5–25. Missoula, Mont.: Scholars, 1977.

———. *Sacred Images: Studies in Jewish Art from Antiquity to the Middle Ages.* Northampton: Variorum Reprints, 1989.

———. "The Second Commandment and the Image in Judaism." In *No Graven Images: Studies in Art and the Hebrew Bible.* Edited by J. Gutmann, 3–14. New York: Ktav, 1971.

Hachlili, Rachel. "Synagogues in the Land of Israel." In *Sacred Realm: The Emergence of the Synagogue in the Ancient World.* Edited by S. Fine, 111–29. New York: Oxford Univ. Press, 1996.

Hahn, Cynthia. "Seeing and Believing: The Construction of Sanctity in Early-Medieval Saints' Shrines." *Speculum* 72 (1997): 1079–106.

Hamburger, Jeffrey. *The Visual and the Visionary: Art and Female Spirituality in Late Medieval Germany.* New York: Zone, 1998.

Hanfmann, George M. A. "The Continuity of Classical Art: Culture, Myth, and Faith." In *Age of Spirituality: A Symposium.* Edited by K. Weitzmann, 75–99. New York: Metropolitan Museum of Art, 1980.

Hannestad, Niels. *Roman Art and Imperial Policy.* Aarhus: Aarhus Univ. Press, 1986.

Hertling, Ludwig, and Engelbert Kirschbaum. *The Roman Catacombs and Their Martyrs.* Milwaukee: Bruce, 1956.

Hollerich, Michael. *Eusebius of Caesarea's Commentary on Isaiah: Christian Exegesis in the Age of Constantine.* Oxford: Clarendon, 1999.

Howard, George, trans. *The Teaching of Addai.* Early Christian Literature 4. Chico, Calif.: Scholars, 1991.

Huskinson, J. M. *Concordia Apostolorum: Christian Propaganda at Rome in the Fourth and Fifth Centuries.* BAR International Series 148. Oxford: B.A.R., 1982.

Jensen, Robin. "Image, Sanctity, and Truth: The Place of the Portrait in Christian Tradition." *ARTS* 13.2 (2001): 26–31.

———. "The Trinity and the Economy of Salvation." *JECS* 7 (1999): 527–46.

———. *Understanding Early Christian Art.* London: Routledge, 2000.

———. "What Are Pagan River Gods Doing at Scenes of Jesus' Baptism?" *BR* 9.1(1993): 35–41, 54–55.

———. "Witnessing the Divine." *BR* 17.6 (2001): 24–31, 59.

Johnson, M. J. "Towards a History of Theodoric's Building Program." *DOP* 42 (1988): 73–96.

Karpp, Heinrich. *Die frühchristlichen und mittelalterlichen Mosaiken in Santa Maria Maggiore zu Rom.* Baden-Baden: Grimm, 1966.

Kartsonis, Anna. *Anastasis: The Making of an Image.* Cambridge: Harvard Univ. Press, 1977.

Kessler, Herbert L. *Spiritual Seeing: Picturing God's Invisibility in Medieval Art.* Philadelphia: Univ. of Pennsylvania Press, 2000.

———. *Studies in Pictorial Narrative.* London: Pindar, 1994.

Kessler, Herbert L., and Gerhard Wolf. *The Holy Face and the Paradox of Representation.* Bologna: Nuova Alfa, 1998.

Kitzinger, Ernst. *Byzantine Art in the Making.* Cambridge: Harvard Univ. Press, 1980.

———. "The Cult of the Image before Iconoclasm." *DOP* 8 (1954): 116–18.

Kleiner, Diana E. E. *Roman Sculpture.* New Haven: Yale Univ. Press, 1992.

Kleiner, Diana E. E. and Susan B. Matheson, eds. *I Claudia II: Women in Roman Art and Society.* Austin: Univ. of Texas Press, 2000.

Koch, G. *Roman Funerary Sculpture, Catalogue of the Collections.* Malibu, Calif.: J. Paul Getty Museum, 1988.

Kollwitz, Johannes. "Probleme der Theodosianischen Kunst Roms." *RivAC* 39 (1963): 191–233.

Koortbojian, Michael. *Myth, Meaning, and Memory on Roman Sarcophagi.* Berkeley: Univ. of California Press, 1995.

Kopecek, Thomas. *A History of Neo-Arianism.* Cambridge: Philadelphia Patristic Foundation, 1979.

Kostof, Spiro. *The Orthodox Baptistery of Ravenna.* New Haven: Yale Univ. Press, 1965.

Kraeling, Carl. H. "The Episode of the Roman Standards at Jerusalem." *HTR* 35 (1942): 263–89.

Layton, Bentley. *The Gnostic Scriptures.* Garden City, N.Y.: Doubleday, 1987.

Lehmann-Hartleben, Karl, and Erling C. Olsen. *Dionysiac Sarcophagi in Baltimore.* Baltimore: Walters Art Gallery, 1942.

Lewy, H. *Chaldaean Oracles and Theurgy.* Cairo: Institut français d'archéologie oriental, 1956.

Liebeschütz, J. H. W. G. *Continuity and Change in Roman Religion.* Oxford: Clarendon, 1979.

L'Orange, H. P. *Apotheosis in Ancient Portraiture.* Cambridge: Harvard Univ. Press, 1947.

———. *Likeness and Icon: Selected Studies in Classical and Early Mediaeval Art.* Odense: Odense Univ. Press, 1973.

Louth, Andrew. *The Origins of the Christian Mystical Tradition: From Plato to Denys*. Oxford: Oxford Univ. Press, 1981.

Lowden, John. *Early Christian and Byzantine Art*. London, Phaidon, 1997.

Lowrie, Walter. *Art in the Early Church*. New York: Norton, 1947.

MacGregor, Neil. *Seeing Salvation: Images of Christ in Art*. New Haven: Yale Univ. Press, 2000.

Malbon, Elizabeth Struthers. *The Iconography of the Sarcophagus of Junius Bassus*. Princeton: Princeton Univ. Press, 1990.

Malherbe, Abraham J. "A Physical Description of Paul." *HTR* 79 (1986): 170–75.

Mancinelli, Fabrizio. *The Catacombs of Rome and the Origins of Christianity*. Translated by Carol Wasserman. Florence: Scala, 1981–.

Maguire, Henry. *The Icons of Their Bodies: Saints and Their Images in Byzantium*. Princeton: Princeton Univ. Press, 1996.

Mango, Cyril. *The Art of the Byzantine Empire, 312–1453: Sources and Documents*. Toronto: Univ. of Toronto Press, 1986.

Mathews, Thomas F. *The Clash of Gods: A Reinterpretation of Early Christian Art*. Rev. ed. Princeton: Princeton Univ. Press, 1999.

Matthews, Christopher. "Nicephorus Callistus' Physical Description of Peter: An Original Component of the Acts of Peter?" *Apocrypha* 7 (1996): 143–45.

Matz, Friedrich. *Die dionysischen Sarkophage* 4. Berlin: Mann, 1968.

Michel, Dorothea. *Alexander als Vorbild für Pompeius, Caesar, und Marcus Antonius, archäologische Untersuchungen*. Collection Latomus 94. Brussels: Latomus, Revue d'études latines, 1967.

Milburn, Robert. *Early Christian Art and Architecture*. Berkeley: Univ. of California Press, 1988.

Miles, Margaret. *Image as Insight*. Boston: Beacon, 1985.

Mitchell, Margaret. "The Archetypal Image: John Chrysostom's Portraits of Paul." *JR* 75 (1995): 15–43.

Morey, Charles Rufus. *The Gold-Glass Collection of the Vatican Library*. Edited by G. Ferrari. Vatican City: Biblioteca Apostolica Vaticana, 1959.

Murray, Mary Charles, "Art and the Early Church." *JTS* 28 (1977): 303–45.

———. *Rebirth and Afterlife: A Study of the Transmutation of Some Pagan Imagery in Early Christian Art*. Oxford: B.A.R., 1981.

Nordström, Carl Otto. *Ravennastudien: Ideengeschichte und ikonographische Untersuchungen über die Mosaiken von Ravenna*. Stockholm: Almquist and Wiksell, 1953.

Olin, Margaret. *The Nation without Art: Examining Modern Discourses on Jewish Art*. Lincoln: Univ. of Nebraska Press, 2001.

Ostrogorsky, Georgije., ed. *Studien zur Geschichte des byzantinische Bilderstreites*. Breslau: Marcus, 1929.

Ouspensky, Leonid, and Vladimir. Lossky. *The Meaning of Icons*. Translated by G. E. H. Palmer and E. Kadloubovsky. Crestwood, N.Y.: St. Vladimir's Seminary Press, 1989.

Pekary, Thomas. *Das römische Kaiserbildnis in Staat, Kult, und Gesellschaft*. Berlin: Mann, 1985.

Pietri, Charles. "Concordia Apostolorum et Renovatio Urbis." *MEFR* 73 (1961): 275–322.

Price, Simon R. F. *Rituals and Power: The Roman Imperial Cult in Asia Minor*. Cambridge: Cambridge Univ. Press, 1984.

Ramage, Nancy, and Arthur Ramage. *Roman Art: Romulus to Constantine*. 3d ed. Upper Saddle River, N.J.: Prentice Hall, 2001.

Rice, David Talbot, and Tamara Talbot Rice. *Icons and Their Dating*. London: Thames and Hudson, 1976.

Roberts, Michael J. *Poetry and the Cult of the Martyrs: The Liber Peristephanon of Prudentius*. Ann Arbor: Univ. of Michigan Press, 1993.

Rorem, Paul. "The Uplifting Spirituality of Pseudo-Dionysus." In *Christian Spirituality: Origins to the Twelfth Century*. Edited by B. McGinn et al., 132–51. New York: Crossroad, 1987.

Rose, Charles Brian. *Dynastic Commemoration and Imperial Portraiture in the Julio-Claudian Period*. Cambridge: Cambridge Univ. Press, 1997.

Roth, Catharine., trans. *St. Theodore the Studite on the Holy Images*. Crestwood, N.Y.: St. Vladimir's Seminary Press, 1981.

Roth, Cecil. "An Ordinance against Images in Jerusalem." *HTR* 49 (1956): 169–76.

Runciman, Stephen. "Some Remarks on the Image of Edessa." *Cambridge Historical Journal* 3 (1931): 238–52.

Sahas, Daniel. *Icon and Logos: Sources in Eighth-Century Iconoclasm*. Toronto: Univ. of Toronto Press, 1986.

Schowalter, Daniel. *The Emperor and the Gods: Images from the Time of Trajan.* HDR 28. Minneapolis: Fortress Press, 1993.

Sieger, Jeanne Deane. "Visual Metaphor as Theology: Leo the Great's Sermons on the Incarnation and the Arch Mosaics of S. Maria Maggiore." *Gesta* 26 (1987): 83–91.

Simpson, Otto von. *Sacred Fortress: Byzantine Art and Statecraft in Ravenna.* Princeton: Princeton Univ. Press, 1987.

Snyder, Graydon F. *Ante Pacem: Archaeological Evidence of Church Life before Constantine.* Rev. ed. Macon, Ga.: Mercer Univ. Press, 2003.

Spain, Suzanne. "'The Promised Blessing': The Iconography of the Mosaics of S. Maria Maggiore." *AB* 61 (1979): 518–40.

Stern, Henri. "Les mosaiques de l'église de sainte-Constance à Rome." *DOP* 12 (1958): 157–218.

Stevenson, James. *The Catacombs Rediscovered: Monuments of Early Christianity.* London: Thames and Hudson, 1978.

Stuart, Meriwether. "How Were Imperial Portraits Distributed throughout the Roman Empire?" *AJA* 43 (1939): 601–17.

Sullivan, Ruth W. "Saints Peter and Paul: Some Ironic Aspects of Their Imaging." *AH* 17 (1994): 59–80.

Taylor, Lily Ross. "Aniconic Worship among the Early Romans." In *Classical Studies in Honor of John C. Rolfe.* Edited by G. D. Hadzsits, 305–19. Philadelphia: Univ. of Pennsylvania Press, 1931.

———. *The Divinity of the Roman Emperor.* Middletown, Conn.: American Philological Association, 1931.

Teske, Roland J., S.J. *The Works of Saint Augustine.* II.2, Letters 100–155. Edited by B. Ramsey. Hyde Park, N.Y.: New City, 2003.

Toynbee, J. M. C. *Death and Burial in the Roman World.* Baltimore: Johns Hopkins Univ. Press, 1971.

Turcan, Robert. *L'art romain dans l'histoire.* Paris: Flammarion, 1995.

———. *The Cults of the Roman Empire.* Translated by Antonia Nevill. Oxford: Blackwell, 1996.

———. *The Gods of Ancient Rome: Religion in Everyday Life from Archaic to Imperial Times.* Translated by A. Nevill. London: Routledge, 2001.

———. *Les Sarcophages romains à représentations dionysiaques.* Paris: Boccard, 1966.

Urbach, Ephraim E. "Rabbinical Laws of Idolatry in the Second and Third Centuries in Light of Archaeological and Historical Facts." *IEJ* 9 (1959): 149–65; 229–45.

Van Dam, Raymond. *Saints and Their Miracles in Late Antique Gaul.* Princeton: Princeton Univ. Press, 1993.

Varner, Eric, ed., *From Caligula to Constantine: Tyranny and Transformation in Roman Portraiture.* Atlanta: Michael C. Carlos Museum, 2000.

Walker, Susan. *Greek and Roman Portraits.* London: British Museum Press, 1995.

Weitzmann, Kurt. *The Monastery of Saint Catherine at Mount Sinai: The Icons.* Vol. 1. Princeton: Princeton Univ. Press, 1976.

Weitzmann, Kurt, ed. *The Age of Spirituality: Catalogue of the Exhibition at the Metropolitan Museum of Art, November 19, 1977–Februrary 12, 1978.* New York: Metropolitan Museum of Art, 1979.

Weitzmann, Kurt, and Herbert L. Kessler. *The Frescoes of the Dura Synagogue and Christian Art.* Washington, D.C.: Dumbarton Oaks, 1990.

Wilson, Ian. *The Shroud of Turin.* Garden City, N.Y.: Doubleday, 1978.

Wolfson, Elliot R. *Through a Speculum That Shines: Vision and Imagination in Medieval Jewish Mysticism.* Princeton: Princeton Univ. Press, 1994.

Wood, Susan. "Alcestis on Roman Sarcophagi." *AJA* 82 (1978): 499–510.

———. *Roman Portrait Sculpture 217–260 A.D.* Leiden: Brill, 1986.

Zadoks-Josephus Jitta, Annie Nicolette. *Ancestral Portraiture in Rome and the Art of the Last Century of the Republic.* Amsterdam: Noord Hollandsche, 1932.

Zanker, Paul. *The Mask of Socrates: The Image of the Intellectual in Antiquity.* Translated by Alan Shapiro. Berkeley: Univ. of California Press, 1995.

———. *The Power of Images in the Age of Augustus.* Translated by Alan Shapiro. Ann Arbor: Univ. of Michigan Press, 1988.

———. "The Power of Images." In *Paul and Empire: Religion and Power in Roman Imperial Society.* Edited by R. A. Horsley, 72–86. Harrisburg, Pa.: Trinity, 1997.

———. *Provinzielle Kaiserporträts. Zur Rezeption der Selbstdarstellung des Princeps.* Munich: Bayerischen Akademie der Wissenschaften, 1983.

Index